Disrupting Education Policy

Disrupting Education Policy

How New Philanthropy Works to Change Education

Marina Avelar

PETER LANG

Oxford • Bern • Berlin • Bruxelles • New York • Wien

Bibliographic information published by Die Deutsche Nationalbibliothek.
Die Deutsche Nationalbibliothek lists this publication in the Deutsche National-
bibliografie; detailed bibliographic data is available on the Internet at
http://dnb.d-nb.de.

A catalogue record for this book is available from the British Library.

Library of Congress Cataloging-in-Publication Data
Names: Avelar, Marina, 1989- author.
Title: Disrupting education policy : how new philanthropy works to change
  education / Marina Avelar.
Description: New York : Peter Lang, 2020. | Series: New disciplinary
  perspectives on education, 2297-718X ; vol 3 | Includes bibliographical
  references and index.
Identifiers: LCCN 2020024403 (print) | LCCN 2020024404 (ebook) | ISBN
  9781787076884 (paperback) | ISBN 9781787077331 (ebook) | ISBN
  9781787077348 (epub) | ISBN 9781787077355 (mobi)
Subjects: LCSH: Education and state--Brazil. | Educational change--Brazil.
  | Education--Social aspects--Brazil.
Classification: LCC LC92.B8 A94 2020 (print) | LCC LC92.B8 (ebook) | DDC
  379.81--dc23
LC record available at https://lccn.loc.gov/2020024403
LC ebook record available at https://lccn.loc.gov/2020024404

Cover design: Pedro Vergani

ISSN 2297-6531
ISBN 978-1-78707-688-4 (print) • ISBN 978-1-78707-733-1 (ePDF)
ISBN 978-1-78707-734-8 (ePub) • ISBN 978-1-78707-735-5 (mobi)

© Peter Lang Group AG 2021

Published by Peter Lang Ltd, International Academic Publishers,
52 St Giles, Oxford, OX1 3LU, United Kingdom
oxford@peterlang.com, www.peterlang.com

Marina Avelar have asserted her right under the Copyright, Designs and Patents
Act, 1988, to be identified as Author of this Work.

All rights reserved.
All parts of this publication are protected by copyright.
Any utilisation outside the strict limits of the copyright law, without
the permission of the publisher, is forbidden and liable to prosecution.
This applies in particular to reproductions, translations, microfilming,
and storage and processing in electronic retrieval systems.

This publication has been peer reviewed.

Contents

List of tables	vii
List of figures	ix
Acknowledgements	
Foreword by Stephen J. Ball	xi
Preface	xvii
Introduction	1

CHAPTER 1
New philanthropy and the global education reform	11

CHAPTER 2
From government to governance: changing relations in society and how to study them	43

CHAPTER 3
Working to shape narratives and frame education policy ideas	81

CHAPTER 4
Working to collaborate in and through networks	119

CHAPTER 5
Working to change structures and institutionalise a reform agenda	151

CHAPTER 6
New philanthropy, education policy networks and issues for a democratic education	191
Bibliography	207

Tables

Table 1.	New philanthropic organisations in Brazil	33
Table 2.	Data collection and analysis with online searches	71
Table 3.	"Research" efforts of new philanthropy organisations	89
Table 4.	Mobilisation for the National Learning Standards institutional supporters	106
Table 5.	New philanthropies' initiatives of formal coordination of networks	125
Table 6.	Examples of new philanthropies events	131
Table 7.	Unibanco Institute 2015 Seminar – List of Speakers	140
Table 8.	Examples of new philanthropies' initiatives aiming at pedagogy	155

Figures

Figure 1.	Analytical heuristic	77
Figure 2.	Analytical frame	79
Figure 3.	GIFE 2016 Conference – social lounge	133
Figure 4.	Connections between speakers prior to the Unibanco Institute 2015 seminar	143
Figure 5.	MNLS's co-affiliation ego network	175
Figure 6.	Composition of MNLS's members between 2015 and 2016	177
Figure 7.	MNLS and MEC – second semester 2015	178
Figure 8.	MNLS and MEC – first semester 2016	179
Figure 9.	MNLS and MEC – second semester 2016	179
Figure 10.	Analytical frame revisited	192
Figure 11.	Analytical heuristic revisited	197

Foreword by Stephen J. Ball

When we think of government and policymaking we tend to conjure up images of elected politicians and career civil servants sitting around tables in a ministry buildings working on rational agendas of policy delivery and reform – driven either by principles, manifesto commitments or ideology. But policy work is not like that anymore. The policy process is distributed across loosely connected arrangements in diverse locations that include agencies, foundations, think tanks and businesses of various kinds, working as contractors, consultants or "interested" parties with their own funding. These arrangements and the many different ties that link them extend across national boundaries in convoluted asymmetrical networks of policy – policymaking has never been particularly transparent, it is now decidedly opaque. This book is about these new modalities of policy and some of the actors local and international who are involved in the contemporary education policy process in Brazil.

Over the last ten years, the methods of network analysis and network ethnography have begun to be used by education policy researchers to trace and make sense of the new convolutions of policy. This deployment of the network as a device for both researching and representing policy has enabled policy researchers to model their methods and analytic practices in direct relation to the global shift from government to governance, what is sometimes called network governance. This shift involves a move away from administrative, bureaucratic and hierarchical forms of state organisation to the emergence of new reflexive, self-regulatory and horizontal spaces of governance – heterarchies. The heterogeneous array of organisations and practices that make up these heterarchies contributes to, reflects, enables, and necessitates the semiotic and technical rearticulation of education and educational governance. The effect is a significant shift in the centre of gravity around which policy cycles move (Jessop, 1998, p. 32). New relations and spaces of governance are under construction that exist and operate above, beyond and between national state systems. Concomitantly, the frame of policy analysis is of necessity also changing: The nation state is no longer a sensible or viable limit to the analysis of policy and governance.

This book addresses exactly this shift in the forms and modalities of the state, in the case of Brazilian and in the example of education policy. It uses network ethnography to identify, map and examine aspects of this shift in relation to specific the international flow of educational forms and normativities.

Network ethnography as a practice is made up of methods, concepts and new research sensibilities to better understand the new actors, organisations, forms of participation and relationships engaging in education policy and, more generally, driving and facilitating the global expansion of neoliberal policy ideas. Network analysis is appropriate here both as a means for the analysis of educational reform and governance, and as a representation of actual social relations and sites of activity within which the work of governing is done. The task/aim of network methodology "must be to identify the actors in these networks, their power and capacities, and the ways through which they exercise their power through association within networks of relationships" (Dicken, Kelly, & Yeung, 2001, p. 93). However, in some respects the work of education policy network analysis has become stuck – many sorts of policy networks are now being researched and mapped in different locations (and between locations) but in many instances the result is no more than a description of network membership and adumbration of network relations. There are relatively few examples of direct research on the effort and labour of networking, or of attempts to "follow" policy through networks, or to address the roles and relationships of key actors or to attend to network evolution. Marina Avelar's book does all of those things. It moves beyond the simple mapping of network relations to analyse network dynamics – how they work, how they change over time, what effects they have on and in the policy process. The book explores a set of inter-locking education policy networks, which are actively engaged with the reform of the Brazilian school system, its educational methods, and forms of educational governance and specifically the construction of a new policy ecosystem – consisting of practices, organisations, infrastructure and incentives imported from elsewhere. This importation is made possible by a mutating infrastructure that supports the movement or mobilisation of policy models, the self-styled "experts" whose involvement in policy model mobility reinforces its embodied nature. The movements outlined in the book involve "experts" from Australia, the UK and USA, hailed and encouraged and funded by Brazilian philanthropic foundations, bringing with them reform ideas, models and forms, to "reform" Brazilian schools. This is surprising and not. The research highlights the existence of an active global market of education policy "solutions" and individuals, organisations and states eager to sell "their" solutions to willing recipients.

As Larner and Laurie (2010) demonstrate in their work on engineers and privatisation, this account indicates the "centrality of multiple and shifting forms of expertise in the reconfiguring of political-economic institutions, ideas and techniques" (p. 224). "Transfer agents" (Stone, 2004), like those described here, are policy experts and consultants whose travels spread "best practice" models, they are members of a growing "consultocracy" who act as mediators of policy knowledge. These are "sociologically complex actors...whose identities and professional trajectories are often bound up with the policy positions and fixes they espouse" (Peck & Theodore, 2010, p. 170). They labour in the interstices of sprawling and expanding international networks to "assemble" political rationalities, spatial imaginaries, calculative practices and subjectivities.

What is evident in this account is local policies made up of "embodied geographies" and their analysis addresses the ways in which ideas travel and orthodoxies become consolidated. At the same time, new kinds of careers, identities and human mobilities are forged within these processes of education policy and education reform. As policies move, and as new sites, new possibilities and sensibilities are established, policy is "talked" and thought and enacted differently, and within new limits. Here the space of policy analysis is not defined by geographical entities, but by the space configured through the labour of policy actors at the intersection of global and local events and relations. Global, regional, national, state and city, local and institutional levels of policy interact, intertwine and diverge. The flows and spaces and recontextualisations that link the local with global give substance to what Appadurai (1996) through his concept of "scapes" describes as "a new global cultural economy ... a complex, overlapping, disjunctive order" (p. 32) which involves "interactions of a new order and intensity" (p. 27) or what Lingard and Sellar (2014) call new topologies of policy, within which policy "space is configured through the intersection of global and situated elements" (Ong, 2007, p. 5).

This is not to suggest that networks can explain all aspects of the policy process; network relations do not entirely displace other forms of policy formation and policy action.

Network ethnography has a dual interest, both in the "structure" of social relations and the interactional "processes" which generate these structures. This necessitates the exploration of the "content" and perception of the network – the "insider" view of the network, and of the construction, reproduction, variability and dynamics of complex and intricate social ties that make it up. Marina Avelar became such an "insider" – attending events, talking with participants, reading and analysing texts, social media, etc. The book draws on her research which uses network ethnography as "an analytic technique for looking at the structure of policy communities and their social relationships"; and as a "conceptual device … used to represent a set of 'real changes' in the forms of governance of education, both nationally and globally" (Ball, 2012, p. 6). The research is made up of a set of techniques that directly engage with the new policy topography. These involved mapping, visiting and questioning, and as Marcus (1995) argues – following policy. That is, following people, "things", stories, lives and conflicts, and "money" (Ball, Junemann, & Santori, 2017). Avelar gives close attention to organisations and actors, and their relations, activities and histories, within the global education policy field, to the paths and connections that join up these actors, and to "situations" and events in which policy knowledge is mobilised and assembled. That is, the "whos" and "whats" but also the "wheres" and "hows" of policy – the places and events in which the "past, present and potential futures of education co-exist" (McCann & Ward, 2012, p. 48). This is ethnography of "awkward scale" (Roy, 2012). It asks: What spaces do policies travel through on the way from place to another? Who is it that is active in those spaces and who moves between them? How is space/are spaces reconfigured as policies move through it/them and how are policies changed as they move? As McCann and Ward (2012, p. 42) explain this means; "staying close to practice" (p. 45).

What is also captured in Marina Avelar's research is one part of a more general re-working of the boundaries of state, economy and civil society in Brazil, and particularly the role of philanthropic foundations in this process. What and who is the state is no longer clear. Where and who makes policy is increasingly opaque. What interests are at stake in the policy process is changing. In all of this education itself becomes subject to the sensibilities and values of the market.

Stephen J Ball
UCL Institute of Education

Bibliography

Appadurai, A. (1996). Global ethnoscapes: Notes and queries for a transnational anthropology. In R. G. Fox (Ed.), *Interventions: Anthropologies of the present. Modernity at large: Cultural dimensions of globalization*. Minneapolis: University of Minneapolis Press.

Ball, S. J. (2012). *Global Ed. Inc.: New policy networks and the neoliberal imaginary*. London: Routledge.

Ball, S. J., Junemann, C., & Santori, D. (2017). *Edu.Net: Globalisation and education policy mobility*. London: Routledge.

Dicken, P., Kelly, P. F., & Yeung, H. W.-C. (2001). Chains and networks, territories and scales: Towards a relational framework for analysing the global economy. *Global Networks, 1*(1), 89–112.

Jessop, B. (1998). The rise of governance and the risks of failure. *International Social Science Journal, 155*(1), 29–45.

Larner, W., & Laurie, N. (2010). Travelling technocrats, embodied knowledges: Globalising privatisation in telecoms and water. *Geoforum, 41*(2), 218–226.

Lingard, B., & Sellar, S. (2014). Representing your country: Scotland, PISA and new spatialities of educational governance. *Scottish Educational Review, 46*(1), 561–567.

Marcus, G. E. (1995). Ethnography in/of the world system: The emergence of multi-sited ethnography. *Annual Review of Anthropology, 24*, 95–117.

McCann, E., & Ward, K. (2012). Assembling urbanism: Following policies and "studying through" the sites and situations of policy making. *Environment and Planning A*, *44*(1), 42–51.

Ong, A. (2007). Neoliberalism as a Mobile Technology. *Transactions of the Institute of British Geographers 32*(1), 3–8.

Peck, J., & Theodore, N. (2010). Mobilizing policy: Models, methods and mutations. *Geoforum*, *41*(1).

Roy, A. (2012). Ethnographic circulations: Space-time relations in the worlds of poverty management. *Environment and Planning A*, *44*(1), 31–41.

Stone, D. (2004). Transfer agents and global networks in the "transnationalization" of policy. *Journal of European Public Policy*, *11*(3), 545–566.

Preface – A critique of false and destructive altruism in the educational and political spheres

Marina de Avelar's original manuscript was the inaugural winner of the Young Scholars' Competition which was developed as part of the Peter Lang Series *New Disciplinary Perspectives on Education*. The text stands out as distinct in terms of its originality, its criticality and the specificity of its focus on the Brazilian context. At the same time, it is also a book which speaks to a more universal and global contemporary moment of crisis.

At root this book is a thoroughgoing critique of what we might term *false altruism*, highlighting the fatal gap between political-educational rhetoric and reality. Avelar demonstrates how the provision of public services is increasingly shared in networks of governance with public and private actors, including business and philanthropy. This effectively represents what she terms a "corporate reform of education", where education comes to be seen as a lucrative global commodity. One of the most original aspects of Avelar's study is how she combines an in-depth analysis of the specifically Brazilian context of the governance of education, while also using an incisive analytical frame to critique how new philanthropists are connected to global networks and participate in global policy mobilities. This critical analysis is both empirically complex and nuanced while maintaining a theoretical rigour and originality which is unusual. This work points to the need to continue to develop the empirical and theoretical models and resources on the Left to properly understand and critique emergent late capitalist developments, rather than simply rely on traditional Leftist theory.

It ends with a powerful plea for a democratic education in method and substance. Avelar shows unequivocally how unelected and in many ways unaccountable voices are having a significant say in determining the contemporary methods, contents and purposes of education, and this is a distorting phenomenon which, while differently expressed in national contexts, also shows a disturbing generality across international networks of comparison.

This research shows that there is an urgent need to make global and national governance of education far more inclusive and far more transparent. Once more, education must move back from private commodity and object of capitalist profit to public and socialist good. Avelar gives persuasive detail on how this contrarian reform of education (*contra* the current corporate dominance especially of tertiary university education) can impact across different spheres of political and social life. In the first instance, this reforming zeal can come from within the new philanthropy where the latter's advocacy practices can be revisited and made more accountable instead of reinforcing what Avelar's great Brazilian compatriot Paulo Freire termed the "culture of silence". Second, and also very much in the spirit of Freire's critical pedagogy, this can generate wider social and civic debates which can "redistribute voice" most especially needed amongst marginalised and disadvantaged groups. Finally, social movements and citizens themselves can both work through strengthened advocacy and activism to demand more democratic and participative processes of policy-making. The multi-disciplinary and multi-level aspect of Avelar's vision is impressive and progressive in its connecting of educational problematics to wider political and social processes and movements. Such an expansive vision gives much greater opportunity and possibility of transformation, identifying varied sites of possible action and of actors, beyond conventional politics and policy sites and beyond the university.

This latter vision of an emergent and radical democracy, often connected to recent social and youth movements (from *Occupy* to *Black Lives Matter* to Greta), is one which is shared across the texts from this Series. While speaking to specific contexts and problems, such particular depth of analysis also allows a more generalised progressive vision to evolve and be articulated against a hegemonic and destructive neoliberal consensus.

Jones Irwin and Stephen Cowden, October 2020.

Preface

The private engagement in education has interested me since the beginning of my work as an educator. In spite of directly working with companies and philanthropies acting in the Brazilian public education, I myself struggled to describe and define how the public-private relationships really worked in practice. I was dazed by the amount of meetings, seminars and events that create opportunities for networking, both amongst philanthropies and between public and private actors; confused to see public servants implementing teacher-training courses that were created and provided by multinational companies; stunned to be with representatives from foundations and governments in meetings to design programs that were later operated as public policies. These public-private relationships are convoluted, fast changing, opaque, in a way that even people involved in them struggle to understand the dynamics they are embedded in.

This intrigue of mine became even more acute when I started researching education policy whilst still working in the non-profit sector in Brazil. In my own professional experience, I could see how education governance was being done with and through complex networks, with many private actors (for-profit and non-profit), with national and international scope, working in unexpected spaces in which policy was being done. Their work concerned both service delivery through public-private partnerships as well as policymaking, through cooperation schemes and meetings (often closed-door ones) with decision-makers and state secretariats representatives. At the same time, my theoretical understanding of education did not give me tools to make sense of the participation of private actors in education and policy. Instead, I worked with the premise that policy was made by the state, within the national space, in response to social problems. I had trouble in connecting my theoretical studies with my professional experience, as I did not see my experience reflected in the books and articles I read or in classes I took, which made things even more perplexing to me.

The private engagement in education governance and policy was not only troubling to me, but it was not known by my friends and colleagues who worked in schools. They experienced education in very different spaces from the ones I was circulating in, and were unaware of the dynamics I witnessed. Contrastingly, these institutions started to gain attention in the press as "experts", and the names of corporate and philanthropic organisations operating in education started to become more familiar to people, and raised the question of how they became so influential in education.

All of this led me to research how big/new philanthropy assembled such a powerful influence over education policy, or how they worked to do so. I was interested in bridging theory and practice, looking at the mundane activities involved in the creation and maintenance of policy networks, and applying and creating theoretical and methodological tools that could help us understand this new messy and opaque scenario. Most importantly, the ultimate goal was to understand the clogs of this system, in order to try and find ways to disrupt an education that follows the "banking" logic, as Freire would put it, and foment a critical education that can truly promote social transformation. The aim was to not only make sense of this, but to share my findings with the education community, so educators can better understand how policy is being done, who the new actors are, what policy spaces are used to assemble these complex networks; and then use this in their own reflexive and critical work. By conducting an ethnographic research and focusing on mundane activities, this book aims to provide a "sneak peek" into the new ways of policymaking, which is now done in complex public-private and cross-national networks, and the role new philanthropy is playing in them. It aims to allow people to "see" what is only seen by those that participate in the policy processes described in this book.

Hence, my PhD research was dedicated to understanding how new philanthropy works to reform education, and how the state itself is being reformed. This is done by paying attention to the "labour" invested by these organisations in networks of public governance. This book presents the findings from this research, as well as contributions to theory and method to try and make sense of the emerging and complex networks that connect

Preface xxi

public and private actors. I hope it provides concepts and tools that can be useful to other researchers.

As it is common in the academic field, a considerable amount of time will have passed between data collection and the time this book reaches the hands of readers. Furthermore, the theme and object of this book is known to be dynamic and fast changing. Lastly, the global context is also noticeably changing, with the rise of ultra-liberalism and ultra-conservatism in many places, together with the COVID-19 pandemic, which consequences are yet to be seen. The data here presented depicts a key period of political transition in Brazil, which was seized by philanthropy to deepen its influence and relationships with the government. Democracy is being shaken globally, and an education that is radically committed to social justice and to equality and that promotes a critical view of power relations is urgently needed. All of this to say that the empirical data of this book will be inevitably outdated, but not the analysis, debates and discussions here presented. I believe understanding the gear working of the neoliberal project for education, which includes new philanthropy, helps us in find creative ways of building up an education that brings about social transformation. I hope this book makes a small contribution in this direction.

Finally, countless people gave me support, help and encouragement in the preparation of this book, for which I am deeply grateful. The CAPES Foundation, Ministry of Education of Brazil and the UCL IOE Centenary Doctoral Scholarship financed the research here presented. Several philanthropic organisations opened doors to me for interviews. Stephen Ball guided me through the entire process. Stephen Cowden, Jones Irwin, Bob Cowen, Sam Sellar, Tristan McCowan and Rob Higham provided invaluable feedback on previous versions, while Toni Verger, Clara Fontvilla and Dimitra Nikita Pavlina provided insight into some of the chapters. Igor gave me the emotional support that I value beyond words.

Marina Avelar
Belo Horizonte, May 2020

Introduction

Philanthropy has a growing global presence in education, despite local and regional differences. In contrast to previous forms of "giving", new philanthropy goes beyond service delivery and is now invested in influencing policy and partaking in public governance. Organisations such as the Bill and Melinda Gates Foundation and the Omidyar Network, as well as the Brazilian examples of Lemann Foundation and Todos Pela Educação, have become active actors and are engaged in diverse areas of education, in spite of their relatively small budgets (compared to domestic or international aid budgets). Drawing from the Brazilian context, this book examines *how* new philanthropy is working to participate in education policymaking and governance, and reform education, paying attention to the daily and mundane activities enacted by foundations in this effort.

New philanthropy, together with other private actors, is central in the advance of an education reform that is being globally implemented, one that employs a managerial paradigm to education and dislocates critical pedagogy approaches and traditional education actors' participation in the sector. New philanthropy is both agent and subject of change in this context (Ball & Junemann, 2012), being reworked with business-like practices while also promoting these practices and discourses in education. This global education policy (GEP) (Verger et al., 2018) agenda implies policies such as the use of standardised curricula, test-based accountability, high-stakes testing, vouchers, charter schools and others. This assemblage of market-based policies has been adopted as an "evidence-based policy agenda", which was created in Anglo-Saxon countries, embedded in the third way and finally spread globally (Sahlberg, 2016). While the work of foundations is typically portrayed in mass media as a selfless generosity, their work poses risks to a democratic education, to its contents, its purposes and how it is governed.

Departing from the "scientific philanthropy" and more traditional forms of charity, new philanthropy is markedly distinct by its use of business methods, logics and language. These organisations draw from the corporate world, venture capital and the Sillicon Valley technology companies and start-ups. While traditional philanthropy tends to focus on service delivery, operating local activities and aiming to offer services complementary to the government's ones, new philanthropy seeks to invest its capitals to disrupt, replace or reshape existing services or sectors. This creates a focus on outcomes and measurable results, a goal of reaching large-scale impact with efficiency, and a "hacker culture" that aims to disrupt entire systems and structures (Avelar & Patil, 2020; Culwell & Grant, 2018). In its work, new philanthropy blurs the boundaries between business and philanthropy, profit and social, and public and private. Part of this involves a search for "return of investment", which can be financial or social. Amongst the many actors involved in this new education arena, such as international development organisations, consultants and "thought leaders", for-profit companies, new philanthropy has a become a central one and has been able to assemble considerable amounts of capital and influence.

At the same time, the state is also changing. In shift that is referred to as from *government* to *governance* (Bevir, 2011; Rhodes, 1996), public management is increasingly being done with complex networks that connect public and private actors. In education, there has been a global surge of public-private partnerships (PPPs, Robertson et al., 2012) with diverse formats that include charter schools, low-fee schools, the provision of auxiliary services and, increasingly, policy services such as consulting. These networks, however, also include more opaque and intangible public-private relationships, such as the "revolving door" phenomenon (Lubienski et al., 2016), with people who build careers in both sectors and spam boundaries between them (Ball et al., 2017; Hogan, 2015). All of these processes are now operationalised in a global scale. Edu-businesses, new philanthropies, consultants, policymakers and other actors now travel across national boundaries, carrying with them policy ideas to reform education (Ball et al., 2017).

New philanthropy's characteristics are deeply related to its work regarding policy. Influencing policy is often regarded by these organisations as an efficient way of leveraging limited resources, reaching greater impact.

However, unlike other actors, new philanthropists tend to bypass traditional ways of policymaking and disrupt structures as they work. With this purpose of changing education policies, new philanthropists in Brazil enact three sets of practices: policy entrepreneurship, networking with public and private actors, and joining heterarchical structures of governance (or becoming "insiders" in education governance).

First, new philanthropists regard "advocacy" as being a fundamental characteristic that separates them from the work of charity, or previous forms of "giving". This involves executing or funding research projects that articulate policy ideas, which are disseminated in different forms, including the press, seminars and directly to policymakers. The efforts and funds foundations invest in advocacy are essential to support their claim of having evidence-based education projects and to be considered "experts". This is the discursive labour invested in framing, articulating and disseminating policy ideas, which is more than mere "advocacy" and is better described as "policy entrepreneurship", or the active work of framing issues and searching for opportunities to push the desired solutions.

Second, new philanthropists articulate relationships with other foundations and supporters of similar policies to mobilise the required resources for large-scale projects. They also foment relationships with decision-makers in governments and public organisations to share their ideas and push for change. This involves having many meetings, small and large, formal and informal, to animate social networks. Networks are not only an organisational structure, but creating connections, maintaining networks, is a deliberate part of foundations work to achieve greater impact in their work.

Finally, new philanthropists work with public authorities of education through collaborative partnerships and relationships (often PPPs, but not only). This is the ultimate space of education governance and reform, and thus being actively engaged in this institutional arena is an imperative goal of many new philanthropies. This work involves developing programmes that can be adopted by secretaries, the provision of consultancy services and a series of meetings to coordinate and negotiate relationships.

These activities depend on large amounts of capital and, together, enable new philanthropists to participate in education policymaking and governance. By being part of these networks, new philanthropist can disrupt education policy, promote the GEP agenda, and undermine efforts and policies of critical education.

Despite the growing role of new philanthropy in education policy and its relevance in the promotion of a global corporate agenda for education, as well as its work in the emergence of a global education policy field increasingly populated by private players, new philanthropy has been severely understudied. While considerable attention has been paid to the understanding of this global corporate agenda for education, and the work of multilateral and international organisations in this context (Gorur, Sellar, & Steiner-Khamsi, 2019), there is still a large gap regarding the work of new philanthropy in education policy. This means researchers have traditionally paid more attention to actors such as the World Bank, UNESCO, the OECD, the Inter American Bank of Development (IABD), USAid and others, but there is a growing need to also examine the work of philanthropic foundations and institutes, edu-businesses, think tanks, funding platforms and social impact businesses – "whose participation in global education policy has been systematically neglected until very recently" (Ball et al., 2017, p. 9).

Addressing this gap is now more pressing than ever. According to the Oxfam, the number of billionaires has doubled since 2008 (Oxfam, 2020). Billionaires are reaching record wealth, while extreme inequality has also reached record levels. Concomitantly, philanthropy has grown a lot in the past years. Although charity and philanthropy have a long history, three-quarters of current foundations have been created in the last twenty-five years (Johnson, 2018). Despite the challenges to collect financial data of this sector, it is estimated that philanthropic foundations have a global assets total of at least USD 1.5 trillion (Johnson, 2018). This group of wealthy elites is now called to solve social issues, amid wider shifts in public management, which are addressed with business techniques. This is done with the expectation that solving social problems can be done while also creating opportunities for business and profit – "doing well while doing good" – or that in addressing social issues returns can also be gained. In this context, education is the largest "cause" or "platform" for these philanthropic efforts (Milner, 2018). However, although philanthropy is perceived as "generous giving", and proponents argue that philanthropy has the potential to innovate in education and find creative solutions for social problems, new philanthropy has been promoting a particular reform agenda for education, one that imports corporate solutions into education and can increase inequality.

Furthermore, the COVID-19 pandemic is likely to deepen inequality and pose new social challenges. While the developments, responses and effects are yet to be seen, there is a risk that privatising solutions might be further disseminated at the expense of social justice. Some studies have documented how emergency or catastrophic situations can facilitate the adoption of pro-market policies that would otherwise experience stronger resistance (Fontdevila et al., 2017; Verger et al. 2016, 2017). The "privatisation by way of catastrophe" advances due to the crisis context, in which external agents have more space and democratic debates are more easily sidelined due the prevail of a sense of urgency. However, these episodes have "amplification potential", the reforms tend to spread beyond the geographical and temporal boundaries of the initial urgency (Verger et al., 2017). The rise of inequality and the related risks to democracy make urgent the discussion of who is making education policy and how this is being done.

With deep and diverse changes in the education arena, new methods are needed to make sense of the growing role of new philanthropy and the shifting terrain of education policy. Thus, besides contributing (empirically and theoretically) to the understanding of how new philanthropy is working to disrupt and reform education, this book also aims to contribute to the development of new methodological tools to address this issue. This book explores the use of network ethnography (Ball & Junemann, 2012), a specific form of ethnography and qualitative social network analysis, combined with techniques of "following policy" (Ball, 2016; McCann & Ward, 2012). This has enabled a focus on policy narratives and discourses in networks, as well as the daily and mundane activities enacted by new philanthropy. The book also conducts a multi-level and *"glocal"* analysis, connecting global trends to local and institutional contexts.

In sum, this book aims to address the research question of *how new philanthropy operates in the networks of education governance*; in other words, how new philanthropy is working to support an education reform that imports business practices into education. It focuses on the "mundane" work of these organisations, the daily activities or what I refer to as the "*labour*" of foundations. I analyse well-connected philanthropic organisations that are working in primary education in Brazil, which are part of a global re-scaling of education policymaking. Though having the empirical setting of Brazilian institutions, the present research analyses networks, policies and discourses that surpass national borders, and considers their "*glocal*" dynamics (or the interrelation of global and local). The book also aims to advance the theoretical and methodological debate of how we can make sense of the new complexities of education policy, namely, the new actors and new scales that are now part of how education policy works.

The first chapter explores the interplay between new philanthropy and the global reform of education, or the new "educational orthodoxy" that imports discourses and practices from the business world into the educational one. It introduces new philanthropy as a fundamental proponent of the corporate agenda for education. Whilst describing global trends, these chapters also present the Brazilian case as a local example to illustrate how these global tendencies are translated into a national context. Thus, some Brazilian new philanthropy organisations are presented, as well as how the global education policy agenda has been translated into this country. In Brazil, this agenda is mainly seen in the use of public-private partnerships, test-based accountability and standardised curriculum, and the later has been especially pushed by philanthropies.

The second chapter explores the on-going shift from government, with a hierarchical state, to governance, which operates with a mix of hierarchy, markets and networks, in which philanthropy works as part of the management of public services. It also discusses the theoretical and methodological challenges of researching and making sense of the slippery, shifting, opaque and messy network governance, with new actors participating in education policymaking, and proposed approaches in response to the shifting terrain of education. Thus, it presents the research methods and theoretical framing of the book, which are intertwined. The research here presented employs a particular version of ethnographic research called network ethnography, prominent among the policy sociology scholars who are interested in the interactions among different groups of public and private actors in education policymaking. Network ethnography combines the basic elements of ethnographic research with techniques from Social Network Analysis (SNA), and here this is combined with the idea of "following policy". The chapter also presents the employed analytical frame, which supports a multi-scalar analysis.

The following three chapters directly address the question of how new philanthropy is working in practice to reform education and how it has assembled an influential position in education policymaking. To do so, they present different aspects of the work foundations enact to reform education, and the three chapters are organised with the same structure. Each chapter analyses one modality of labour, namely, the labour to frame ideas (Chapter 3), the labour to relate (Chapter 4) and the labour to institutionalise policies and relationships (Chapter 5). The chapters follow the structure of the analytical frame, so they start with the analysis of one modality of labour within the overall Brazilian new philanthropy network, drawing mainly from five pivotal foundations and their connections. This first chapter section aims to provide an account of the wide new philanthropy context in the Brazilian education, with rich and varied examples, with analytical width. At the same time, it aims to build up analytical concepts, heuristic devices that are operated as tools to make sense of the data. Second, the chapters advance the analysis by exploring the labour modalities in the work of the Mobilisation for the National Learning Standards (MNLS). This second section offers a detailed analysis of how one significant advocacy coalition (organised by philanthropies) enacts each modality of labour. It thus provides analytical depth, with one in-depth case that connects the elements explored by the heuristic through the chapters. In other words, it illustrates how the three labour modalities are interconnected and how a single actor enacts them in different moments, places and spaces. Finally, each of the data chapters analyse the MNLS's global networks within the chapter's labour modality. The third section provides a *glocal* perspective with insights on how the global actors and discourses interact with the local and the cross-scalar aspects of the data (Peck & Theodore, 2010). Therefore, throughout these three chapters, the analysis goes back and forth, zooming in and out of networks, to connect global, national and local contexts.

The third chapter analyses the labour of new philanthropy in framing, defending and disseminating education policy ideas. To make sense of this labour modality, I draw from the policy entrepreneurship literature, especially in addressing the labour that goes into assembling legitimacy in a policy arena. It first analyses how new philanthropists have been operating as policy entrepreneurs in Brazil, creating a claim of being heard, sharing ideas in many spaces and investing different kinds of resources in this endeavour. Second, the Mobilisation for the National Learning Standards (MNLS) is introduced. The chapter explores how this group works as a policy entrepreneur and frames education inequality as a policy problem and a standard curriculum in Brazil as the appropriate policy solution. Such ideas are persistently shared in many venues and channels to gain support. Finally, MNLS's labour to frame ideas, or its policy entrepreneurship, is analysed internationally, and the chapter especially considers its use of global consultancies and benchmarking. To conclude, I ponder on how new philanthropy actively participates in policymaking through efforts of shaping policy problems and solutions. New philanthropies have been building up their position of legitimate policy actors by claiming "expertise" in education, and forging a space for corporate actors to enact policy entrepreneurship.

The fourth chapter[1] focuses on how individuals labour to animate policy networks and, within this, it carefully looks at the relevance of events for the creation and maintenance of global education policy networks. To make sense of this labour modality, I draw from the policy networks literature, namely concerning the interdependence and coordination of network actors. The chapter offers an overview of some of the pragmatic and mundane activities that are carried out for the construction of network relationships. Namely, it focuses on the interdependence of actors in networks, as well as the "on-going chains of effort" (Fenwick, 2011) to coordinate policy networks. One seminar is closely examined to offer a glimpse of the complexities, meanings and relationships present in a single event. The seminar "Education Management", organised by one corporate

---

1   Some parts of this chapter have been published at Avelar, M., Nikita, D. P., and Ball, S. J. (2018). Education policy networks and spaces of "meetingness": a network ethnography of a Brazilian seminar. In Verger, A.; Altinyelken, H.K.; Novelli, M. (Eds.). *Global Education Policy and International Development* (2nd ed.). London: Bloomsbury Publishing Plc.

institute, is analysed with an exploration of its relevance for the policy debates at the time, for the mobilisation of MNLS and the coordination of global networks.

The fifth chapter[2] resorts to "heterarchies" as a more defined concept to discuss how foundations participate in governance and closely collaborate with public authorities in the management of specific programmes and projects. I refer to these as the labour invested in institutionalising policy ideas and relationships. To make sense of this labour modality, I draw from the governance literature concerning heterarchies, namely the messy and uneven and on-going aspects of this organisational form. New philanthropies now build a series of different relationships with public authorities that vary in format and intensity. These can involve pedagogical services and materials, as well as policy-focused services, that resemble consultancies. Thus, the chapter analyses how MNLS has built a profoundly intertwined network with the Ministry of Education, creating new policymaking spaces. Finally, it discusses how Lemann Foundation made possible an international triad between MEC, the Australian Curriculum, Assessment and Reporting Authority (ACARA)[3] and MNLS, and built global policy pipelines for a policy mobility between Australia and Brazil. Together, these sections illustrate how heterarchies work in practice first by discussing how foundations and governments collaborate in many ways in governance through many partnerships, second how individuals connect public and private sectors, third how new policymaking spaces are created and fourth how global heterarchies make policy mobility possible. The chapter concludes with a reflection on how heterarchies work in practice.

To conclude, the book finishes by reflecting and connecting the previous chapters to discuss the findings of how, after all, new philanthropy

---

2 Some parts of this chapter have been published at Avelar, M., and Ball, S.J.. "Mapping new philanthropy and the heterarchical state: The Mobilization for the National Learning Standards in Brazil." *International Journal of Educational Development* (2017).

3 The Australian Curriculum, Assessment and Reporting Authority (ACARA) was created in 2008 and its "functions include development of national curriculum, administration of national assessments and associated reporting on schooling in Australia" (ACARA website).

works to partake in education policymaking and governance. It ponders on the complex networks that connect these actors and challenge our understanding of how policy is being made in practice, not necessarily offering answers, but opening up a set of issues (Lingard, Sellar, & Savage, 2014). Finally, it considers the implications for practice, focusing on the dangers for democracy in face of the growing role of philanthropic actors in education governance.

CHAPTER 1

New philanthropy and the global education reform

New philanthropy is not about "giving", it is about "social investment", "impact investment", "return of investment", "measurable impact" and win-win solutions – these are all business terms now used in philanthropy. Philanthropy increasingly operates like the market, and there is now a plethora of concepts used to describe, discuss and analyse the changes that are happening in this sector. In the context of philanthropic organisations operating in education, authors have named these new actors as *new philanthropy* (Ball & Junemann, 2011, 2012; Ball & Olmedo, 2011; Olmedo, 2016, 2017), *corporate philanthropy* (Au & Ferrare, 2015), *venture philanthropy* (Adrião, Pinto, Adrião, & Pinto, 2016; Saltman, 2010), *philanthrocapitalism* (Bishop & Green, 2010), and yet other names like strategic, entrepreneurial, catalytic, high impact or muscular philanthropy. The numerous names mirror the complexity and diversity of the empirical scenario, reflecting how it has become challenging to describe the new types of philanthropic organisations, as well as how diverse and non-homogeneous the field is.

In spite of the diversity of terms, there are some characteristics of new philanthropy that are markedly different from the twentieth century philanthropy, or "scientific philanthropy" (Saltman, 2010). Drawing from the for-profit sector practices, philanthropy is transforming in the context of new public governance, in a way that it is both an agent and subject of change. This means it is an important device in the reform of the state (Ball & Junemann, 2012), so much so that it is becoming an "explanatory variable to understand the recent changes and directions of national and international political agendas in different parts of the world" (Olmedo, 2016, p. 46). At the same time, its practices, discourses and priorities are changing by the transfer of business practices into philanthropy (Saltman, 2010) to solve social "wicked" problems (Ball & Olmedo, 2011). In spite of the philanthropic work not being new, contemporary philanthropy differs from previous modes of giving in some aspects, and "its functions and position within the social space have changed substantially" (Olmedo, 2016, p. 47).

This new philanthropy is key in the promotion of a global reform of education. In the last years, education has been subjected to similar reforms across the globe, with a discourse that has been characterised by a managerialist paradigm and increased emphasis on the delivery of "outcomes". In spite of variations, this is a "particular educational reform orthodoxy" that has emerged since the 1980s (Sahlberg, 2011), which relies on the transfer of practices and solutions from the corporate to the educational world. Many terms have been used by the authors to describe this global trend, such as the "education corporate reform" (Apple, 2006; Au & Ferrare, 2015; Freitas, 2012; Ravitch, 2011), the "global education policy" (GEP) (Ball, 2012; Rizvi & Lingard, 2010; Verger et al., 2018), the global education reform movement (GERM) (Sahlberg, 2011, 2016) and "enterprise education policies" (Burch & Smith, 2015). Despite divergences[1], it is well accepted there is a neoliberal set of education policies and discourses that is increasingly becoming global in scale, while also going through translations and re-contextualisations to particular educational contexts (Cowen, 2009; Verger, Lubienski, & Steiner-Khamsi, 2016).

This chapter discusses the interplay between new philanthropy and corporate reform of education. Both are related to the dissemination of

---

1   When comparing the terms, the concept of GERM stresses the developments of the standardisation of education and is more specific about which policies are involved in it, but it does not account sufficiently for the wider social and political contexts and actors that enable the GERM to arise. The corporate reform and the entrepreneurial reform of education, differently, stress the neoliberal context, with the economisation of education and importing of business solutions, while being somewhat less specific about what policies might look like. Finally, the GEP stresses the new scales of such policies, and understands it as a field. In this book I consider the global education reform movement (the specific education policies, the agenda) as part of the corporate reform of education (the wider shift of values and discourses in education), which is related to the emergence of the global education policy (the rescaling of education policy, with these policy solutions moving around the globe); but these are sometimes used interchangeably.

neoliberalism, and the adoption of business-like practices and discourses. While new philanthropy is perceived as a generous activity and part of the solution for persistent social problems, it also poses risks to education, which are explored in what follows.

New philanthropy: Importing business practices into philanthropy

Philanthropy has a long a history, as ancient as Greece. Throughout its history, with several development stages and trends that were intimately related its social and historical conditions, philanthropy has been deemed *new* and *innovative* a number of times. Namely, it was termed "new" for its secularisation in the sixteenth century, in the nineteenth century for its work with the state in the provision of welfare services, later in the twentieth century for its use of scientific methods, and now for the use of business practices, which have been enthusiastically celebrated as new and as innovative solutions for the most persistent social problems. At the same time, some debates have been ever present, such as the concern about the power relations embedded in giving, which criteria should be used to separate the worthy from the unworthy receivers, if faith and philanthropy should merge, and regarding the existence or irrelevance of boundaries between public and private (see Cunningham, 2016 for a historical overview).

Concerning the more recent developments, the early twentieth century philanthropy was marked by big philanthropic foundations fuelled by vast fortunes, such as The Carnegie, John D. Rockefeller Sr., the Edward Harkness and the Russell Sage Foundations. This was the so-called "scientific philanthropy". Claiming to "giving wholesale, not retail" (Sealander, 2003, p. 221), it did not give towards individual poverty, but large problems, such as the "eradication of disease or the improvement of agricultural yields" (Cunningham, 2016, p. 52). It aimed at reforming deep-rooted problems, with support of science and research. This is the rationale for universities and research institutions often being key beneficiaries, especially in the social sciences.

More recently a new "new philanthropy" emerged with the criticism of welfare states, which started in the 1970s and grew exponentially from the 1980s onwards. It coincided with a marked increase in inequality, and in the relative wealth of the very rich, as high taxation levels disappeared with the argument that they prevented investments, risk-taking and hard work. As a result, wealthy people had "ready money in the pockets" and it "gave a new confidence to philanthropists that they had a role to play and the money with which to play it" (Cunningham, 2016). Thus, this "new philanthropy" imports business practices and discourses into philanthropy, such as the logics of investment and "impact" with measurable results. Some of its proponents, enthusiasts of the potential of using business tools for social purposes, refer to it as "*philanthrocapitalism*" and see it as capable of solving the world's most persistent problems, while also having some return for it – "doing well by doing good" (Bishop & Green, 2010).

Fundamentally, what characterises the "new" new philanthropy is that its institutions now function like business (Olmedo, 2014), meaning "philanthropy is being reworked by the sensibilities of business and business methods" (Ball & Junemann, 2011, p. 657). This is done in such a way that philanthropy is not about "giving" anymore, but rather "investing". Donors are seen as investors and donations as investments that must bring return (mostly social in the case of philanthropy, but this can increasingly involve financial returns as well, with the blurring between for-profit and non-profit activities). Social projects or implementing institutions might be rated according to how secure they are for investment, or how they can guarantee outcomes, and intermediaries institutions may be responsible for rating organisations and managing the philanthropic investment portfolio of donors. Philanthropies can also operate impact investing, and fund for-profit organisations that aim to tackle social problems (or social businesses).

Drawing from business, venture philanthropy and tech companies, new philanthropy is focused on impact and measurable outcomes. To do it efficiently, it aims to leverage limited funds to reach large-scale effects, which is related to a "hacker culture", or the search for innovative ways to disrupt current structures and services (Mclean, 2020). It aims at systemic change, operating in different scales of intervention, engaging diverse actors and focusing on innovation (OECD, 2014).

In the context of the blurring between business and philanthropy, or profit and social, it is understood that charity can be profitable or, at least, can propel a company's reputation (Bishop & Green, 2010). This new language is used in new philanthropy, and is particularly clear within venture philanthropy. In spite of a lacking clear definition, venture philanthropy operates in similar ways to venture capital, usually offering the capital needed for the expansion of activities (of either non-profit or for-profit organisations) and being actively engaged with technical and management assistance (OECD, 2014). It often tackles "impact investment" – in which "the idea behind impact investing is that investors can pursue financial returns while also intentionally addressing social and environmental challenges" (Bugg-Levine & Emerson, 2011).

The win-win idea of doing philanthropy while also having "returns of investment" (social or financial) is central in new philanthropy, and is at the core of Giridharadas' (2018) criticism towards it. The author of the best seller "Winners Take All: The Elite Charade of Changing the World" describes how problematic is the idea of changing the world with a "win-win" approach, without losing any privileges or profits. He explains how changing social structures necessarily means better wealth distribution, reducing inequality, improving working conditions, increasing taxation over the super wealthy and multinationals (as some sociologists and economists have been arguing for long).

The blurring between profit and non-profit activities has made possible confounding arrangements, such as the creation of "for-profit philanthropy" (Brakman Reiser, 2018). Saltman (2018) argues that while the application of business ideals, corporate culture and private sector approach to charity are characteristics of new philanthropy and venture philanthropy, *philanthrocapitalism* takes a step further in the direction of blurring lines between for-profit and non-profit efforts and declares a for-profit company itself as a philanthropy (Saltman, 2018). Examples include the Omidyar Network and CZI, Zuckerberg's Limited Liability Company (LLC) company and so-called philanthropy. Differently from non-profit organisations, in the USA LLCs do not need to release tax reports on the use of money and can conduct lobbying (Brakman Reiser, 2018, Saltman, 2018). For example, the Omidyar Network is

> free to make for-profit investments as well as philanthropic donations to pursue its mission of "individual self-empowerment" […] "After a few years trying to be a traditional philanthropist, I asked myself, if you are doing good, trying to make the world a better place, why limit yourself to non-profit?" he explains. Although there is a separate chequebook for the foundation, his "investment team" is free to put his money in either for-profit or non-profit projects. The team's main criterion is whether the investment will further the social mission. (The business of giving, 2006)

The blurring between market and philanthropy relies on a double shift, an "economic rationalisation of giving" (Saltman, 2010) together with a "moralisation of economic action" (Shamir, 2008). The first leads to an "increasing use of commercial and enterprise models of practice within new forms of philanthropic organisation and investment (e.g. venture philanthropy, due diligence, accountable donations, micro-finance, etc.)" (Olmedo, 2016, p. 47). The second aims to foment "a kind of rehabilitation for forms of capital that were subject to 'ill repute' in the public imagination" (Ball & Junemann, 2012, p. 32). This double shift obscures how wealthy donors are actually part of the creation and maintenance of the social problems their donations claim to address, what Olmedo (2016) calls the "irony" in new philanthropy:

> portraying themselves as morally compromised agents, the new philanthro-capitalists thin out the relationships between, on the one hand, the processes through which they amass their fortunes and, on the other, the roots of the social problems that they seem willing to address. That is, there seems to be no critical reflection on the "contribution" of capitalism, and, within it, the business practices of their own companies worsening of old and the creation of new forms of inequality and social injustice across the globe. (Olmedo, 2016, p. 48)

Besides, and resulting from, the central characteristic of translating business into philanthropy, new philanthropy has some marked practices. First, "givers" are directly involved in the philanthropic action. New philanthropists adopt a more "hands-on approach" and want to be personally involved in decisions (Ball & Junemann, 2012). Jorge Paulo Lemann is an unarguable example of personal involvement. The richest Brazilian citizen is among the richest people in the world, with an estimate net worth of more than USD 24 billion (at the end of 2019), and invests one third of his time in philanthropic activities at the foundations Lemann and *Estudar*[2] ("Study"). He and his two business partners personally take part in the selection of scholarship grantees, who will receive financial support to study in "global top ranking universities" (Correa, 2013). Lemann, Harvard alumnus himself, also makes use of his personal network in his philanthropic work. He acts as a "kind of ambassador" of *Fundação Estudar* in other countries. It is in great part due to his contacts in foreign universities that *Estudar* regularly brings representatives of elite universities to offer lectures to Brazilian students. For instance, in 2011 the president of Harvard, Drew Faust, went to Brazil at the invitation of Estudar (Correa, 2013).

This direct involvement is a considerable difference between scientific and new philanthropy, as "there was a distance between the donors and the end uses made of the donated money in education—once given, the money was not closely controlled and directed in its uses" (Saltman, 2010, p. 63). New philanthropists want to ensure funding is used in ways and for causes they support, in an attempt to have greater control over how the money is spent, making sure it promotes the intended reform (Saltman, 2010, p. 72). As a result, new philanthropists have become important and active actors in all policy processes, including design, negotiations and delivery processes, which implicate in the reorganisation of public services, civic action and community development (Olmedo, 2016, p. 47). There has also been a larger concentration in philanthropic funding and action, because in spite of the hegemonic role played by philanthropy in the twentieth century, it was not unified in its approaches. Instead, it "offered funding for a wide variety of initiatives and projects that were not restricted to the conservative side of the political spectrum" (Saltman, 2010, p. 72).

The mobilisation and use of one's own capitals, in its many forms, is also part of the hands-on approach. New philanthropists, like Bill and Melinda Gates or Jorge Paulo Lemann, are willing to mobilise their own "economic, cultural and social capitals in order to pursue their charitable agendas" (Olmedo, 2014, p. 585). In mobilising their different resources, elite actors who engage in philanthropy are called hyperagents by Schervish

---

2   Foundation created by him and his two partners, Sicupira and Telles.

(2005; 2003), which have "the enhanced capacity of wealthy individuals to establish control of the conditions under which they and others live" (Schervish, 2005, p. 62). In other words, hyperagents are "individuals who can do what it would otherwise take a social movement to do" (Bishop & Green 2010, p. 51).

In an illustrative example of hyperagency, in 2015 there was a conflict between Viviane Senna and education associations[3]. Viviane Senna, sister of the racer Ayrton Senna, is the president of Instituto Ayrton Senna, one of the biggest institutes in Brazil, which is active in every state of the country. She is part of Todos pela Educação governance board, is influential in the national press and was listed amongst the "Ten most powerful businesswomen in Brazil" by Forbes. She is a clear example of how philanthropic work has been turned into a "status symbol" (Handy, 2007), allowing Viviane Senna to be a well-regarded public figure. On June 2015, in an interview with Folha[4] (Brazilian newspaper) and the BBC[5], she stated education is "still based on opinions rather than being 'scientific based'". Less than a month later, six public education organisations replied in an open letter critiquing her statements. A small note was published in Folha, but not the entire content of the letter or an interview with a representative. Viviane Senna, as a "hyperagent", could have a presence in the press, and have her voice heard, in a way that not even a social movement – with six representative entities – could. This is also an example of how "new philanthropy is taking a more protagonist role in political terms, which is already contributing to the re-dispersal of political and moral authority" (Olmedo, 2016, p. 48).

The focus on "return" leads to an extreme attention to measurable outcomes. Evaluations and metrics to measure and demonstrate impact became a widespread practice among foundations. Institutional reports exhibit the results of assessments and are used to attract new "investors" and offer accountability to donors (Ball & Junemann, 2011). As Ball and

---

3 <http://www1.folha.uol.com.br/educacao/2015/06/1643231-educacao-e-baseada-em-achismos-nao-em-ciencia-diz-viviane-senna.shtml>.
4 <http://www1.folha.uol.com.br/paineldoleitor/2015/07/1653031-presidentes-de-associacoes-de-educacao-protestam-contra-viviane-senna.shtml>.
5 <http://www.bbc.com/portuguese/noticias/2015/06/150525_viviane_senna_ru>.

Junemann (2012) put it, new philanthropies now "use forms of business research and due diligence to identify or vet potential recipients to monitor the impacts and effects of donations on social problems" (p. 52). Decisions are made based on the "idea that resources should be used in a targeted and rational way based on data in order to identify and scale successful social programmes" (Rogers, 2011, p. 378). In the past few years, this focus on outcomes has also led to the emergence of new forms of financing social initiatives, with "results-based financing", which refers to the payment being conditional on achieving a measurable outcome, instead of the traditional format of funding inputs and processes (Oxman & Fretheim, 2009).

New philanthropy also differentiates itself from previous modes of giving with global action. Both the agenda and work of philanthropic organisations have been globalised. These institutions act upon global "grand challenges", which draw from development agendas, with scalable solutions that are "applied independently of context as generic, technical solutions" (Olmedo, 2014, p. 587). And "perhaps, nothing succinctly illustrates this better than the incessant call for 'what works' (Saltman, 2010, p. 74). The search for "what works" creates and reinforces global networks as new philanthropists have the wish to tackle "grand challenges" by using "silver bullets" (Ball & Olmedo, 2011, p. 85). In this context, "silver bullets" focus on generic solutions that can be scalable and implemented in spite of local, national and international contexts (Ball & Olmedo, 2011). As foundations move, they create "generative nodes", or spaces that create connections between public and private actors, which are "new sites of 'policy mobilisation' and 'globalising microspaces' that operate between and beyond traditionally defined areas of policy formulation, such as localities, regions and nations" (Ball & Olmedo, 2011, p. 86).

The globalisation of agendas and solutions is related to new philanthropy's global reach through the international connection of elites as well, with technologies of communication and travel that made it easier to sustain a "networked life" (Urry, 2003). The spaces of "meetingness" (Urry, 2007, see Chapter 4) are fundamental for the activation of global networks through formal and informal meetings. In this scenario, new philanthropy and policy networks have a global reach and ideas and discourses flow, in and out and around Brazil. Besides new actors, the GEP and the work of new philanthropy bring about new scales into education policy. In the past years, the framing of policy discourses and texts has extrapolated the nation, in a way that now the "context of policy writing" is multi-layered across the local, national and global (Lingard & Rawolle, 2010, 2011; Rizvi and Lingard, 2010). With disputes and power struggles, this "field is far from a flat terrain", actors have different capacities of mobilising different types of capital, which are needed to advance their interests and ideas (Verger et al., 2018, p. 9). In the GEP field, some actors have greater chances in framing policy problems and solutions, namely "key international players and policy entrepreneurs, *with the capacity to transcend different scales at any moment*, have more chance of introducing their ideas, preferences and languages in this field" (Verger et al., 2018, p. 9, added emphasis). This rescaling of policies, and the "capacity to transcend scales" is explored and made explicit throughout the chapters in the second part of this book. The third session of each chapter, which makes explicit the multi-scalar and global work of some foundations, connecting cities and schools, policymakers and new philanthropists in Brazil, the USA, England, Australia and other countries.

New philanthropy and education policy

Finally, a fundamental change in philanthropy concerns how working with the state and acting in policymaking became a major goal of new philanthropists. Whilst previously philanthropic work would be mainly circumscribed to service delivery, like in traditional NGO's work, foundations now participate in policymaking work of various kinds, working in the "context of influence" and "context of text production" (Bowe & Ball, 1992). They have become key political actors that go beyond delivery and work in "advocacy and negotiation of policy processes" (Olmedo, 2014, p. 583). Part of this interest of new philanthropists on policymaking is based on "the idea that the wealthy, particularly the super wealthy, should take greater responsibility for using their wealth for the common good" (Rogers, 2011, p. 378), or the "moralisation of economic action" (Shamir, 2008) explored previously. In this idea, private institutions must work to solve "wicked problems" (Ball & Junemann, 2012). As the former Executive Secretariat of GIFE said: "In other words, the solutions will go through a new balance in this composition between public and private" (Interview, GIFE, 2016).

The corporate values of new philanthropists have implications for the way they work and at the same time their agenda in education. New philanthropy has been promoting a specific reform assemblage that is now seen globally. The corporate reform of education has been supported by new philanthropy, and is at the core of its agenda for education. Foundations not only "talk the talk", but also "walk the walk", they "practice what they preach" by operating with the corporate practices they aim to ensue schools with. In fact, this connection is historically set, as the beginning of the shift from scientific to venture philanthropy strongly coincides with the wider neoliberal shift in education (Saltman, 2010, p. 70). There is a deep alignment between the corporate reform of education and new philanthropists, as both have a focus on "strategy, efficacy, and method, eschewing underlying concerns with the overarching values and goals of public schooling as well as with the contested ideological positions animating particular reform initiatives" (Saltman, 2010, p. 74).

This global education reform is part of the wider context of neoliberalism, here understood as a theory and a set of policies, which have both material and discursive consequences. First, as a theory, it proposes that "human well-being can be best advanced by the maximisation of entrepreneurial freedoms within an institutional framework characterised by private property rights, individual liberty, unencumbered markets, and free trade" (Harvey, 2007, p. 22). Second, it is also:

> an ensemble of economic and social policies, forms of governance, and discourses of ideologies that promote self-interest, unrestricted flows of capital, deep reductions in the cost of labor, and sharp retrenchment of the public sphere. Neoliberals champion privatisation of social goods and withdrawal of government from provision for social welfare on the premise that competitive markets are more effective and efficient. (Lipman, 2013, p. 6)

This means the current education reform reframes and reworks structures and discourses. Regarding the first, the management structures are reorganised, in a way that the neoliberal state is departing its commitment and authority over public education, leaving it to be occupied by a network that is populated by corporate interests related to the neoliberal project (Au & Ferrare, 2015, this aspect is further explored in Chapter 3). Here, marketplace principles are the model for public management and public policy, where third-party organisations have a more central role, which is a "government-endorsed role in designing, providing and evaluating government services. Government agencies become nodes in a market-driven network of vendors" (Lipman, 2013, p. 193). As for the discursive shifts, neoliberalism is not only manifested in macro social structures, but there is also "a neoliberal common sense". There is a reshaping of the discourse of education along the lines of businesses and narrowing of education purposes to economics. This advances "policies guided by free market assumptions" and "funding of organisations and projects in line with a neoliberal policy agenda" (Au & Ferrare, 2015, p. 9). The discourses, or the ideals and common sense, of education are also reworked in this context, where "market principles of competition and consumerism" have become "accepted policy strategies for improving social outcomes" (Burch & Smith, 2015, p. 193).

In practice, in a broad agreement amongst scholars and activists[6], it is understood that these reforms usually involve outcomes-based management that use standardising teaching and competitive evaluation with high-stakes testing, deregulation of educational labour practices, access to public education as market, defunding public education, private accumulation of public money via marketisation, and reliance on non-democratically elected bodies to determine and implement education policy. This reform agenda can be traced back to the outcomes-based education, which became popular in the 1980s and was later followed by standard-based education policies in the 1990s, especially in Anglo-Saxon countries. Policymakers believed that "setting clear and sufficiently high performance standards for schools, teachers, and students will necessarily improve the quality of desired outcomes" (Sahlberg, 2011, p. 178). Consequently, from this belief were introduced centrally prescribed curricula with detailed performance

---

6   See e.g. Apple, 2006; Au and Ferrare, 2015; Fabricant and Fine, 2013; Hursh, 2000; Lipman, 2013; Saltman, 2010, among others.

targets, external testing and evaluation systems. Literacy and numeracy are seen as core subjects in the curriculum, and central targets of policies and tests, leading to a curriculum narrowing. The performance of schools then became closely attached to processes of inspecting, accrediting, ranking, rewarding or punishing with test-based accountability policies. Arguably, this has led to increased control of schools, with a narrowing of teachers' autonomy and creativity and the reliance over low-risk teaching methods (Sahlberg, 2011). In sum, the GEP revolves around the transfer of ideas from the corporate to the educational world, with a standardisation of education and test-based accountability, which lead to a focus on the subjects of literacy and numeracy, low-risk teaching and increased control of schools (Sahlberg, 2011).

It is important to stress, however, that the GEP is manifested in different places with different characteristics, it can be materialised in different formats, "as it moves, it morphs" (Cowen, 2009). This policy assemblage does not travel in complete packages, there is no comprehensive and single list of policies and practices that ultimately define this new educational orthodoxy. Nor is there a "threshold or objective criteria for determining the point at which a reform trend becomes a GEP" (Edwards & Moschetti, 2019, p. 2). Instead, this is a trajectory of reform, with some key discourses, ideas, arguments, rationales and narratives about education, about its role in society and how it should be managed. At its core lies the use of corporate techniques to education, as Saltman describes:

> The cultural aspect of corporatizing education involves transforming education on the model of business, describing education through the language of business and the emphasis on the "ideology of corporate culture" that involves making meanings, values, and identifications compatible with a business vision for the future. The business model appears in schools in the push for standardization and routinization in the form of emphases on standardization of curriculum, standardized testing, methods-based instruction, teacher de-skilling, scripted lessons, and a number of approaches aiming for "efficient delivery" of instruction. The business model presumes that teaching, like factory production can be ever-more speeded up and made more efficient through technical modifications to instruction and incentives for teachers and students, like cash bonuses. (Saltman, 2010, p. 22)

This agenda has been strongly supported by its proponents and advocates as being "evidence based" and technical (as opposed to "political" or "ideological"). However, the findings and evidence around these policies are at least inconclusive, and there is evidence these policies can have undesired and harmful effects (Verger et al., 2018). For example, among the many identified issues raised, GEP policies and their market mechanisms often lead to increase of inequality and social segregation, reduction of collaboration between schools and teachers, curriculum narrowing and transfer of public funds to private organisations and investors (Au, 2007, 2009, 2016; Au & Ferrare, 2015; Carnoy & Marachi, 2020; Darling-Hammond, 2007; Edward & Moschetti, 2019; Freitas, 2012; Miller & Almon, 2009; Nichols & Berliner, 2007; Ravitch, 2016; Sahlberg, 2016; Saltman, 2012, 2018). These policy effects illustrate how the use of business assumptions to public matters is problematic, as these assumptions are not "universally beneficial". Instead, they only benefit some, the ones at "the top of the business", contradicting how public institutions "have a mandate of being universally beneficial" (Saltman, 2010, p. 78).

At the same time the GEP reworks the "content" of education policies, the methods of policymaking are also changing, within a congested and disputed arena in which policy is treated as a technical matter, not political. This approach leads to the exclusion of traditional education actors, such as teachers and unions (Ball et al., 2017). Thus, democracy and social justice are often raised as extremely relevant issues in the context of harmful market-based policies and growing participation of corporate actors in policy and governance. The new policy networks with private actors create layers of "corporate policy influence that are complex and connected to large political and institutional forces" (Burch & Smith, 2015, p. 205). In these spaces, there are some "deeply disturbing state-corporate ties that can serve to 'lock in' the privileging of commercial interests as part of 'public' policy". These ties overlap in many points, and create commercial spaces in education settings and, thus, work "against the democratic purposes of education" (Burch & Smith, 2015, p. 191).

Amid the complex and opaque networks, that connect public and private actors, there are few, if any, mechanisms for accountability and civic control:

> one of the central issues with this type of governance by corporations, corporate interests, and non-governmental organisations is that there is absolutely no mechanism for holding them accountable for what they do to public institutions, including public education. [...] They are reconstructing public education along the lines of the neoliberal model, with many private entities making massive profits at the expense of public assets, and we have no way to recoup our losses and fix what they have done. This is the nature of network governance in the neoliberal state. (Au & Ferrare, 2015, p. 10)

Hence, in spite of recognising the importance of understanding new philanthropists' motivations, this research is concerned about the *hows* of new philanthropy's work, not the *whys*. I agree with Saltman who argues that "the intentions of the venture philanthropists are less important than the *effects of their actions on public education*—how it transforms not only the control and ownership of it, but the very meaning it might have and its role in a society committed to public democratic values" (Saltman, 2010, p. 41).

As it is explored throughout this book, the GEP agenda has been supported by private actors, specially philanthropy. New philanthropists tend to support education projects that draw from a corporate worldview, leading to a continuous expansion of neoliberal language, practices and reasoning in public education. This includes a growing use of business terms to describe education policies such as "choice, competition, efficiency, accountability, monopoly, turnaround, and failure" (Saltman, 2010, p. 64). Education is treated as a "social investment" that requires a business plan, quantitative measures and be brought to scale (Saltman, 2010). New philanthropists, however, disregard fundamental differences between foundations and schools, especially the social purpose of education. All of this means that a fundamental characteristic of new philanthropy in education is that the "public and civic purposes of public schooling are redescribed" in "distinctly private ways" (Saltman, 2010, p. 64).

In this endeavour, new philanthropy concomitantly engenders "new methods of policy" and introduces new policy programmes (Olmedo, 2016). It involves new policy methods and contents, policy *hows* and *whats*. Regarding the methods or *hows*, new philanthropies engage "new players to the field of social and education policy, repopulating and reworking existing policy networks" (Olmedo, 2016, p. 49). So while new philanthropies operate in the education field, they rework the field itself and its discourses, and provide "legitimacy to the role of business in the solution of social problems" (Olmedo, 2016, p. 49). Concomitantly, they directly participate in designing and delivering of policy programmes. In this regard, "new philanthropy is at the forefront of a right-wing movement to corporatise education at multiple levels" (Saltman, 2010, p. 1), with a reform programme that was presented in the first chapter. However, there is an imbalance between the power and controversy of the super wealthy in policy-making and the attention this has been receiving in research. As Rogers (2011) put it: "The most controversial aspects of philanthrocapitalism are related to the policy-making and agenda setting powers of the new global elite" (p. 377). Still, there is a relevant growth of studies being conducted about the topic.

Although new philanthropy has become a fundamental policy actor, and has been receiving attention from the press and public in general, it has not been receiving enough attention from researchers. The investigation of the work of new philanthropists in the governance of education has been limited to approaches that are "looking at only some of the places in which policy is being done" (Ball, 2012, p. XII). As a result, education studies still "pay little attention to the role of advocacy and philanthropy networks (apart from NGOs) in the flow and influence of policy ideas, but these groups and individuals often have very specific and very effective points of entry into political systems" (Ball, 2010, p. 162).

Making sense of the participation of new philanthropists in networks of education governance is relevant not only for theoretical purposes, but also for strengthening democracy. Contradictorily, "educational philanthropy that appears almost exclusively in mass media and policy circles as selfless generosity poses significant threats to the democratic possibilities and realities of public education" (Saltman, 2010, p. 1).

The corporate agenda for education replaces and pushes away the critical approach to education, in content and in political participation in the education policy arena. The focus on measurable outcomes – that leads to standardised practices, conservative pedagogy, narrowing of the curriculum – replaces a holistic view of education, with its commitment to liberating people with a critical view of the power relations around them. As Saltman describes:

> Holistic, critical, and socially oriented approaches to learning that understand pedagogical questions in relation to power are eschewed as corporatization instrumentalizes knowledge, disconnecting knowledge from the broader political, ethical, and cultural struggles informing interpretations and claims to truth while denying differential material power to make meanings. (Saltman, 2010, p. 22)

A corporate approach to education creates a fundamental tension (or irony, as Olmedo, 2016 says), where children are not to be taught to think critically about the power relations present in society, which are often maintained by the very organisations/companies/foundations that propose such education reforms. They "offer no way to critically analyse such representations and the visions and values that they propose" (Saltman, 2010).

In this managerial approach, there is no space for a critical pedagogy that "insists on the centrality of the questions about the purposes of these institutions, who designs and decides what is taught, who is permitted access". One that is "fundamentally concerned with the ethical basis of teaching and learning" (Cowden & Ridley, 2019). As Freire puts it, "it would be naive to expect the dominant classes to develop a form of education that allows dominated classes to perceive social injustices in a critical way" (Freire, 2018). It important to stress this tension between projects and agendas, because whilst it is assumed in critical pedagogy that education is inherently political (Freire, 2018), the GEP supporters, including new philanthropy, argue it is solely "evidence based", a technical matter. Additionally, the narrative that new philanthropy is a generous attitude and part of a collective effort towards the common good covers the deep differences in social and educational agendas and projects, and the consequent intense disputes in the education arena.

Indeed, in spite of the global advance of this corporate reform agenda, its growth happens amid resistance, and even a renewed interest in critical approaches. The present research analyses the work of new philanthropy in promoting a corporate reform of education, which results in a lack of analysis of dissident voices as a "self-evident and self-fulfilling" (partly due to the method and approach, see Chapter 3) (Ball et al., 2017, p. 9). These voices are nonetheless present in other places and spaces, and include teachers, students, parents, workers' unions, scholars, journalists, activists, NGOs and other third sector organisations (sometimes even funded or related to corporate philanthropists), that work for alternative and more democratic education projects. Thus, although this research does not include the analysis of resistance to the corporate and philanthropic actors and networks, it is fundamental to temper the present account with a brief note concerning the resistance to such corporate reforms described so far in Brazil.

First, in spite of privatising efforts and advances, public education (as offered by the state) in Brazil is still free of charge and available to all. This is established by the Brazilian legislation through the Constitution and the fundamental education bill LDBEN 1996. This is the case throughout the entire educational system, from early years education to universities.

Second, many actors, namely teachers, students, unions and researchers have publicly displayed resistance to corporate policies (such as funding cuts and the current curriculum reform). As an example, a series of teacher strikes have been frequently organised all over the country and in different spheres[7] (Basic and Higher Education). Students have also organised protests, especially through the "occupation" of schools. This form of protest gained prominence after students occupied more than 200 schools in São Paulo in 2015 to resist a regional reform of middle schools that would result in a higher ratio of students per teacher, as well as a federal reform of middle schools curriculum[8]. In the first year of the Bolsonaro government, the largest protests in the countries were organised by higher

7   <https://novaescola.org.br/conteudo/10655/greves-de-professores-atingem-5-estados>.
8   <https://www1.folha.uol.com.br/saopaulo/2016/07/1787761-fortalecidos-apos-ocupacoes-secundaristas-de-sp-renegam-entidades-estudantis.shtml>.

education teachers and students[9]. Teacher unions and organisations such as the Brazilian Campaign for the Right to Education (BCRE) have continuously worked to resist the policies described so far, while also promoting and proposing alternative ones. A central example has been the BCRE's long work in the area of education financing and their project of the *Custo Aluno Qualidade Inicial* and *Custo Aluno Qualidade* ("initial student-cost quality" and "student-cost quality"). These initiatives bring about a different way of conceptualising the education budget, focusing on the cost of the necessary inputs for quality education, opposing views of austerity and a reductionist focus on outcomes.

Third, there is evidence of struggles and disputes within the government itself, including at federal spheres. For instance, after a long process of formulation, Cesar Callegari, former president of the Learning Standards Commission at the CNE, quit the position in July 2018[10]. He claimed the new learning standards would increase inequality in Brazil and argued it should be completely reviewed and discussed (see Chapter 6 for further discussion on the relationships between the Ministry of Education and MNLS amid the curriculum reform).

Finally, researchers are continuously writing about the corporate reform of education, aiming to analyse the dangers and pitfalls of these policies. With a critical approach to education studies, scholars in Brazil present strong criticisms towards these policies and are often engaged in social activism.

In sum, when considering the widespread efforts of new philanthropies in education, one might think this is a complete "take-over" or hegemony of private actors in education governance. These forms of resistance are a reminder that this is not the case. Nonetheless, it is also relevant to stress that in face of this resistance, new philanthropies have put in place extraordinary efforts to circumvent democratic processes and accomplished remarkable results, as the following chapters expose.

---

9   <https://brasil.elpais.com/brasil/2019/05/15/politica/1557950158_551237.html>.
10 <https://avaliacaoeducacional.files.wordpress.com/2018/06/carta-aos-conselheiros-do-cne.pdf>.

New philanthropy and education reform in Brazil

Since the 1990s there has been a growth in number and relevance of the third sector in Brazil. In spite of similarities between the Brazilian and US philanthropy (especially regarding the shift towards new philanthropy), the overall field is quite different, which must be taken into account during analysis. Some of the main differences concern the amount of funding that is mobilised, the corporate nature and type of investment done by organisations, which are discussed below. Besides this, there are also differences concerning terminologies. Instead of the term "philanthropy", the most commonly used term in Brazil is "social investment" or "private social investment" (Hartnell & Milner, 2018). This is the term used by the Group of Corporate Foundations and Institutes (GIFE in Portuguese). GIFE became institutionalised in 2009, after being an informal group since 1989, and it brings together 129 institutions including businesses and philanthropy from corporate, independent, family and community backgrounds. This organisation, which is central in the Brazilian corporate third sector, adopted this term in 1995 to distinguish the "impact" activities from the charitable ones (referred to as "philanthropic" at the time).

The philanthropic field in Brazil mobilises a relevant amount of resources, but it is much smaller than the US one. Together, the 113 GIFE survey respondents have invested BRL 2.9 billion a year, or USD 830 million at the currency exchange of 2016 (almost 20 per cent less than in 2014) (GIFE[11] Survey, 2016). These values are considerable, although much smaller than the amount of USD 60.1 billion invested in the USA in 2014 by US foundations, which increased to USD 62.8 billion in 2016 (Foundation Centre). Nonetheless, the budget mobilised by philanthropy in Brazil is

---

[11] GIFE surveys its members biannually, which is one of the few instruments available to assess the third sector in Brazil. Since 2016, GIFE publishes a key facts report, comparing some data regarding philanthropy in Brazil and the USA, using data from the Foundation Centre (USA). The data here presented also includes some comparison between the Brazilian and US scenario, as most of the literature produced about philanthropy and philanthropy in education comes from that country.

50 per cent larger than the budget of the Ministry of Culture (which was BRL 1.9 billion, but the Ministry of Culture has been dismantled by the Bolsonaro government). In spite of more than 25 per cent of GIFE members having a budget greater than USD 8.5 million in 2014, the total investment is quite concentrated. The top 13 investors[12] (with a budget larger than USD 20 million) accounted to about two-third of the total at that year. Furthermore, the top investor of that year, not disclosed, has invested the prominent value of BRL 537,311,200.00 (approx. USD 1.69 billion). This last information was not available in the 2016 survey.

Second, philanthropy in Brazil is much more corporate than in the USA, and grant-making is not a disseminated practice. In Brazil, 53 per cent of organisations are corporate associations and foundations, against only 3 per cent in the USA (GIFE Survey, 2016). Contrastingly, in the USA 92 per cent are independent and family foundations. This information becomes even more relevant to the theme of this book when paired with the data regarding how this money is invested. While in the USA most philanthropic money is distributed as grants (96 per cent primarily fund the project of civil society organisations), the GIFE members have a markedly "hands-on approach". Only 16 per cent of respondents primarily fund other civil society organisations, 43 per cent run their own programmes and 41 per cent do both. Between 2014 and 2016, donations to civil society were reduced to 21 per cent of the social investment – from BRL 894 million to only BRL 594 million. According to the Network of Philanthropy for Social Justice (Rede de Filantropia para a Justiça Social), the reasons for the philanthropies' preference for running their own programs involve the lack of trust regarding the NGO sector, the wish to have direct control over resources and the taxation over donations.

Finally, amongst GIFE's members, 84 per cent have education as their priority investment (against 80 per cent in the US), 89 per cent claim their work is somehow related to public policy and 58 per cent aim at influencing or supporting policymaking. Regarding the ones that invest more

---

12   More than BRL 100 mi: one company, two family foundations, two corporate foundation. Between BRL 50 to 99,99 mi: two companies and six corporate foundations.

than USD 20 million, 75 per cent claim to aim at policy (GIFE, 2014). In sum, there is considerable social investment from philanthropy in Brazil, which is mainly focused on education and aims to influence policy. Along these lines, the former Executive Director of GIFE argued in an interview that "to understand the social investment in education is to understand the private social investment in Brazil" (Interview, GIFE, 2016). This exposes how these new philanthropic organisations have a considerable budget that is mobilised to steer education policy.

In spite of data limitations in this comparison (due sampling and definition of terms), there are some reflections that can be made. The Brazilian philanthropy is far more corporate and hands-on than the American one, which is more family-based and grant-making. The contrasting profiles reminds us that although network governance and philanthropy are growing internationally, they are manifested in different places with different characteristics, thus raising different issues and concerns. Besides the usual matters around philanthropy, regarding elite's power and if it contributes to social change or social reproduction, the Brazilian profile makes these debates more pressing. In Brazil, philanthropy seems to be about companies and businessman "investing" in their own "philanthropic" activities that follow their own agendas, which highlights issues around accountability, transparency and democracy. All of this also raises challenges for research, as to how we can investigate and understand this field. While in the US researchers have been "following" the money, investigating who receives philanthropic grants, in Brazil it is imperative that one studies the work of foundations, as they implement their own projects. Here, the sharing of "labour" – collaborating in networks – is just as important as sharing money, which reaffirms the need to analyse the work and practices of the biggest organisations directly, as this book does, instead of advocacy funds.

In this context, some philanthropic organisations are central in the education arena, as network nodes that are active in framing debates, connecting institutions and people, and investing considerable amounts of money in their own efforts. These organisations will be analysed throughout the book, and are presented in Table 1.

Table 1. New philanthropic organisations in Brazil

Todos pela Educação (TPE)	Todos pela Educação (TPE) was created in 2006 and claims to aim to "contribute to ensuring an education with quality in Brazil until 2022 (the 200th anniversary of independence)". In 2014, it became an OSCIP – an "*Organisaçao da Sociedade Civil de Interesse Público*" (Civil Society Organisation with Public Interest). Claiming to be "a movement from the Brazilian society", the TPE is not connected to any political party and has representatives from all social sectors, including public managers, educators, parents, students, researchers, media representatives, businessmen and professionals from social organisations that are "committed to the guarantee to the right to quality education". TPE, unlike the other foundations, does not maintain or execute any projects of its own (with public-private partnerships, for example). Instead, it focuses on policymaking, and operates like a think tank. It was created to gather different social sectors in favour of education, but has established itself as a corporate movement (Rossi et al., 2017, p. 360).
Lemann Foundation	Lemann Foundation is non-profit family organisation that was created in 2002 by the businessman Jorge Paulo Lemann, who is currently the richest Brazilian citizen and was amongst the 30 richest billionaires in the world in 2019, according to Forbes. He has graduated in economy at Harvard University and worked for the Credit Suisse. His fortune was built with different investments, but he is currently known as one of the main holders of AB InBev, the biggest beer company in the world (with Belgium Interbrew and Budweiser). He usually does business with his two partners Marcell Hermann Telles and Carlos Alberto Sicupira, also amongst the richest Brazilian citizens and his collaborators in philanthropy. The foundation develops and supports "innovation programmes in education", does research to "support public policy", offers training to education professionals, maintains networks of like-minded professionals, amongst other activities. Its goal is to contribute to "innovative and high quality solutions for education, aiming to reach 30 million people, more than 200,000 teachers that will ensure learning for every student, and 65 leaders, that will promote social transformation of high impact" (Lemann Foundation website, 2018). It has a sector to influence education policy, which argues that "in order to information and evidence is always accessible to these who do education policy, here we make available research and data to support the daily practice of public managers ahead of education".

(continued)

Table 1. Continued

Ayrton Senna Institute (ASI)	Created in 1994, the Ayrton Senna Institute has worked with more than 1300 cities in Brazil through public-private partnerships, or 25 per cent of Brazilian municipalities (Comerlatto & Caetano, 2013). After the death of the Formula 1 pilot Ayrton Senna, the institute was created and directed by his sister, Viviane Senna. The institute claims to act through "social solutions directed for human development, research and production of knowledge to enhance the quality of education". The organisation has a council made of several corporate sectors in national and international level (Peroni e Cormerlato, 2017). In its "education solutions", the organisation uses large-scale solutions to entire cities and states, with a control of teaching method and contents that is supported by online management system. With global connections, the ASI is integrated in the education network of UNESCO, as Chair in Education and Human Development (since 2004).
Unibanco Institute	Created in 1982, the Unibanco Institute is one of the largest foundations operating in the Brazilian education. It is a corporate philanthropy, whose funding comes from an endowment managed by the bank Itaú. It is focused on "improving the results and production of knowledge about high schools". So the organisation "produces and implements management solutions – in the education system, in the school and in the classroom" (Unibanco Institute website, 2018). It offers teaching methodologies, as well as school management technologies, mostly focused on secondary education. The institute has been working towards the endeavour to transform its programmes into public policy, by becoming a Federal Government partner, and then expanding it to the entire country. Through public-private partnerships, its programs are adopted and implemented with state level governments.

Natura Institute	Natura, a Brazilian beauty products company, created the Natura Institute in 2010 with the rationale that "every company has the commitment with society that goes beyond its corporate action" (Natura's website, 2018). The Institute aims to enlarge the social investments of the company that have been enacted since the 1990s (Natura's website).[a] The institute's funding come from the selling of one line of products named "Crer para Ver" (Believe to See). It works with education projects through public-private partnerships and supporting third-party initiatives. It focuses on "improving educational systems" by "incorporating best practices into the Brazilian education systems, also supporting the re-design of public education management systems" (Natura's website). It also aims to "radicalise education models" by proposing "innovation in educational practices", and to "mobilise society for education", "being a pro-active actor that articulates, connects and integrates an immense network of relationships that works for life-long learning" and "a network that waves together and aims at a legitimate transformation of education" (Natura's website).
Mobilisation for the National Learning Standards (MNLS)	The Mobilisation for the National Learning Standards defines itself as a "non governmental group of education professionals", which has been advocating for a national standard learning standard since 2013. It promotes "debates, studies and researches with head teachers, teachers and students, and investigates cases of success in many countries" (MNLS website). It is funded by the Itaú BBA bank, the Lemann Foundation and the Natura Institute, and brings together a network with representatives of new philanthropy and business, as well as representatives from federal, state and municipal governments. In spite of being organised and funded by private organisations, the MNLS has worked as a boundary-spanning node in the learning standards policy network.

[a] <https://www.natura.com.br/a-natura/sociedade/instituto-natura>.

In Brazil, the corporate reform of education does not sustain a privatising model with charter and academy schools, or vouchers found in places like the USA, England or Chile (or not yet). Nor does it focus on low-fee schools found in low-income countries (see Srivastava and Walford, 2016; Srivastava, 2016a, 2016b). However, the GEP in Brazil does include the key characteristics of a results-oriented education management, with a standardisation of education, large-scale assessment and focus on STEM disciplines (Arelaro, 2007; Krawczyk & Vieira, 2008).

Since the 1990s, corporate education policies have been gaining currency in the country. In spite of particularities of the Brazilian state[13], large-scale assessments and managerial principles work as important guidelines for the work of the state in education (Rossi, Bernardi, & Uczak, 2017). Large-scale evaluations, PPPs and the establishment of national learning standards are highlighted as the most relevant policies within the spectrum of the corporate reform of education in Brazil. In this scenario, there has been a shift in the forms and intensity of relationship between public and private organisations in education in Brazil, especially after the 1995 State Reform (see Peroni & Adrião, 2008 for a detailed analysis of the public/private relationship in the Brazilian education, and for a historical analysis see Pires, 2015).

First, large-scale evaluations became central in the Brazilian education since the 1990s (Bonamino & Sousa, 2012; Coelho, 2008; Freitas, 2004; Hypólito, 2008; Hypolito & Jorge, 2020). The formulation and enactment of these evaluations are organised in a system[14] created in 1988 and implemented in 1990. It changed its format and priority during its

---

13 The Brazilian political system is organised at a number of levels in set of a complex federal relations, within which the national government interacts with 27 states and 5570 municipalities. In this arrangement, the Brazilian educational system is complex and large: in 2017 there were more than 35 million students in primary and secondary public schools, in a system that combines municipal, state and federal levels of management.
14 System of Assessment of the Basic Education (*Sistema de Avaliação da Educação Básica* – SAEB).

first decade, from a formative assessment, with participation of teachers in its formulation, to the production of a comparative indexes (Lima, 2016). From 1995 it became a central policy in education, with support of the World Bank and funding from the United Nations Development Programme Development (UNDP) (Lima, 2016). It gained strength in the last years, through the implementation of other exams and assessments in the system, as well as attachment these tests to indexes[15] and ranking. This policy mobilises an expressive amount of financial resources from the government, and involves a great number of state and non-state actors (Lima, 2016, p. 35).

Second, PPPs have been increasingly used as a tool for public education management (Adrião, 2018; Adrião, Peroni, & da Costa, 2005; Antunes & Peroni, 2017; V. M. Peroni & Adrião, 2008; A. Rossi, Helo, & Uczak, 2012). The most common formats of PPPs concern the provision of early years education through a voucher-like system, and the provision of a complete school management model with teaching material and assessments (Adrião, Garcia, Borghi, & Arelaro, 2012). However, private actors, from business and philanthropy, have also been active in policymaking. They partake both in the provision of services, or the "rowing" in governance, as in the decision-making, or the "steering" (Peroni & Comerlatto, 2017; Rhodes, 1996). For instance, the positioning of Todos pela Educação has been decisive in the formulation of the National Plan of Education of 2007, issued at the same time as the Plan of Goals of the Commitment All for Education (A. J. Rossi et al., 2017), which indicated an assimilation of the corporate movement at the time (Evangelista & Leher, 2012; Oliveira, 2009; Saviani, 2007).

Third, the Brazilian Learning Standards have been formulated and approved amid the growing relevance of large-scale assessments and participation of private actors in education policy. Although the debate around a national curriculum in Brazil is not new, the current document has been formulated and approved in Brazil between 2015 and 2017. The discussion around a national curriculum was initiated in 1997, during the government

---

15   Index of Development of the Basic Education (*Índice de Desenvolvimento da Educação Básica* – IDEB).

of Fernando Henrique Cardoso. The proposed reform was named at the time National Curricular Parameters (NCP, *Parametros Curriculares Nacionais* – PCNs in Portuguese). In a broader context, at the time there was an international movement towards centralised curricula in Europe (Ball, 2013; Bowe et al., 1992), Australia, and the USA (Apple, 1993, 2006), with similar debates evident in parts of Latin America and Africa (Macedo, 2016). In these latter regions the World Bank and the Inter American Bank of Development (IADB) wrote documents with guidelines that clearly encouraged the centralisation of curriculum and assessment (Macedo, 2015). However, in Brazil there was resistance to such measures, especially from academics and teachers' unions. The biggest issue was that decentralised policies were seen as more democratic amid the context of the process of "redemocratisation" (the military dictatorship officially ended in 1985 and the new Federal Constitution was written in 1988) (Arretche, 1996). The National Council of Education (CNE in Portuguese[16]), then, developed a somewhat generic document with curricular guidelines that were proposed but not imposed on local authorities, thus maintaining states and municipalities' autonomy over their curricula (Macedo, 2015, 2016).

Later, between 2008 and 2010, MEC created more detailed instructions in the form of a five-volume document named "*Indagações Curriculares*", although it did not articulate a comprehensive "curriculum" as such (Macedo, 2016). At the same time, the National Plan for Education was being discussed, a national document with aims and goals for the following ten years. After a long debate with a wide participation of civil society, the National

---

16   The Ministry of Education (MEC in Portuguese) is responsible for education management at the federal level, and creates the national guidelines for all other entities, for example, regulations on funding and the National Plan for Education. The federal level also holds the main responsibility for higher education. MEC has two main decision-making spaces, the Minister's Office and the National Council of Education (CNE in Portuguese), with a functioning that mirrors a president and a house of representatives. The CNE is composed of two chambers, the chambers of 'basic education' and 'higher education', and there are eleven members in each one. In MEC's hierarchy, below the Education Minister and CNE, there are six secretariats, amongst which the Secretariat of Basic Education (SEB) is the most significant in relation to the learning standards that have been recently approved with strong support of new philanthropy.

Plan for Education was signed in 2014 with an apparent consensus about the need of national learning standards: "Thus, 20 years after the first attempt of establishing a national curriculum in Brazil, it seems the dispute is coming to its end. [...] Although the federal system has its set of shared responsibilities, the process of national curricular centralisation seems to have become hegemonic" (Macedo, 2016, p. 6).

From 2014, after the National Plan for Education had established the National Learning Standards (NLS) as a "strategy for improving education in Brazil" the debate about the form and content of the NLS gained momentum and increased public attention. The NLS is strongly supported by new philanthropies in Brazil, who have been concerned with standardising the curriculum in order to make it comparable across the country, facilitating large-scale evaluations and the control of teachers' work. This case echoes how

> the venture philanthropists' approach to schooling emphasizes standardized testing, standardized teaching, and the standardization of curriculum at the expense of an emphasis on individual and social contexts, the relationship between knowledge and authority, and the possibilities for acts of interpretation, dialogue and debate to form the basis for social intervention and social transformation. (Saltman, 2010, p. 9)

It also points to how the corporate reform assumes standards that describe what teachers should do are sufficient to lead to education improvement. In this sense, it "assumes that the most effective way to improve educational systems is to bring well-developed innovations to schools and classrooms from outside, often from the business world" (Sahlberg, 2016, p. 137). In this case, new philanthropists support the NLS with the expectation this will enhance education in Brazil, in spite of the resistance of teachers, researchers and representatives from unions, exemplifying how the corporate reform can lead to a de-professionalisation of education and teaching.

The creation of the learning standards is strongly supported by new philanthropy in Brazil, especially through the group named Mobilisation for the National Learning Standards (MNLS, or simply "Mobilisation"), one of the most prominent participants in this debate. The MNLS is one of many new "complex and contradictory spaces ripe for critical interrogation" (Peck & Theodore, 2012, p. 21). Throughout the book I examine what this group is, how it was created, its goals and agendas, and its composition. Other well-connected and influential foundations are also examined, all supporters of MNLS, namely Todos Pela Educação, Lemann Foundation, Ayrton Senna Institute, Unibanco Institute and Natura.

As it will be explored throughout this book, this education reform agenda has been supported by private actors. From the 1990s onwards, Brazilian businessmen started to mobilise and present an interest to build up an education reform agenda to create a competitive economy and workers with the necessary skills for it (Rossi et al., 2017). In this effort, corporate reformers have been working towards consensual education goals in Brazil, which have been historically supported by social movements. However, such goals have been reframed and shifted with corporate methods, as Rossi et al. (2017) explain:

> Working with the discourse of "education for all and all for education", they incorporated and re-signified historic demands of the fight for the democratisation of education, giving it a new framing. They present proposals for the sake of improving education's quality, defending more time in schools, the universalization of schooling, large-scale assessment, promoting external partnerships to support educational activities, among others. This discourse of qualifying and amplifying the schooling is a social consensus and refers to historic demands from social movements. Businessmen, however, included them, proposing a different way of executing them, having as a method the corporate management. (Rossi et al., 2017, p. 360)

The implications of private actors in education for the democratic management of education in Brazil are specially concerning, with two aspects that aggravate the issue. According to the Federal Constitution of 1988 and the fundamental education law, LDBEN 1996, education should follow the principles of "democratic management", which means that school management should be locally determined in partnership with local authorities and schools' communities (Peroni, 2013). Thus, authors emphasise the contradiction between corporate policies, with standardised measures and a managerial model, and democratic management, mandated by the national legislation (Arelaro, 2007). Further, this contradiction is intensified by the national context of a hugely unequal population and educational system (Arelaro, 2007). Brazil is greatly diverse and unequal, making the use of standardised solutions, such as the ones presented by Ayrton Senna Institute and Unibanco Institute more problematic.

Thus, researchers have been addressing the question if such institutes, with a "managerial" approach to education, can support and enact a democratic management of education, established by legislation in Brazil (Peroni & Comerlatto, 2017, p. 10). This discussion, critique and investigation are especially relevant in the current scenario of a conservative turn. Since 2016, when the former president Dilma Rousself was impeached under controversial circumstances, in what some authors have been referring to as a parliamentary coup (Arelaro, 2017), severe austerity measures (namely the PEC 241/55, which limits the public expenditure for twenty years) and further corporate education policies have been put in place (namely approving a standard learning standard, reforming the curriculum and organisational structure of middle schools). The situation became even more precarious with the election of Jair Bolsonaro in 2018, with severe budget cuts in primary and higher education, as well as the promotion of an ultra-conservative agenda (suppressing a critical education, especially with debates around gender and race, and supporting military schools). In spite of the resistance of social movements, new philanthropy has reacted to austerity measures with silence, and supported authoritarian corporate reforms in education. The data presented in this book focuses precisely on this transition period in Brazil.

A better understanding of new philanthropy in education governance in Brazil can contribute to the field of education policy, not being limited to the interest of Brazilian authors and practitioners. As a regional leader in Latin America and one of the largest economies of the world (yet brutally unequal), Brazil is not a simple "emulator" of global trends, but an active participant in global mobilities of policy. On the one hand, global actors aim at taking part in the network governance of education in Brazil, sometimes with profit goals. For instance, companies like Google and Pearson are already operating in the country, often in partnership with Brazilian foundations. A recent example concerns Sir Michael Barber, a well-known traveling technocrat or "thought leader" that has been working with Pearson (see Hogan et al., 2015), who went to Brazil in May 2018 to speak at an event by invitation of the Lemann Foundation[17]. On the other hand, Brazil also takes part in the mobility of ideas and people beyond its boundaries. An example is REDUCA (*Red Latinoamericana por la Educacion*), a corporate/philanthropic network, which brings together actors of the region that work towards a corporate reform of education. Todos pela Educação, a central actor in Brazilian education policy, was the creator of this network. In spite of their relevance and international reach, efforts like these are under researched (see Martins, 2019). Thus, understanding how new philanthropy works in and around Brazilian networks of education governance fits in wider efforts of understanding global mobilities and trends of education policy. Furthermore, analysis and accounts from low and middle income countries are urgently needed, as most of the literature regarding new philanthropy in education addresses the topic from the (so-called) global north perspective.

---

17 <https://fundacaolemann.org.br/noticias/sir-michael-barber-fala-sobre-gestao-publica-de-resultados>.

CHAPTER 2

From government to governance: Changing relations in society and how to study them

In spite of the growing participation of private actors in the governance of public matters, our imaginary of how governments work is still very much bureaucratic and hierarchical, as we imagine ministries, secretaries, top-down decision-making and so on. It is challenging to make sense of how new philanthropy is part of the education reform if we understand the state and governments as bureaucratic, static and rational organisations. If, however, we comprehend how the state is increasingly working with and through dynamic networks, which include private actors as part of the structure that manages public services, then we can begin to grasp how policy is being done in practice. This is what authors have been referring to as a shift from *government* to *governance* (Bevir, 2011; Jessop, 2002, 2011; Rhodes, 1996). The shift from hierarchical governments to networks of governance has brought a new mix of actors into the provision and management of public services. This chapter discusses the changes from government to governance, as well as the theoretical and methodological shifts necessary to make sense of the changes in how policy is being done.

Governance and networks have become "buzzwords" that are used in different fields to reflect different situations, and can thus mean different things. There is an extensive literature around governance, which has developed different theories with different epistemologies. This "ubiquitous term", as Bevir (2011) puts it, has been used in the disciplines of development studies, economics, geography, political science and sociology. It may refer to management practices, organisational issues and even global debates, such as the climate change that claims to be an issue of "global governance". Governance is then a disputed term and a loosely used one, permeated by theoretical, epistemological and methodological discussions, which generally mirror broader debates in social sciences (Rhodes, 2007).

Nonetheless, in this research *governance* refers to the changes in public management that have been taking place since the end of the twentieth century (continuing up to today) and draws attention to the complexity of patterns of ruling (Bevir, 2011). As a result of public sector reforms initiated in the 1980s, states increasingly share governing with societal actors (like private companies, non-governmental organisations, non-profit service providers). Decision-making processes and implementation systems that used to be mainly executed by the state are increasingly dispersed in a complex network of institutions. In other words, centred on processes of deregulation, privatisation and competition, these reforms have "contributed greatly to the broad shift from direct service provision by government to more complex patterns of governance incorporating markets, networks and private and voluntary sector actors" (Bevir, 2011, p. 9). Thus, hybrid patterns of management and a fragmentation of service delivery arose by incorporating private and voluntary providers in what used to be the public sector's activities. Despite theoretical and methodological debates in the research field, *government* is considered to be done through hierarchical bureaucracies, and *governance* is accomplished through diverse and flexible networks (Ball & Junemann, 2012). Finally, in spite of considerable variation, this changing relationship between the state and society is regarded as an international phenomenon (Bevir, 2011).

The new governance is characterised by a hybrid working, with a multi-jurisdictional dynamic and plural stakeholders (Bevir, 2011). First, it combines established administrative arrangements with features of the market (market mechanisms and non-profit organisations). While previous hierarchical and bureaucratic structures still remain, new forms of public-private, or only private, regulation are being developed, creating a new balance between hierarchy, market and networks. Second, its processes combine people and institutions across different policy sectors, levels of government and are often transnational. The multi-jurisdictional aspect means that "the dominant mode of governance is characterized by networks that are formed by a hybrid mix of actors (individuals, companies, foundations, NGOs, governments, etc.) embedded in a system of national, sub-national, supra-national, intergovernmental, and transnational relations" (Olmedo, 2016, p. 58). Third, even though interest groups have long been present in policymaking process, now there is an increasing participation of non-governmental actors involved in policymaking. Arguably, there has been an increase of advocacy groups, third-party organisations delivering public services and expansion of philanthropic work (such as the Brazilian foundations presented in the previous chapter). This hybrid and multi-jurisdictional organisation, with multiple stakeholders, is linked through networks (Bevir, 2011). This is of great relevance for the study of education policy because "in policy practice, all this translates into changes in the way in which public services are designed and delivered" (Olmedo, 2016, p. 52), with a complex mix of "strategic alliances, joint working arrangements, networks, partnerships and many other forms of collaboration across sectorial and organizational boundaries" (Williams, 2002, p. 103).

While the public/private relationship wasn't inaugurated in this particular time; on the contrary, boundaries between them have always been a thin line (Peroni, 2013), those relations have assumed a new shape and intensity (Ball & Junemann, 2012) with the expansion of "neoliberal modes of governance" (Olmedo, 2017). A new mix between state, market and philanthropy is being created, in which the three elements are also reworked. The state is being reworked as a market-maker, commissioner of services and performance monitor. The market is expanding to increasingly subject the social and the public to the rigours of profit. Philanthropy is being reworked by the discourses and sensibilities of business, adopting, for example, practices of impact, scale, assessment, focus on outcomes, efficiency and competition (Ball & Olmedo, 2011; Bishop & Green, 2010). All these "transformations represent new forms of governmentality and power regimes and are deeply rooted within the political economy and political philosophy of neoliberalism" (Olmedo, 2016, p. 46).

Reflecting these empirical shifts, there are also theoretical and analytical movements. The concept of governance also represents a change in the theoretical perspectives about the work of governments. In all different perspectives and approaches, governance is opposed to the concept of the state as a monolithic actor or institution. So *governance* also refers to "various new theories and practices of governing and the dilemmas to which they give rise. These new theories, practices and dilemmas place less emphasis than their predecessors on hierarchy and the state, and more on markets and networks" (Bevir, 2011, p. 1). The "reified concepts of the state" are challenged, and "theories of governance typically open up the black box of the state" (Bevir, 2011, p. 1). Thus, the complexity, and often messiness, of the policymaking process is embraced in the analysis. Different actors, interests and processes that take part within and beyond the state are analysed, in opposition to a concept of a state as a unitary and cohesive actor with unified interests and strategies. The governance literature accepts the challenge of revisiting the boundaries between the state, market and society, and to explain the complexity of its functioning with its many different participants. Relatedly, there are diverging interpretations of the implications for democracy, and authors have been engaging in the controversial discussion around the social implications of the network governance. While some see potential for a democratic participation in such new ways of governing, others argue new governance creates a "democratic deficit", "as the processes of policy and governance become more dispersed and less transparent" (Olmedo, 2016, p. 58). A central issue is that "alongside the introduction of new actors and organizations, the shift to polycentrism also involves the displacement of some others, like trade unions and professional associations" (Junemann & Ball, 2013, p. 425).

Heterarchies: An organisational form between hierarchy and networks

Considering how the idea of governance may now have too many meanings and thus mean little, the concept of heterarchy becomes useful to better conceptualise some aspects of the changes towards governance. It can help us go beyond the "babylonian variety of policy network concepts" (Börzel, 1998, p. 1) and "specify a set of dimensions, characteristics, relationships and functions that are embedded in new forms of governance, and the relations of power and actors roles that animate the work of governance" (Ball and Junemann, 2012, p. 137). Heterarchies make it explicit that these are not "just networks" (Parker, 2007); but "latent structures that are taking on an expanding and evolving range of policy tasks and public service delivery roles" (Ball & Junemann, 2012, p. 137).

A heterarchy is, first, an organisational form. The governance literature traditionally distinguishes three main organisational forms: market, hierarchy and network. These forms have different "coordination models of reciprocal interdependence", which differ to each other regarding their rationale and logic – namely exchange, imperative coordination and reflexive self-organisation (Jessop, 2011). The market is an example of a formal rationality that is "impersonal" and aims at an "efficient allocation" of resources to competing ends. A hierarchy, of a firm or government, is different and has a "substantive rationality", which is "goal-oriented" and prioritises the "effective" pursuit of organisational or policy goals. Finally, a network is a "reflexive self-organisation", with "on-going negotiated consent to resolve complex problems in a corporatist order or horizontal networking to coordinate a complex division of labour" (Jessop, 2011, p. 113). In social network terms, these three organisational forms of markets, hierarchies and networks can be represented as dyads, chains and triads, respectively. Markets can be thought as being a series of dyadic connections (two parties). Hierarchies can be understood as a "chain" of nodes, with "command based in authoritative control with a well-identified leadership". Finally, a network is "a connection between three or more people" (Stephenson, 2016, p. 141).

However, heterarchies have been gaining prominence as a fourth organisational form, "an organisational form somewhere between hierarchy and network that draws upon diverse horizontal and vertical links that permit different elements of the policy process to cooperate (and/or compete)" (Ball & Junemann, 2012, p. 138). In social network terms, heterarchies can be seen as a "connection between three or more hierarchies engaged in asymmetric, repetitive and sustained collaborations. Participating hierarchies intermittently lead and follow, suppressing a competitive drive in lieu of a collaborative ethos that benefits the whole network" (Stephenson, 2016, p. 141).

Jessop (2011) focuses on the complexities of the functioning of heterarchies and goes beyond organisational description towards a deeper understanding of how heterarchies operate. He argues a heterarchy is a:

> reflexive self-organisation [that] is concerned to identify *mutually beneficial joint projects* from a wide range of possible projects, to redefine them as the relevant actors attempt to pursue them in an often *turbulent environment* and monitor how far these projects are being achieved, and to organise the material, social, and temporal conditions deemed necessary and/or sufficient to achieve them. It *does not require actors to accept substantive goals defined in advance* and from above on behalf a specific organisation (e.g. a firm) or an imagined collectivity (e.g. the nation). Instead it has a substantive, procedural rationality that is concerned with *solving specific coordination problems*, on the basis of a *commitment to a continuing dialogue to establish the grounds for negotiating consent, resource sharing, and concerted action*. To distinguish such an approach from the anarchy of the market and the hierarchy of command, governance in this narrow sense is often referred to as *heterarchich*. (Jessop, 2011, p. 113, added emphasis)

In this diverse, temporary and ever-changing organisational arrangement of heterarchies, the messiness, unevenness and complexity are inherent characteristics, in opposition to the assumed order of hierarchies. They have characteristics of assemblages, such as being loosely coupled, temporary and uneven. They bring together different elements, which may converge at points, and work differently according to local circumstances (Ball & Junemann, 2012). They are "to an extent imaginative and experimental and, to an extent, polyvalent, and often involve considerable stumbling and blundering" so "they are a policy device, a way of trying things out" (Ball & Junemann, 2012, p. 138). These aspects help us in reframing our imaginary of how governments work, and help us to accept, embrace and understand the complexities and often messiness of how education policy is being done.

Complex heterarchies do not erase more traditional policy actors and sites. Instead, "new linkage devices and lead organisations are created over and against existing ones, excluding or circumventing but not always obliterating more traditional sites and voices" (Ball & Junemann, 2012, p. 138). Thus, in heterarchies, public sector organisations may adopt many roles, sometimes as "clients", others as "contractors", sometimes "partners" or even "competitors" (Ball & Junemann, 2012, p. 139). In the following chapters, some of these different possible roles become clear through the cases explored. What this means is that public services are not being "taken away" from public sector control, but are being organised "through collaborations of various kinds with the public sector, although some are more meaningfully collaborative than others and not all rest on shared objectives or a balance of influence" (Ball & Junemann, 2012, p. 139). These partnerships open a way for flows between sectors, flows of "people, information and ideas, language, methods, values and culture" and in this context the work of governance is increasingly dispersed and opaque (Clarke & Newman, 2009). All of this also involves the creation and use of new policy spaces, "in spaces parallel to and across state institutions and their jurisdictional boundaries" (Skelcher, Mathur, & Smith, 2004, p. 3). This can be specially seen regarding the work of MNLS and its operation as a policymaking space in its own right, operating parallel and across the Ministry of Education (see Chapter 6). In this new mix of markets, networks and hierarchies, new personal and professional connections across different institutions and sectors – public, private and voluntary – are established. Careers are forged in movement between and across these sectors by boundary-spanners, people who bring "unlikely partners together" break "through red tape", and see "things in a different way" (Williams, 2002, p. 109).

Governance in Brazil: Tensions and advances of social rights in neoliberal times

The current Brazilian Federal Constitution, signed in 1988, and the 1995 State Reform are stressed in the literature as the turning point towards governance in Brazil. The 1988 Constitution is regarded as a significant advance in the social rights scenario in Brazil, while also accepting principles of public/private cooperation in public services. Seven years later, in 1995, the State Reform plan was signed and is considered a critical moment towards governance in the country.

The Federal Constitution (*Constituição Federal*) is the fundamental legal document in Brazil. After a number of previous constitutions[1], the current one was signed in 1988 and is considered to be the most democratic constitution in the Brazilian history. Referred to as the "Citizen Constitution" (*Constituição Cidadã*), it introduced novel civil, political and social rights in the country (Carvalho, 2001). After twenty-one years of military dictatorship in Brazil, the 1988 Constitution (CF/88) was signed amid a struggle for "redemocratisation", when popular movements and civil society organisations were mobilised for social rights (Peroni, 2013).

Education was established as a social right in the Constitution's second item, titled "Fundamental Rights", together with health, work, leisure, security, social pension, protection to maternity and childhood. Remarkably, "for the first time in our constitutional history, the Social Rights Declaration is made explicit, with primacy to education" (Oliveira, 1999, p. 61). Education is further addressed on Section 1 of Chapter 3. In the article 205, education is ratified as a right to all, and a duty of state and family, which should be promoted in collaboration with society. Further, article 213 states that "public resources will be assigned to public schools, and might be allocated to community, confessional or philanthropic schools", as long as they are non-profit organisations.

However, the democratisation process did not unfold without contradictions. By the end of the military dictatorship, in the 1980s, neoliberal[2]

---

1   Brazil has had several National Constitutions: 1824 (Brazilian Empire), 1891 (First Republic), 1934 (With social rights), 1937 (Vargas Dictatorship), 1946 (Democratisation), 1967 (Golpe in 1964) and 1969 (Amendas a antiga) and finally 1988, when "Social rights were integrated for the first time in a Brazilian Constitution as fundamental rights" (Pires, 2013, p. 164).
2   Here understood as: "Neoliberalism is a theory of political economic practices proposing that human well-being can be best advanced by the maximisation of entrepreneurial freedoms within an institutional framework characterised by private property rights, individual liberty, unencumbered markets, and free trade" (Harvey, 2007, p. 22) and "an ensemble of economic and social policies, forms of governance, and discourses of ideologies that promote self-interest, unrestricted flows of capital, deep reductions in the cost of labor, and sharp retrenchment of the public sphere. Neoliberals champion privatisation of social goods and withdrawal

policies and state reforms were under way in many western countries, which influenced the Brazilian CF/88 document. While introducing social rights not previously present in the Brazilian legislation, public/private partnerships (PPPs) are presented as commendable tools for managing public services, which were further encouraged seven years later with the 1995 State Reform. Thus, some authors claim that while the CF/88 established education as a fundamental right and presented great progress in relation to previous documents, it also asserted that education would be provided by the state in collaboration with private actors (Oliveira, 2009; Peroni, 2013; Peroni et al., 2013).

Being written in a context of national "redemocratisation" and, concomitantly, the international rise of neoliberalism, the CF/88 ensures both: a "democratic management" of education (*gestão democrática*) with the participation of local communities in the making of education and school management, and also opens space for the participation of private providers of educational services, especially the "confessional sectors" (Pires, 2013). The CF/88 internal disputes are related to an international context of neoliberalism and also a tense national consensus around the "democratisation" of the country. In spite of agreeing upon the value of "redemocratising" the country, right and left wing groups did not necessarily agree upon the terms of the transition (Carvalho, 2001). Further, it should be marked that the allowing of private providers of education in the Constitution is not necessarily evidence of neoliberalism. The running of schools by non-profit private entities has been present through history in Brazil as in most countries. Some challenges of analysing and interpreting change and permanence, similarities and differences, regarding governance, philanthropy and education reform are further discussed below.

Not long after the promulgation of the new Constitution, Fernando Henrique Cardoso, from the PSDB[3] party, was elected in 1994 amid an economic crisis and social instability. One year later, the Ministry of

---

of government from provision for social welfare on the premise that competitive markets are more effective and efficient" (Lipman, 2013, p. 6).

3   Partido Social Democrata Brasileiro (Brazilian Social Democratic Party), a centre-right-wing party.

Administration and State Reform (MASR) signed a state reform, which is recognised as a turning point of the shift from *government* to *governance* in Brazil. Both the President Cardoso and the Minister of the State Reform, Besser Pereira, were advocates for the Third Way (Peroni, 2013). A "new" state definition was announced by this reform through the document Director Plan of State Apparel Reform (DPSAR) ("*Plano Diretor de Reforma do Aparelho do Estado*"). It stated "the state reform should be understood within the context of *change of the state role*, which *ceases to be directly responsible* for economic and social development through the production of goods and services, to become stronger in the *function of supporter and regulator* of this development" (Ministério da Administração Federal e Reforma do Estado, 1995, p. 17, emphasis added). Thus, the reform aimed to change the state role from "direct responsibility" to "regulation" in more complex networks of governance with new actors.

This state reform project indicated three privatising strategies to be adopted throughout all ministries: outsourcing (*terceirização*), privatising (*privatização*) and publicising (*publicisação*). The first is the transfer of auxiliary services to private sector providers and the second is the selling of state companies to private owners. Most importantly, the third, "publicisation" refers to the transfer of social and scientific services previously executed by the state to non-state institutions, indicated in the document as "non-state public sector" (Peroni, 2013, p. 20). The education sector (with schools, universities, research centres and child care facilities) was amongst the services partially transferred to the "third sector", composed by non-governmental institutions. As a result, the principles of network governance were also manifested in the education legislation. In 1996, the Law of Guidelines and Bases for Education was signed (LDBEN 1996) and presented the state as a provider of education together with civil society (Krawczyk & Vieira, 2008; Monteiro, 2013).

After the 1995 reform, the Brazilian third sector went through an intense growth of 215 per cent between 1996 and 2005. It later slowed down to 8.8 per cent between 2006 and 2010 and reached 290,700 non-profit private foundations and associations in Brazil in 2010 (FASFIL, 2010), and this number has reduced to 237,000 in 2016 (FASFIL, 2016). Besides introducing three privatising strategies, the state reform project also reinforced the general principle of managing public services according to market ideals: "These are competitive services and can be controlled not only through managerial administration, but also and mainly through social control and the constitution of quasi markets" (Bresser Pereira, 1997, p. 12). The 1995 reform was later reaffirmed with a change in the constitution in 1998 (the 1998 *Emenda Constitucional*). Both documents advance the premise that the state should not be the main (or only) promoter of social services and policies. Instead, it should work with civil society though public/private partnerships (Pires, 2013).

Studying global policies imposes challenges regarding the analysis and interpretation of changes and permanence, differences and similarities, between times and places. There are some remarks to be made regarding the study and analysis of education network governance in Brazil – like in many low and middle income countries – which present dangers and challenges to make sense of change and permanence, of similarity and difference in this context.

First, there is a danger in overstating the "change" in governance and the "new" participation of private actors. It is important to stress that the participation of private actors (including corporate ones) in education was not a novelty of the end of the twentieth century (in Brazil or in other countries). For instance, in 1821, Dom João, King of Portugal and Brazil ("United Kingdom" at the time), established that any citizen could open a primary school (Peroni, 2013). Cury (2008) explains that the public body, considered "insufficient" to universalise primary teaching, authorised partial funding of private school offer at the time. Since then, Brazilian legislation has considered legitimate the freedom of teaching, while at the same time reaffirming the state as the fundamental power that authorises and grants school education (Peroni, 2013). In another public-private dynamic, during the military dictatorship corporate actors participated in educational matters and were influential in education policymaking, especially through the organisation IPES (*Instituto de Pesquisas Economicas e Sociais*, or Institute of Economic and Social Research) (Souza, 1981). In this realm, one should be careful with interpreting any non-state action in education as neoliberal. There were private actors in education before neoliberalism, and there are now, in neoliberal times, private actors that resist neoliberal reforms. What we see now, however, like in other contexts, is a new form and new intensity of public/private relationships (Ball & Junemann, 2012).

Second and contrastingly, there is a danger in overstating similarities and not seeing differences between Brazil and the places where the literature on governance has been produced, namely the United States of America and Europe, especially the United Kingdom. The shift from government to governance in Brazil happened in a very different context from these countries. While the Brazilian state is also changing its role and seeking to share social responsibilities with other actors from civil society and the market, new governance in this case does not indicate a shift from a "welfare state", as portrayed in the Anglo-Saxon literature. Instead, the turning point of the change in the means of governing takes place in a context in which the country was – and is – struggling with strengthening democracy and ensuring universal social rights, and when social movements had high hopes for the promises of the 1988 Constitution. So while in 1988 the UK was signing its new Education Act, regarded as an important turning point towards a corporate reform of education, with accountability measures (Ozga, 2009), in Brazil, at the same year, the new Constitution was being signed, which is regarded as a relevant moment of social rights advancement, in spite of the changes later propelled by the 1995 State Reform. Thus, if on the one hand there are similarities and analytical insights to be drawn from the European and North American literature, on the other there are empirical specificities that must be attended, which cannot be overwritten with theoretical concepts from elsewhere.

One might ask then if it makes sense to talk about a "shift" from government towards network governance in Brazil. I would argue that if such a shift is understood to refer to a change from bureaucratic forms of social management to heterarchical ones, then it is a useful and coherent concept. However, there is a caveat to be made about what a hierarchical "government" looks and looked like, as it would be a mistake to imagine European-like welfare state before a shift towards governance in Brazil. Hence, the concerns, debates and dangers regarding the participation of business and philanthropic organisations in the governance of education are different and, perhaps, more intense in contexts like the Brazilian one in contrast to (so-called) western / global north countries. Nonetheless, there are several echoes and connections between different places, including the fundamental aspect of a growing philanthropy, that has become a decisive stakeholder and social actor in education, which supports a reform of education that draws from a corporate worldview.

The need of new methods and theories to make sense of new actors in education

The shifting terrain of education policy, with new actors playing new roles in dynamic and global networks of governance, poses a series of theoretical and methodological challenges. In fact, "taking globalisation seriously means the revision of the core questions that frame education policy research agendas and projects" (Verger et al., 2018, p. 9). However, in spite of the growth of corporate and philanthropic action in public education, there still is "an enormous gap in the research field of education policy" (Ball, 2012, p. xii). Most research is still bounded by the nation state and "policy-as-government paradigm" (Ball, 2012), preventing us to understand how policy is being done, as we do not see the participation of new private actors and the new global scale of policy. Despite the growing participation of business and philanthropy in relation to public sector reforms, the role played by these policy actors is underestimated in most academic research (Frumkin, 2008; Olmedo, 2014). Thus, drawing from Ball et al. (2017), the method of network ethnography (NE) and following policy (McCann & Ward, 2012; Peck & Theodore, 2012) are intertwined in the approach of this research, and stem from the recognition that "the portrayal and analysis of these complex, translocal, evolving and multimedia social relations requires an appropriate method of research" (Ball, 2017, p. 32).

With an intense mobility of goods, people, ideas and policies, the world is increasingly globalised. As a result, the relationships between the global and the local are changing, and notions of nationally bounded phenomena are troubled. While education researchers often frame the policy analysis within nation states, now many policies actually have their origins and influences from elsewhere, such as the corporate reform of education described before, which can be mediated and influenced by international organisations, international consultants, or with funding from philanthropy, and so on. This means there is an emergence of "new transnational spaces of policy and new intra-national spaces of policy", with new relationships between these spaces, and policies that move "across and between these spaces" with "relationships that enable and facilitate such movement" (Ball et al., 2017, p. 12). New research strategies, methods and perspectives are needed to account for the participation of new actors in the policymaking arena and the globalisation of policy. Limiting education policy analysis within nation states is no longer sensible, this is the fallacy of the "methodological territorialism" (Ball, 2012, p. 93).

There are several theoretical and methodological challenges that must be addressed, and three can be highlighted: the perspectives of *"educationism"*, *"statism"* and *"nationalism"* (Dale & Robertson, 2009; Verger et al., 2018). The first is an approach that tends to analyse education policy without taking into account wider social contexts. The second is limited to the state in the analysis of policies, without considering other groups and actors that partake in policymaking. And the third analyses policy within the national boarders, without pondering the movement of people and ideas that do not abide by such boundaries. These perspectives are limited to make sense of the current complex global networks of governance (Ball et al., 2017). It becomes necessary to "think outside and beyond the framework of the nation state to make sense of what is going on inside some nation states" (Ball et al., 2017, p. 12). This implies "extending the limits of our geographical imagination", and "attempting to grasp the joining up and reworking of these spaces in and through relationships" (Ball et al., 2017, p. 17).

Addressing these limitations implies epistemological and ontological shifts, with less interest in structures and more emphasis on flows and mobilities (Ball, 2012, p. 5). The network and mobilities approaches to policy studies seek to remediate some of these analytical limitations. They focus attention onto the new actors that operate within governance, the mundane work of policymaking, the movement of people and ideas, and avoid "methodological territorialism", or "the practice of unreflectively understanding the social world through the lens of territorial geographies" (Larner & Le Heron, 2002, p. 754). Policy is considered something that extends beyond the boundaries of the nation state and makes possible the tracing of the global movement of policies. Additionally, the policy mobility approach offers a critical perspective on the global movement of policies, by drawing attention to the power relations and the labour invested in mobilising policy across countries. The analytical focus then lies on the "various network strategies through which durability and mobility is achieved, always focusing attention on the tiny, often mundane exchanges going on within the complex commotion of materials and human action that we think of as educational life" (Olmedo, 2017, p. 117). In other words, "we need a more careful tracing of the intellectual, policy, and practitioner networks that under-pin the global expansion of neoliberal ideas, and their subsequent manifestation in government policies and programmes" (Larner, 2003, p. 510). By paying attention to the apparently mundane practices, the labour, invested in (global) networks of governance, it becomes possible to offer "descriptions of the circulatory systems that connect and interpenetrate 'local' policy regimes" (Peck & Tickell, 2002, p. 229), and understand processes of "*glocalisation*" and the "actually existing neoliberalism" (Brenner & Theodore, 2002).

In these lines, the policy mobility approach has been developed by researchers from the field of human geography to understand how policies move globally (McCann & Ward, 2012; Peck & Theodore, 2010, 2012). This is part of a "new generation of critical policy studies" (Peck & Theodore, 2010, p. 169). Though heterogeneous, these critical policy studies are rooted in critical epistemologies and assume that:

> policy actors and actions are understood to be politically mediated and sociologically complex. As such, the beliefs and behaviours of policy actors are embedded within networks of knowledge/expertise (many of which are translocal and transscalar), as well as within more "localised" socioinstitutional milieux. (Peck & Theodore, 2012, p. 23)

Despite the relevance and contribution of other approaches, this perspective opposes itself to "orthodox views of policy transfer" (Peck &

Theodore, 2010), which assume rational-choice on the part of policy actors, with a tendency for good policies to drive out bad ones. Further, the research methods these approaches tend to be positivist (Peck & Theodore, 2010). So policy mobility differentiates itself from the concepts of policy transfer, convergence or learning. The first, policy transfer, focuses "on decision-making dynamics internal to political systems" and aims to "address the role of agency in transfer process" (Stone, 2004, p. 547). The second adopts the concept of "convergence" to attribute policy transfers to structural forces "driven by industrialization, globalization or regionalization forcing a pattern of increasing similarity in economic, social and political organisation between countries" (Stone, 2004, p. 547). Lastly, policy learning has been linked to epistemic communities (Haas & Haas, 1995), advocacy coalitions (Sabatier, 1988, 1991) and is articulated by Stone (2004) as a process that "occurs when policymakers adjust their cognitive understanding of policy developments and modify policy in the light of knowledge gained from past policy experience" (p. 548).

Peck and Theodore (2010) have enunciated some key characteristics of the policy mobility perspective. First, it is assumed that policy formation and transformation are socially constructed processes and fields of power. Second, actors are not seen as "lone learners", but members of epistemic communities. Third, mobile policies rarely travel as "complete packages", but are moved in bits and pieces. Fourth, policies move in a "complex process of non-linear reproduction", mutating and morphing as they move. And fifth, mobile policies do not move across a flattened space of transaction, but they move in "cross-scalar and interlocal" spaces, increasingly complex within new forms of uneven economic development. In sum, "in contrast with the orthodox literature on policy transfer, the governing metaphors in critical policy studies are not those of transit and transaction, but of mobility and mutation" (Peck & Theodore, 2010, p. 170).

While not assuming straightforward and lineal exercises of policy borrowing, the policy mobility aims to "identify the surface traces of policy flows or instances of circulating policies" (Olmedo, 2016, p. 57). This process happens in what can be referred to as the "'local globalness' of urban policy transfer" (McCann, 2011, p. 107). The analysis then aims to attend to the "complexities of *glocalization*—the interplay of global *forms* [...] with local circumstances" (Ball, 2017, p. 30). This means the

> analysis rests on the need to think both about ways in which the "global" impacts on the "national", and at the same time acknowledge the extent to which the national is critical in the formation of global policy agendas. That is, the interdependency of actors and the movement of ideas across local, national and global settings. (Ball et al., 2017, p. 11)

This approach is contrasted with a "nationalist" one (Verger et al., 2018) or "methodological territorialism" (Larner & Le Heron, 2002). In this case, the analytical framing is not defined by geographic categories and entities (a city, a state, a country...), but by the space configured by the very intersection of global and local elements (Ball et al., 2017). This requires we "acknowledge that global activity can take place at multiple levels and on multiple scales, through complex, evolving network relations, with 'domestic' policy actors acting globally in their own right" (Ball et al., 2017, p. 12).

The study of the mobility of policies is not abstract. Instead, besides highlighting the power relations present in the movement of policies, the mobility turn also emphasises the role of *mundane* activities of policy work, the *labour* involved in the movement of policy. Thus,

> "instead of conceiving of the global economy as a disembodied and disembedded set of supra-human forces", "the analytical approach to what is referred to here as 'the global' responds to the set of discrete, identifiable and traceable practices (connections, transactions, meetings, travels, influences, and impositions, etc.), through which international economic and political relationships are enacted". (Olmedo, 2016, p. 46)

This approach follows the calls by Larner (2003), McFarlane (2009) and McCann (2008), among others, who urge us to look at "*mundane*" practices to understand how policy is being made, or the "*labour*" invested. Larner argues we need to be aware of "the apparently mundane practices through which neoliberal spaces, states and subjects are being constituted in particular forms" (2003, p. 511). McFarlane urges us to pay greater attention to "the labour of assembling and reassembling sociomaterial practices that are diffuse, tangled and contingent" (p. 562). McCann (2008) invites us to look at the role of expertise and apparently mundane practices in contemporary government. In other words, this is "actually existing neoliberalism" (Brenner & Theodore, 2002), because "what we are dealing with here are new ways of 'neoliberalism in action', that is a set of practices and processes, structures, and relationships, which constitute what could be understood as 'doing neoliberalism'" (Olmedo, 2016, p. 59).

All of this means shifting "from the study of mobile policy to the study of the practices through which policy is made mobile" (Roy, 2012, p. 35), and "this involves both giving attention to the labour of policy actors and concomitantly thinking differently about the labour of policy researchers—how we research policy" (Ball et al., 2017, p. 43). It is "by paying attention to these agents of neoliberalism [that] it becomes possible to think about how power and 'expertise' flow between nations and how policy entrepreneurs, NGOs, think tanks and commercial providers of education 'do' globalisation" (Exley, Braun, & Ball, 2011, p. 213). Drawing on these authors, throughout the book I refer to mundane practices invested in the maintenance of networks and the mobility of policies as "*labour*".

Part of this labour revolves around movement, travelling and meetings. The mobility turn emphasises movement in its multiple configurations and variations, from physical movement of materials and people to digital or virtual movement of other goods (e.g. information, ideas, even of power). It "connects the analysis of different forms of travel, transport and communications with the multiple ways in which economic and social life is performed and organized through time and across various spaces" (Urry, 2007, p. 6). Thus, the movement and labour invested in different activities, including policymaking is stressed. This allows us to consider how "very 'costly' meetings, communications and travel through time-space" are central to networks, and are "necessary to 'form' and to 'cement' weak ties at least for another stretch of time" (Urry, 2007, p. 231). By "meetings" Urry refers to "both the highly formalized with 'agendas', structure and timetables and the informal to where the specific space and time are planned in advance to where they are negotiated en route" (Urry, 2007, p. 232). In these spaces of meetingness, "network members, from a range of backgrounds, come together, where stories are told, visions shared, arguments reiterated, new relations made, partnerships forged, and commitments made" (Ball, 2017, p. 35). The large seminars and small meetings described in this book are examples of how "the bases of such [physical, corporeal] travel are new ways in which social life is apparently 'networked'", that is "life is networked but it also involves specific co-present encounters within certain times and places" (Urry, 2003, p. 156). In this sense, "meetingness, and thus different forms and modes of travel, are central to much social life, a life involving strange combinations of increasing distance and intermittent co-presence" (Urry, 2003, pp. 155–56). Urry's *mobilities paradigm*, although primarily applied to social networks, pertains to "an alternative theoretical and methodological landscape" (Urry, 2007, p. 18), which can prove fruitful once applied to policy analysis.

In paying attention to people and policies in movement, mobilities research requires methods that allow us to observe social relationships and interactions. This means "observing directly or in digitally enhanced forms mobile bodies undergoing various performances of travel, work and play" (Sheller & Urry, 2006, p. 217). Options would include "mobile ethnography", "time-space diaries" and "cyber-research", methods that stimulate the memory or methods that would capture the "atmosphere of place" or "transfer points" (Urry, 2007). The method of network ethnography, described below, not only works with the cross-fertilisation of social network analysis (SNA) and ethnography, but also draws from and echoes these aspects of the mobilities research.

This requires looking at the mobile people, policies and places (McCann & Ward, 2012),[4] or the "whos" and "whats" and "wheres" of policy (Ball et al., 2017). The first, people or "whos", means asking who mobilises policy, implying that "our work asks how policy actors circulate policies among cities, how they draw on circulating policy knowledge and how and for whom they put these engagements to use as they assemble their own 'local' policies…" (McCann & Ward, 2012, p. 42). The study of "whos" can be done by traveling or with documentary evidence of travelling, in "paying attention to the way stories about places and policies are told" (McCann & Ward, 2012, p. 48). Second, the policies or "whats", means asking how policies are made mobile and what situations, "transit points" and "sites

---

4   See annexes for McCann and Ward (2012) table that systematises the approach.

of persuasion" policies move through (McCann & Ward, 2012). This can be done through tracing movement and mutation of policies with documentary evidence, following policy models or policy actors, conducting oral histories of the spread of policies and attending "relational situations" like conferences. Third, the places or "wheres" requires asking how places become attached to models, and attending to the places and events in which the "past, present and potential futures of education co-exist" (McCann & Ward, 2012, p. 48). As regards the "wheres", both "following policies and 'studying through' the sites and situations of policymaking" are recommended. Part of it is concerned with how education is assembled "through policy actors' purposive gathering and fixing of globally mobile resources, ideas, and knowledge" (McCann & Ward, 2012, p. 43).

Following policy "involves close attention to organizations and actors within the global education policy field (and their movement), to the chains, paths and connections that join up these actors, and to 'situations' and events in which policy knowledge is mobilized and assembled" (Ball, 2017, p. 32). All of this requires "staying close to practice" (McCann & Ward, 2012, p. 45), in such a way that network ethnographers become what Burawoy calls global ethnographers, that is, they "become the living embodiment of the processes we are studying" (Burawoy et al., 2000, p. 4). As network researchers we travel, we attend, we meet and we network – in order to research networks. Our practice is homologous to/with the networks researched. But it also means that we "examine policy in many forms: written policies, policy models and best practices, policy knowledge, policy responses to specific concerns, and the sociospacial manifestations of policy work", in a way it "challenges policy as technical, rational, neutral, and apolitical" (McCann & Ward, 2012, p. 42).

Thus, although this research began in Brazil, concerned with Brazilian new philanthropy, in conception and execution, global connections and dynamics constantly cropped up in data collection and analysis. The dynamics of contemporary education policy in Brazil, which are narrated and analysed in this book, are shaped and shape the global movement of policies and ideas. So to understand how new philanthropists are operating on and within networks of education governance in Brazil, it was necessary to look at much wider global people, policies and places. To do that, I follow the whos, wheres and whats of policy.

In practice, the use of NE to attend to these shifts in perspective and framing entail extensive and exhaustive online searches, interviews, and the participation and observation of events. NE is a toolbox that education policy scholars have been employing to tackle "the proliferation of policymaking sites and activities around the world and the increasing mobility and flow of education policy" (Ball et al., 2017, p. 18). It is used as an appropriate method to investigate the interactions among public and private actors in education governance (Ball et al., 2017; Ball & Junemann, 2012; Hogan et al., 2015; Olmedo, 2014, 2017). It is an assemblage of research tactics and techniques that addresses both the organisation and processes of network relations. Attention is given to new configurations of social life and relations, which are increasingly "networked" (Urry, 2003). The method follows the general principles of qualitative research, such as working in natural settings, with studies being subject to on-going design and redesign, a concern with social processes and meaning and data collection and analysis occurring simultaneously (Ball et al., 2017).

More specifically, NE proposes an ethnographic approach to networks, drawing from ethnographic research and Social Network Analysis (SNA). The NE method enables researchers to capture details and meanings of policy relations, as well as interactions, practices and meanings policy actors share, together with their participation in the policy process (Ball & Junemann, 2012). The NE approach echoes the "inside-out" perspective of Riles (2001), with both network graphs and an analysis of the social relations that constitute the network, with an awareness of contexts and "an appreciation of the perception of the network from the inside and an appreciation of the content of the ties in terms of quality, meaning, and changes over time" (Edwards, 2010, p. 24). It involves the "identification and analysis" of both the "creation and operation of global education policy networks and the connections that constitute them" (Junemann, Ball, & Santori, 2018, p. 458). By identifying, analysing and paying attention to the insider relations and the overall network, NE "allows for greater attention to the power relations that constitute the dynamic flows of material and symbolic resources" (Au & Ferrare, 2015, p. 15).

In combining elements from formal SNA and an anthropological take, networks present a triple usage: as methodological tools, as metaphors (or analytical abstractions) and as descriptions of empirically identifiable social forms (Knox et al., 2006). First, as a method, the network is used for data collection and analysis. Unlike other tools and objects, the network presents an opportunity to mix qualitative and quantitative methods. Second, as a metaphor, "the strength of the network metaphor has been to encourage us to rethink questions of relatedness, and to consider how the implications of distance(s) of different kinds might be addressed by the network" (Knox et al., 2006, p. 134). In the case of current education policy networks that reach new places, spaces and scales, using networks as metaphors can challenge assumptions of relatedness. Third, as a model, "the importance of the network is that it can be both a model and an object, that it can be turned, as Riles puts it, inside out. The inside of the network (the social relationships of which it is composed) is at the same time the outside (the representation or visualization)" (Knox et al., 2006, p. 133). In some circumstances, "heterarchies" are used in this book (see Chapter 6) as a very specific version this "form", as "analytical abstractions and descriptors of empirically identifiable forms" (p. 135). Thus, the "network", that is "uncanny" in including in itself multiple meanings (Knox et al., 2006), supports the rethinking of relatedness, distance and space, while also providing a way to go about the complexity of empirical policy settings.

With this the anthropological approach to networks, all three "usages" of networks are employed, and it aims to analyse narrative and discursive aspects of networks. These aspects are so relevant that the process of research is reversed in comparison to formal SNA procedures. Thus, instead of identifying "boundaries" and "populations" first, the researcher starts with the discourses and narratives of a social group. In this sense, "the boundaries for such domains can be identified only through the 'stories' which are associated with them, with discourse identifying the 'insiders' as those who belong to networks, their roles and identities" (Knox et al., 2006, p. 129). Then, as one follows and explores the discourses and narratives, the description of the networks already constitutes its analysis, as it plays out the complexities and hybridities of the networks. From the analytical description, the researcher can also develop a critical analysis that considers power relations, or "the place of discourse and narrative through which networks are produced" (Knox et al., 2006, p. 132). In this case, the interest is less in defining or delimiting networks, but rather "in tracing these definitions and operationalisations of the 'network' as an ideal-type or form of relating" with "detailed ethnographic description of the ways in which people articulate their relationships with one another as network relations, and are able to envisage those relationships through the use of pictorial and diagrammatic representation of networks" (Knox et al., 2006, p. 133).

The formal procedures and concerns of SNA become less important in this approach and perspective. Measures, identification of boundaries, appropriate sampling and missing data are not the primary concern. It could be argued such interests are likely based on a modernist assumption of discovering the truth or fundamental structures of networks. In a structuralist epistemology, missing a node or an edge would jeopardise all measures and explanations of a network analysis. Instead, here it is assumed there is no one truth to be discovered, but meanings, senses and interpretations to be made sense of within the inevitable limits and distortions of access to data. The researcher has access only to traces of unstable, opaque and ever-changing networks, with which one can make some sense of how they work. So networks are addressed "narratively" and "discursively". There is a focus on the network histories and their evolution. The graphs are used as research tools that support the "following" of people and tracking of policy developments. A network is not a research "product", "output", or the end point of analysis in itself, it is not simply a matter of finding network structures and applying measures as in more orthodox versions of SNA (Avelar, Nikita, & Ball, 2018).

Within this design, the analytical effort was rendered in a systemic approach to data collection and analysis (with tables and graphs), but with no imposing of order for the sake of order, and the prioritising of meaning and interpretation rather than numerical indicators and measures. Thus, formal SNA graph rules were disregarded when considered unsuitable, such as having graphs with only one kind of node (people *or* institutions), or only one kind of edge (partnerships *or* events). Namely, the analysis of the MNLS's supporters (Chapter 6) benefits from a more formal approach to networks, with attention to affiliation and co-affiliation network relations and the related transformation of data (Borgatti & Halgin, 2012). The analytical procedures and assumptions embedded in affiliation networks (such as the understanding that institutions with higher co-affiliation share information), were fundamental to systematise the MNLS data and achieve the meaningful findings about the interactions between MEC and MNLS. Network ethnographers might benefit from pushing for further cross-fertilisations between formal SNA and the anthropological take, while SNA scholars can benefit from a narrative take on networks (as proposed by Knox et al., 2006).

This book experiments with a "narrative" and "discursive" take on networks. In both cases, there is no focus on language or literary theory. Instead, an analysis of policy networks with focus on discourses and narratives is "heavily focused on illuminating mechanisms in policy practice, rather than on trying to generate laws", because "the insistence on the social rationality of power and meanings is typical for the analysis of narrative and discourse" (Hajer & Laws, 2006, p. 262). Although an analysis of narratives and discourses meet and share characteristics in ways that it is not always easy to differentiate them (Hajer & Laws, 2006), this book focuses more on the first. Instead of drawing on Foucault's governmentality in which "the discourse analytical methods have been employed to expose power regimes in policy domains" (Hajer & Laws, 2006, p. 262), such as the work of Dean (1999, 2017), this book focuses more on narratives, understanding that "a narrative offers one interpretation of events and social relationships" (Marsh & Smith, 2001, p. 531). Hence, narratives are analysed through interviews and pieces of news to track networks evolution and change in time. This is done, for example, with a focus on one event (the Unibanco Institute Seminar in Chapter 5) and the network of one advocacy group (the MNLS in Chapter 6). The analysis aims to address the question of how these networks were developed, how these people came to know each other, from which spaces and contexts they are drawn, and what discourses brought them and holds them together (in other words, why certain speakers were selected for the seminar, and how one advocacy coalition brought together civil servants with new philanthropists).

In regard to the narrative study of networks through time, there is both a methodological and substantive contribution. First, a considerable part of the data is collected through identifying past meetings and seminars. These gatherings are the scattered, yet "traceable", evidence of the evolution of these networks. Thus, the findings are generated through a systematic following and tracing of meetings as part of the object of study. Second, the "tracing back" illuminates and illustrates how policy networks have a history. They are the product of "on-going chains of effort" (Fenwick, 2011). Hence, examining the changes and evolution of education policy networks can be a way to tackle the problem of fixity and flatness pointed by authors in the field (Ball et al., 2017; Hogan et al., 2015). Thus, this book seeks to offer "a more ethnographic approach that highlights the importance of combining and comparing publically accessible materials with the more private stories that make up personal biographies and careers" (Larner & Laurie, p. 220). Chapter 5 in particular works with this combination. The first part of the chapter addresses the official accounts of institutional partnerships, with data from the foundations' institutional websites and reports. The second and third sections of the chapter provide glimpses of the embodied aspect of neoliberalisation, carefully analysing "personal biographies and careers" with a focus on some of the people that are part of the MNLS.

Despite the potential, the use of networks presents limitations and dangers. First, there is a long-term tension between formal and anthropological approaches to networks. So it does not offer a coherent and simple theoretical foundation (Knox et al., 2006). For instance, while cultural SNA writers still strive to formalise their understandings of networks with support of mathematical techniques, anthropological writers do not share this concern (Edwards, 2010). Second, network metaphors present the danger of becoming "descriptors of structures rather than heuristic devices", or an "explanatory device" (Knox et al., 2006, p. 134). Third, the network, used to play out mobility, might in turn create new fixities and rigidities, in a different form. In this sense, networks "can challenge the received understanding of the spatial and relational dimensions of social life but, […] as soon as it stops challenging and starts prescribing, then the productive capacity of the network is diminished" (Knox et al., 2006, p. 134).

Network ethnography and following policy in practice

In practical terms, NE involves four main activities, as outlined by Ball and Junemann (2012): internet searches, interviews, field observation and graph building. These activities do not imply fixed steps in a neat process. Instead, as the studied networks are "always in the process of being made ... never finished; never closed" (Massey, 2005, p. 9), the method must be able to accommodate the complexity of the networks and its permanent changes. Network ethnography is then "necessarily open and flexible" (Olmedo, 2014, p. 576) in its operation, as the researcher needs flexibility to explore relationships in the network as one finds them during data collection. Indeed, "the method is appropriate inasmuch as it is flexible, evolving and adaptive in bringing ethnographic sensibilities to bear to the portrayal and analysis of the complex, translocal, evolving and multimedia relations that constitute global policy networks" (Ball et al., 2017, p. 19). The flexibility, adaptability and responsiveness of the method is also reflected in its understanding of settings and boundaries. Here, "in understanding a global policy network, the natural setting of the research study is neither geographically fixed nor singular - settings are multiple, fluid and evolving, in part virtual but also with moments of 'meetingness'" (Ball et al., 2017, p. 16).

First, the process starts with extensive and exhaustive internet searches around the primary actors of the studied network. The use of online data stems from the "recognition that as our research settings are multiple, fluid and evolving, they are also to a large extent virtual" (Ball et al., 2017, p. 18). In this book, NE involves deep and extensive Internet searches focused on institutes and foundations operating in the network governance of the Brazilian education, especially the ones that specifically aim at participating, influencing and steering education policy, as well as their partners and collaborators. This requires visiting countless webpages (webpages of foundations, the Ministry of Education – MEC, the National Council of Education – CNE, universities, etc.), personal CVs (especially from actors highly connected and the "*boundary-spanners*", subjects that move or moved between public and private sectors), newspapers and related social media, blogs and documents (such as official notes from MEC, CNE and the Deputy Chamber). MNLS's institutional website was also examined with support of an Internet archive[5] to access the list of the MNLS's individual members in different points in time. Network graphs were created and worked on throughout this stage and guided the work of following stages (and are open to changes).

The conduct of these Internet searches resembles a "snow ball" procedure from webpage to webpage. At first, exploratory searches are conducted with no specific concerns, searching for traces of relationships. Once something is identified (a person, an institution, a policy, a story, an event...), this is followed in an attempt to gather data, with details, evidence and versions of it. Moving forwards on an online search can mean following a link that is available at the page, or conducting a new search with an Internet search tool.

Data collection and analysis then happen simultaneously, since choosing what should be followed already constitutes data analysis. Besides taking screenshots, saving PDF files, highlighting them and adding information in spread sheets, there are questions being asked and decisions being made regarding where to proceed. When visiting webpages, I try to understand the organisation at stake – what it does, what are its values, who works for it and with whom they collaborate. In this process, finding and understanding connections and relationships is just as important as understanding the institutions and people themselves. The names of people and institutions are not very telling at first, as the researcher does not know them *a priori*. However, as one visits webpages and lists the people and organisations, some patterns start to arise and key actors start to be repeated. This is one fundamental benefit of drawing on SNA. It is important to stress here, however, that the identification of such actors does not necessarily rely on quantitative methods, on identifying, for instance, nodes with higher values of density or centrality – although I did pay attention to both in reviewing and analysing the network graphs. Instead, it is a qualitative perception of relevance that is to the fore. One identifies relevant actors by seeing them repeated in different relevant situations, reports, boards,

---

5   internet archive <waybackmachine.org>.

events and policy stories. This also serves to identify institutions that often work together, and on what type of initiatives, with what type of strategies and mobilising which discourses. At the same time, graphs are built, but with no weights on edges or directed edges. It is a simple way of visualising connections that on tables are messy and unreadable.

In Table 2 the online data sources are presented with some questions that are asked in the process. These questions are not limited to the online searches. Instead, they informed, and are carried, to the other activities as well.

Second, interviews are conducted with individuals and institutions identified as highly connected, or relevant and influential. The interviews aim to add meaning and context to the data collected online. With semi-structured interviews, policy actors are not asked the same questions, but rather interrogations that are based on the online findings, namely about the projects and relationships they foster. Online searches are thus vital for the creation of relevant questions and collection of pertinent and meaningful data. Nonetheless, there are themes and topics that cut across most interviews concerning how institutions create and maintain partnerships and how they use meetings to animate networks.

Additionally, each interview influences the following one as the researcher progresses with data collection. There is no assumption or intention of keeping oneself unaffected by previous conversations. In fact, some interviews are chosen and carried out with basis on anterior questionings, including recommendations from interviewees about who should be interviewed next. As one progresses, some themes become clearer, and the relevant actors are usually confirmed while on fieldwork, as interviewees continually point to the same set of institutions. In this case, Lemann Foundation, Todos pela Educação, Natura Institute, Unibanco Institute and Ayrton Senna Institute were often mentioned as references or as partners.

Third, researchers participate in and observe events as key sites of policymaking and network maintenance. The relations analysed here are so opaque in blurry networks that one cannot attempt to make sense of them without "entering" them. And one only enters them by partaking in the very spaces and relations one is studying (Ball & Junemann, 2012). Following policy, with network ethnography, involves the observation of

Table 2. Data collection and analysis with online searches

Types of online data source	Data collection and analysis
Institutional webpages - Public and private institutions	The analysis of institutional websites involves the exploration of numerous pages, including the goals and aims, the vision and mission, the projects, the partnerships, the videos, the available materials, and others. It also involves the search for people, names that are often repeated and names of the people in directive roles (foundation board, directors and executive secretariats). Questions: What does this organisation do? What projects does it execute? What are its goals and aims? Which discourses are mobilised? Who is part of it? What are its partners? What events are organised by it? How are projects conducted in collaborations, or how are tasks divided between partners?
Institutional Reports - Mainly from foundations, usually published yearly	The analysis of reports enabled a better understanding of the work of new philanthropists, namely the projects they execute, partners involved and the discourses and policy stories that are mobilised. Reports are written with an extremely positive language and narrative, which retells only success cases and does not acknowledges limitations and problems. It is a piece of data that clearly articulates discourses and narratives. Questions: What did this organisation do this year? What projects were executed, and how did change from previous years, and why? How are the results presented? Who participated in the initiatives? Who is the intended audience of projects and of reports? What events were attended and organised?

(*continued*)

Table 2. Continued

Types of online data source	Data collection and analysis
Personal CVs - Well-connected people, boundary-spanners, head of foundations, speakers at events	Personal CVs were used to make sense of who are the people identified in other sources. This is not about having an "objective" list of work placements. Instead, CVs are also analysed as discursive pieces of data, in which people create a narrative of their career trajectory and the relevance of things they have done. Questions: Where has s/he worked? What are the connections between these former institutions? Has s/he, spanned boundaries between public and private, and how? How are new careers being created?
Event programmes - Meetings and seminars	Event programmes have been relevant to identify connections between people and institutions. In opaque networks, these events are spaces in which traces of relationships temporarily surface to the researcher. Questions: Who are the speakers? Why these, and not others? What connects them? What are the topics of discussion, and how are they framed?
Newspapers - Pieces of news about meetings and events, policies and new philanthropy projects	Newspapers were used to follow up on the findings of previous sources, with snapshots of momentary and opaque relationships. Newspapers often cover seminars and launching of PPPs, and to do so they offer a brief description of context, such as the involved partnerships and next steps. They also offer small glimpses of interviews, which can be useful to understand the people and discourses at play. They provided alternative narratives of new philanthropists' projects and events, and supported the tracing of networks developments. Questions: What is being covered, and why? How is it presented? Who is involved in it?

large events, small meetings and observing the space of foundations (the ones I visited/conducted an interview in). These fieldwork observations provide an ethnographic experience that allows the researcher to better understand the culture of new philanthropy by observing the spaces, the corporate decorations of offices and events, the small talk held in between seminar talks and how people behave in philanthropic spaces. Field notes and pictures are used in the analysis, together with the data collected online and with interviews.

When participating in meetings and events, the fieldwork involves paying attention to the institutions and people that have funded the event, observing the physical organisation of the conference space (with stands, publicity, folders...), listening to the references mentioned in the presentations and in informal conversations during the conference. Concomitantly, informal dialogues are also helpful and can support data collection decisions, such as identifying some references and leaders of the network. These events also help the researcher in developing a vocabulary that can ease interviews: Foundations have their very own set of words to refer to practices and discourses named differently in academic research, such as "alignment" (between philanthropy and business, and philanthropy and policy), partnerships, advocacy and so on. This can support the creation of a non-threatening environment for interviews, and relatable and intelligible interview questions. Indeed, one becomes part of the network oneself is researching (Burawoy et al., 2000). Besides physical visits, some events were "attended" or watched virtually. Some events I attended, for others I analysed the programme and watched the videos made available online.

Throughout the three activities, policy network graphs are built as tools to identify relevant individuals, institutions and relationships in relation to specific policies or networks. In these activities, the researcher pays "close attention to organisations and actors within the global education policy field, to the chains, paths and connections that join up these actors, and to the "situations" and events in which policy ideas and methods are mobilised and assembled" (Ball et al., 2017, p. 19). The graphs are fundamental to keep track of the relationships found between people, institutions, policies and events. Graphs can make possible the visualisation of the emergence of connections and more defined communities in messy and complex networks, which then inform the following choices on how to proceed with data collection and analysis. As data collection demands a continuous back and forth movement, the graphs also support the identification of what is relevant and the pursuit of a route, or following these people, institutions and policies. In this research, the data spread sheets were analysed with Gephi software.

In network ethnography, the graphs are often used with flexibility. Unlike formal SNA, in NE graphs are research tools to support data collection and analysis, so these networks can "be viewed as descriptive devices rather than analytical representations" (Hogan et al., 2015, p. 44). This should be stressed for two limitations. First, the networks in this book do not follow the rules and rationales of formal SNA, but instead work with a qualitative take on networks, within the logics of NE and "following policy". So there is not a formal concern with measures, edge's weight and formulas. Second, I agree with Ball (2012, p. 144) and Hogan et al. (2015) who point out that "network maps of this kind freeze flows and flatten asymmetries of power" (p. 44). These graphs are limited to represent a complex, fluid, unequal and ever-changing reality:

> It is worth re-stating the artifactual limits of our network. It is a heuristic for understanding policy mobility and the construction of a new policy dispositif. It is not exhaustive. That is, in good part, as Temenos and McCann point out, a consequence of limited resources set over and against the evolving, dynamic and mutating nature of the network. With more time and more money we could have *followed* links and relationships further, through more disparate nodes, to more distant and more local points. These limitations also explain the absence here of any robust quantitative indicators of connectivity or concentration in our account. Any claims made on the basis of such indicators would be vitiated by the failure to exhaust the connections and establish a clear network boundary; although we would also claim that such a boundary is inappropriate here. The relationships and connections involved are continually expanding in number, scope and location. Which points up a further limitation of our network portraits and analyses. These are primarily static and inevitably dated by the time you read this. (Ball et al., 2017, p. 11)

Although limited, the graphs not only have a pragmatic role of informing data collection and analysis, but they also operate in a symbolic and creative way that "foregrounds the importance of network connections"

(Hogan et al., 2015 , p. 44). Network graphs remind us how connected and cross-scalar education governance is now, and in spite of limitations, are still useful, especially if compared to text and tables.

Thus, searching for better ways to use network graphs, I studied, tested and practised different types of graphic representation. Some of them disappointingly became confusing and did not represent what I wished to visualise. There were graphs that informed following research steps, but were later reformed and incremented with new data. Two types of graph were specially employed, straightforward partnership graphs (formal partnerships between institutions, see Chapter 5) and affiliation networks (see Chapter 6).

In SNA, the term "affiliations" usually refers to membership or participation data and co-affiliations are "opportunities for things like ideas to flow between actors", and "affiliations data consist of a set of binary relationships between members of two sets of items" (Borgatti & Halgin, 2012, p. 417). So data is represented in two sets, in this case a set of people and a set of institutions, with a relation that connects them, in this case "*being a member of*". In affiliation graphs, there are only connections across sets, and no connections within a set. So a person can be connected to many institutions (as "being a member of" many institutions), but not to other people. Similarly, institutions can be connected to many people, but not directly connected to other institutions. Here, in Chapter 6 the affiliation data concerns MNLS individual members and the institutions to which they are affiliated through professional work, which has been collected online in a variety of websites (mainly institutional websites and publicly available personal CVs). In this regard, "an important advantage of affiliation data, especially in the case studying elites, is that affiliations are often observable from a distance (e.g. government records, newspaper reports), without having to have special access to the actors" (Borgatti & Halgin, 2012, p. 417)

When one is interested in the relationship between one part of the set, such as the relation between institutions – rather than between people and institutions – "we can in fact construct some kind of tie among members of a node set simply by defining *co-affiliation* (e.g. attendance at the same events, membership on the same corporate board) as a tie. Thus, affiliations data give rise to co-affiliation data, which constitute some kind of tie among nodes within a set" (Borgatti & Halgin, 2012, p. 423). Accordingly, in Chapter 6 a dual-mode network (person-by-institution) was converted into a co-affiliation one-mode network (institution-by-institution), assuming that two institutions that have a member in common have a significant chance of ideas being exchanged from one to the other.

Identifying and categorising these affiliations was challenging at times. These professionals have mobile and boundary-spanning careers (Larner & Laurie, 2010), some pursue more than one occupation, and others change jobs rather quickly. Thus, the graphs are a static oversimplified representation of complex and fast-changing network relations (Ball & Junemann, 2012). The affiliations considered refer to the individual's main employment, but in some cases two affiliations for one individual were included when these were meaningful policymaking roles (such as a being part of a municipal consultative body).

The effort of following people, analysing networks and focusing on practices allowed for the identification of three aspects of non-state actors' work to participate in education policymaking, or "labour" modalities: the discursive, the relational and the institutional. These aspects are presented in Figure 1.

These elements have been organised here as a heuristic device. This means it does not attempt to be a typology, but can be used as starting point to guide investigations. It is not an all-encompassing description or explanation. Nor does it propose a clear-cut separation between practices, or labour aspects and modalities. New philanthropists do all three things; they are policy entrepreneurs, work in networks and partake in heterarchies. All practices involve discourses, relationships and institutions, with some policy entrepreneurship, networks and heterarchies in different ways, partly because of the empirical nature of the phenomenon, with blurry and opaque networks, partly because of the adopted theoretical perspective, with a focus on flows, mobilities and labour, instead of structures and explanatory models.

This can be applied to research in other contexts, to shed light on the many areas of influence and types of activities invested. It offers a theoretical and methodological contribution to better understand how

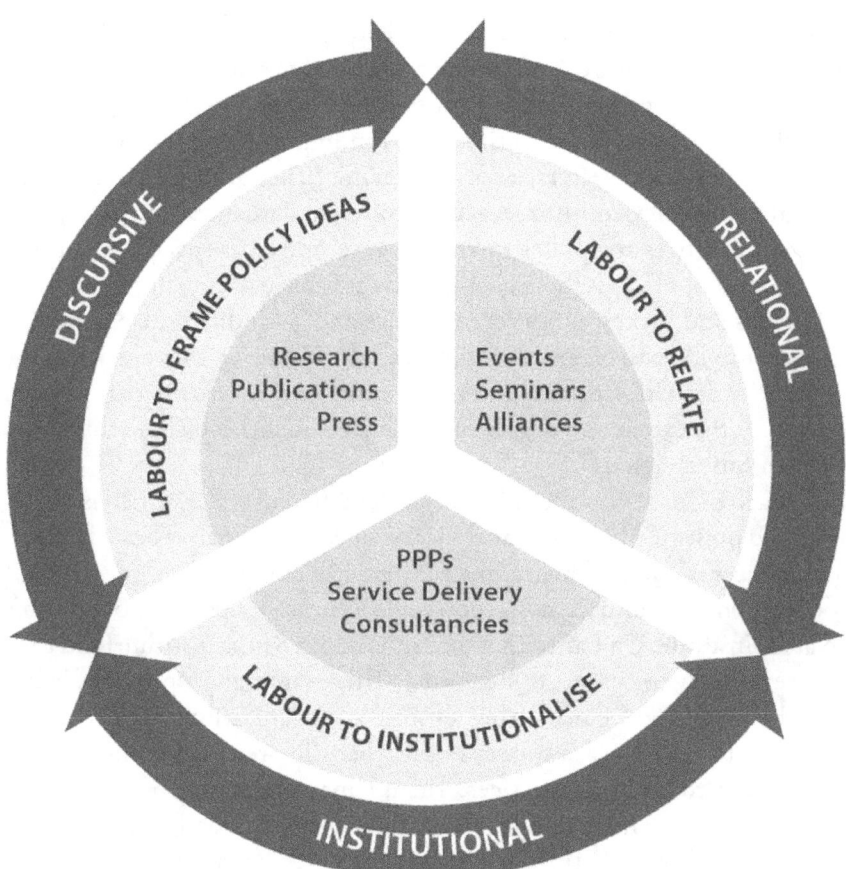

Figure 1. Analytical heuristic

new philanthropies are working to frame ideas around education policy, building cross-scalar (from local to global) and multi-jurisdictional relationships (public and private, market and not-for-profit, among others), and temporarily stabilising policy ideas and relationships in heterarchies by institutionalising these arrangements.

The description of the foundations work in this book may seem somewhat scattered, or perhaps messy at times. At points it is deliberately left like this, in an attempt to not inscribe order where there is hardly any, to overwrite messiness with simplicity, and provide the reader a vivid account of how new philanthropy is participating in education policymaking. All of this labour happens at once – promoting events, participating in social meetings, campaigning with the press, funding studies, creating partnerships with different secretaries of education... They are diffused, operated in different policy contexts, reaching different audiences, impacting discourses, practices and policies in a cross-level and cross-space fashion. The sheer amount of work these foundations are able to carry out, in a variety of arenas and spaces, on different topics and with different partners, is indeed too large to encompass in one study. However, I would argue the volume of activities, the ubiquity of foundations, is actually part of what produces the extent and degree of influence philanthropy has achieved in the education arena.

Each modality of labour is analysed in different scales, which is organised and presented here as an analytical frame. First, I analyse how these sets of practices are enacted in networks of Brazilian new philanthropy, focusing on five central foundations – Todos pela Educação, Lemann Foundation, Natura Institute, Unibanco Institute and Ayrton Senna Institute (and their contexts, networks and connections). This examination provides width for the analysis for considering a group of organisations with different projects, thus a rich variety of examples that still presents significant similarities regarding these practices. Then, I analyse how the same practices can be found in one more specific case, the Mobilisation for the National Learning Standards (MNLS), which is supported by the five studied foundations. This provides depth of analysis, in which I can look at the data with more detail and attention to specific moments, spaces and situations of policymaking and governance. Finally, the practices are analysed amid the global connections of the same case, the MNLS, which makes possible a "*glocal*" analysis, which considers the transnational connections of this group. The analytical frame is presented in Figure 2.

The analytical frame made possible a cross-scalar analysis of complex networks, which was particularly fruitful. Starting the analysis of data with a whole network provided an understanding of the wide context and network dynamics. It also made possible the identification of key analytical themes (practices, discourses and narratives). Then focusing on one in-depth case and its connections provided an exhaustive account of

From government to governance

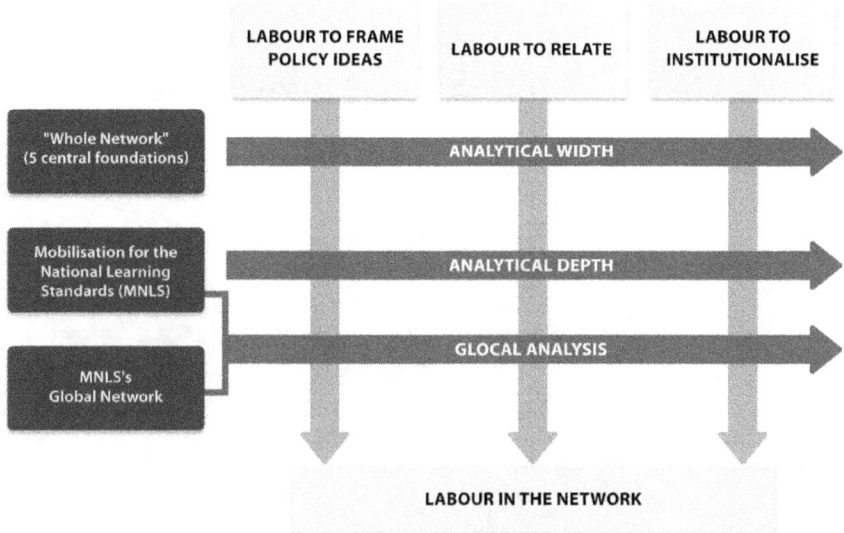

Figure 2. Analytical frame

personal connections, use of meetings and creation of discourses. Finally, in deliberately tracing global connections around this case, it was possible to identify the formation of "glocal" partnerships and relationships, with global discourses being shared by consultants and in meetings, and the creation of policy pipelines for policy mobility.

Although cutting the data to make it fit in a text has the risk of over simplifying and deforming it, this frame is used to organise the messy and overwhelming data. The limitations of the device are perhaps remedied with the MNLS section in each chapter, which provides a more bounded, in-depth and cross-theme analysis. Nonetheless, the MNLS scale is also challenging due to its global reach. Global networks of education governance are overwhelming, and impossible – and probably inadvisable – to be flattened and tidied up in simplistic typologies or explanations. What the analytical heuristic and frame set out to do, instead of an explanatory model or typology, is a tentative way to make sense of complex policy relationships, opening a way for questionings and reflections, and not closing down tidy accounts.

CHAPTER 3

Working to shape narratives and frame education policy ideas

> "I am a producer of education policy, so it is a proper work of advocacy. We try - but sadly it is not us who are writing the Learning Standards - but we try to produce inputs to help the ones who have the pen in their hands. It is about having influence over people with these inputs we produce."
>
> Interview, Lemann Foundation, 2016

In a room full of people from business and philanthropy, he said, "if you look at the strategic plan of most of the organisations in the sector, you'll see that they do not position themselves as substituting the state, but to help building policies". This happened during the 2016 GIFE Conference, when Denis Mizne, the Executive Secretary of the Lemann Foundation, described how the work of foundations has been changing in the past years. He narrated how foundations have been changing their work from "charity", with the provision of services that should be offered by the state, towards a focus on policymaking. This change in focus revolves around "policy entrepreneurship", with many activities that aim to create a new image for philanthropists, and this allows them to be active and effective in the education policy arena. New philanthropists partake in policymaking as actors that defend certain policy ideas and frame problems and solutions in the process. This effort, referred to as policy entrepreneurship (Kingdon, 1984), revolves around investing resources to frame and share policy ideas, as well as participating in processes of policy change (Capella, 2016). In spite of the work of policy entrepreneurs not being new, and the existence of an extensive literature around policy entrepreneurship, the work of new philanthropists as policy entrepreneurs is somewhat new and still understudied.

This chapter analyses the discursive and political labour of new philanthropy to frame, defend and disseminate education policy ideas. This work is about framing what is a social problem that deserves attention, what is the best policy solution to it, and convincing people about it. Contrasting to a "technical" and depoliticised understanding of policy, that takes social problems and solutions for granted and a simple matter of "evidence", here it is understood that this process of "advocacy" is inherently political, it is about choosing some agendas while displacing others, selecting certain "solutions" while taking the attention away from alternatives. While this is done, discourses are also reworked, redefining what is "thinkable" and "unthinkable", or considered logic and rational or utopian and ideological, and who is legitimate in this arena.

This chapter first analyses how new philanthropists have shifted from charity to a focus on policy, operating as policy entrepreneurs. Within this, it explores how successful entrepreneurs assemble an "authoritative voice" (Ball, 1993), with a claim to be heard, sharing ideas in many spaces and investing different types of resources in these endeavours. Part of it involves "defending" policy ideas through knowledge mobilisation. Second, the Mobilization for the National Learning Standards (MNLS) is introduced, and I explore how this group has been effectively working as a policy entrepreneur and framing education inequality as a policy problem and a standard curriculum in Brazil as the best policy solution. MNLS persistently shares policy ideas in many venues and channels, and gathers and gains support from other policy actors in the process. Finally, MNLS's policy entrepreneurship is analysed internationally, with its use of global consultancies and benchmarking. To conclude, I ponder on how new philanthropy actively participates in policymaking with efforts to shape policy problems and solutions. New philanthropies build their position as legitimate policy actors by claiming "expertise" in education, and create a space for corporate organisations and actors to participate in education policymaking.

Policy entrepreneurship in education: From charities to authoritative voices

Among philanthropic organisations, both corporate or grass-roots, a contrast is drawn between the ones that execute charitable service provision, or insular social assistance, and the ones that aim at policy, as described by the former executive secretary of GIFE:

> It is a diverse group. In spite of being perceived as homogenous, it is not. There are institutions with very different characteristics. So there are institutions that fundamentally work in a "charity" way, and there are institutions that work with a type of activity, which is absolutely strategic, of *policy change*. So you have a large dispersion, with a unitary vision or a vision of *transforming the country*. (Interview, GIFE, 2016, added emphasis)

As explained by the interviewee, aiming at some kind of policy effect is not characteristic of all GIFE members, and being a corporate foundation does not necessarily imply aiming at policy change. Nonetheless, partaking in policymaking is now not just one part of new philanthropies' activities, but the fundamental goal of some well-connected foundations. This is illustrated by the 2014 biannual survey conducted by GIFE, in which 89 per cent of respondents claim their work is related to public policy, and 58 per cent aim at directly influencing or supporting policymaking. Moreover, amongst the largest organisations, which invest more than USD 21 million per year, 75 per cent aim at influencing policy. However, there are corporate foundations that do execute "charity-like" services. For instance, Bosch Foundation, in spite of being a "corporate foundation" created and funded by a large international company, operates as a local organisation that delivers services and does not seek to participate in policymaking. As a corporate foundation, but not a policy entrepreneur, this contrasting example sheds light on its opposite, of how large foundations work as policy entrepreneurs.

Bosch is a multinational German company, "supplier of technology and services", with more than 400.000 employees in different countries, and generated sales of 78 billion euros in 2017 (Bosch site). The company was founded in 1886, and taken to Brazil in 1954. Now it employs more than 8,500 people in the country, with a liquid revenue of BRL 4.4 (Bosch Brazil website).[1] Its Brazilian office is at the state of São Paulo, in the city of Campinas. The Bosch Foundation is in the same estate as the company, next to the "Bosch Club", a space with barbecue areas, tennis courts and gym for the employees. The Bosch Foundation was created as a part of the corporate structure to care for employees and offer them motivation and a positive impression of the company, a classic example of Corporate Social Responsibility (CSR). The institute works locally in the cities in which Bosch operates. With a relatively small budget, reportedly BRL 1 million a year (Interview, Bosch Foundation, 2016), the foundation worked with only a few schools in Curitiba and a single school in Campinas, which is geographically close to the foundation. This school was the only one that welcomed Bosch's social project when the foundation sent out a call for applications through emails and phone calls. According to the interviewees, there was a lot of resistance from head teachers once they learnt "the partnership proposal came from a philanthropic institute" (Interview, Bosch Foundation, 2016). The school in Campinas that accepted the partnership invitation went through a series of meetings to identify the most pressing school issues. Having identified a reportedly weak relationship between teachers, parents and students as the largest problem, the foundation proposed a series of activities to promote bonding, including a day of games and a collective refurbishment, to which Bosch Foundation supplied materials and the community planned and executed the work.

The work of this philanthropy contrasts with the one conducted by some highly connected and prominent foundations, which describe policymaking as a fundamental aspect of their work. The Executive Secretary of the Natura Institute asserts: "In general we believe one of the main roles of the third sector is to positively influence public policy. So in practically all we do we have a desire that it may become a public policy" (Interview, Natura Institute, 2016). Policy is both means and end for these institutions: They aim to partake in policymaking, and use influence and definition

---

[1] <https://www.brasil.bosch.com.br/nossa-empresa/bosch-no-brasil/>.

of social problems and their policy solutions as ways of achieving the reform of education, in various forms and along different dimensions (curriculum, leadership, pedagogy, technology…).

New philanthropists refer to this work around policymaking as "advocacy". However, this shift in philanthropy is more than that. The idea of advocacy falls short in accounting for the efforts invested here and the dynamics in the arena. Namely, "advocacy" captures only the political (and more visible) aspect of policy work, concerning the convincing of audiences through the framing of issues in persuasive ways and building support networks. It does not capture the discursive aspects of policy entrepreneurship, which stress the active framing of problems and solutions in a way that demands action, and makes certain policies thinkable and unthinkable (Ball, 1993). Second, "advocacy" implies that the advocates, in this case new philanthropists, are somewhat "outsiders" to the policymaking process, who aim tirelessly to convince "insiders", or members of the government of ways of doing policy differently. As discussed throughout the chapter, and indeed the book, this outside/inside, or public/private, division is not as clear as one would imagine. New philanthropy now participates in "all aspects of the education policy cycle, from agenda setting, through policy production and implementation to evaluation" (Hogan et al., 2015, p. 61), and collaborates in networks of blurred public-private boundaries.

Instead of "advocacy", foundations do *policy entrepreneurship* to reform education through policy. They aim to bring about or contribute to large-scale changes in the country through influencing education policy according to an agenda of corporate reform of education (as discussed in Chapter 1). This involves assembling an "authoritative voice" (Ball, 1993) to participate in the discursive and political definition of policy problems and solutions, and philanthropies are able to mobilise and invest large amounts of resources, such as money, time, and social capital to frame policy problems and solutions (Capella, 2016; Kingdon, 1984). They can use different investments in the hope of future returns (Capella, 2016).

"Entrepreneurship", like governance, has become a buzzword that is now used by businessmen, social influencers, in the media, and so on. The study of "entrepreneurship" and "entrepreneurs" has been growing in the past decades in areas such as administration, economy and political science. The concept was first employed by Schumpeter (1983), who regarded the entrepreneur as an innovator, someone who does things differently. So an entrepreneur was not necessarily someone with financial investments, but with an idea and ability to turn it into something powerful and lucrative. The concept later shifted from economics to politics with the term "political entrepreneur" (Wagner, 1966), used to "designate individuals who employ time, energy and financial resources not only because they are concerned with the group's goals, but also because they see an opportunity to transform this investment into something personally gratifying" (Shepsle, 2006, in Capella, 2016, p. 488). In this sense, "the [political] entrepreneur makes possible the collective action through its expertise, knowledge and timing about the right moment to act, realising the potential for collective action, which would not happen without its intervention" (Capella, 2016, p. 488). The "entrepreneur" has also been studied in the field of organisational studies, with the institutional entrepreneur, which is associated with the work of Paul DiMaggio (1988) within organisational new institutionalism. For the author, entrepreneurs promote changes in institutional arrangements to pursue their own interests intentionally. They have the required resources to do so, which can be analytical, political or cultural skills that allow one to develop new alliances and stimulate collaboration. The literature highlights the discursive aspect of this work, considering how language and narratives are used to convey beliefs and values to gain support for ideas. For some authors, such as Battilana et al. (2009), the institutional entrepreneur not only participates in inciting change, but is actively engaged in the very process of enacting the changes advocated.

Finally, drawing upon these former usages, the term has been employed in policy studies in the form of the *policy entrepreneur*, which gained attention in the 1980s. John Kingdon (1984, 2013) was one of the first authors to use this concept. With his model of "multiple streams", which is focused on agenda setting, he pointed to the relevance of individuals that defend and promote policy ideas, policy entrepreneurs.[2] This policy model

2   For brevity, the terms policy entrepreneur and entrepreneur will be used interchangeably in this text.

considers there are three policy dimensions, or policy streams, that concern problems, solutions and political dynamics. It claims that policy agendas change when the three streams converge, which creates concrete possibilities of shifts. In these moments, named "policy windows", "a problem is recognised, a solution is available, and the political conditions make the moment appropriate for a change" (Capella, 2016, p. 491). The policy entrepreneur acts in this process, by shaping the understanding of policy problems and solutions, and partaking in political relationships to create appropriate conditions for policy change (Capella, 2016).

In sum, a policy entrepreneur is an actor that participates in policy-making, investing resources to defend particular policy ideas and gaining support for such ideas. In this process, policy problems and solutions are framed discursively, while at the same time the entrepreneurs define themselves as legitimate policy actors, part of the solution. A definition of policy entrepreneurs is not dependent on one's affiliations, as they can be in different places in, out and around government (Kingdon, 2013). Instead, the policy entrepreneur is characterised by their activity around policy, as Kingdon (2013) put it:

> but their defining characteristic, much as in the case of a business entrepreneur, is their willingness to invest their resources - time, energy, reputation, and sometimes money - in the hope of a future return. That return might come to them in the form of policies of which they approve, satisfaction from participation, or even personal aggrandisement in the form of job security or career promotion. (p. 122)

To achieve success in policy entrepreneurial efforts, part of new philanthropy's labour revolves around assembling the required resources and capabilities to frame and disseminate ideas. This involves practices and discourses that redistribute "voice" in the education policy arena, as Ball (1993) explains: "Policy as discourse may have the effect of redistributing 'voice' [...] so that it does not matter what some people say or think, only certain voices can be heard as meaningful or authoritative" (p. 15). The redistribution of voice is part of the "politics of truth", in which "advocates and technicians of policy change" (Ball, 1993, p. 15) partake. To assemble an "authoritative voice", policy entrepreneurs invest some efforts, which will be examined in what follows. First, they establish a "claim to hearing"

(Kingdon, 2013), meaning to have credit in the eyes of the general public and be seen as "legitimate" policy actors. Second, entrepreneurs foster political connections and employ skills of presentation and persuasion through which they articulate and disseminate their policy ideas. Third, entrepreneurs are persistent and are willing to invest considerable financial resources in the policy process, in all of its aspects.

Producing "evidence" and becoming "experts": The work to become a legitimate voice in the public debate

To assemble a "claim to hearing" (Kingdom, 2013) new philanthropists invest in the production of "evidence" through their own funded research, by making links with and disseminating ideas through the press and other media and collaboration with chosen "experts" – those "on-message". There has been a growth in the production of "research" by new philanthropies in Brazil since 2013. Before that year few reports had been produced, and since then most well-connected foundations have been investing in the production of "evidence". These studies are done in an array of formats and sizes, including small exploratory efforts and large-scale and heavily funded studies, which can include universities and scholars. In the first case, the research projects can be executed as a preliminary stage within a larger project, like Institute Natura did with the project "Full-time Schools". A representative from this institute affirmed that conducting exploratory research is a "necessary first stage of a project" (Interview, Natura Institute, 2016). On the other hand, studies can be more ambitious, executed by an internal "research" department in foundations or by a contracted partner. Ayrton Senna Institute and Lemann Foundation have mostly executed their own studies, usually in partnership with other institutions. Natura Institute, Unibanco Institute and TPE have contracted out reports to research organisations. Some examples are organised in Table 3.

Table 3. "Research" efforts of new philanthropy organisations

Institution	How research is done	Examples (since creation of org.)
Lemann Foundation	Partnerships with universities	Harvard, MIT, Stanford, Teachers College – Columbia University, University of Illinois, University of Southern California, Oxford (formerly Yale and UCLA)
	Develop their own studies (with partnerships)	Excellency with equity, Life Project and Conselho de Classe (with Itau BBA, Credit Suisse, TPE)
Natura Institute	First stage of project	Full-time schools
	Contracting out reports	Mapeal (with CIPPEC)
Ayrton Senna Institute	Develop their own studies (with partnerships)	Alfabetismo e competencias, Construindo uma Educação de Qualidade
	Partnerships with universities	University of Ghent, Insper
Unibanco Institute	Contracting out reports	School management (for racial equality, and for gender equality)
Todos Pela Educacao	Presenting papers	68 presented articles in seminars, including academic events
	Writing papers	19 articles published in journals and proceedings
	Studies and research (including policy analysis and government documents)	Over 100 documents
	Other productions	Over 60 publications

The findings and results of these studies are usually presented in well-designed reports, with colourful outlines and info graphics. To disseminate "research evidence", these organisations promote regular publications. For instance, the Unibanco Institute has a fortnightly publication, the *Boletim Aprendizagem em Foco*. Created in 2015, its readership goal is focused on school head teachers and it aims to "deepen the debates about the Brazilian education context and bring to the agenda relevant themes for public policy. With a fortnightly publication, it is anchored in empirical evidence, disseminating research, studies and national and international experiences" (Unibanco website).

However, the evidence produced or selected is not "neutral". It is politically mediated both in its production and how this "evidence" is taken up in policymaking. First, philanthropic studies tend to prioritise and reinforce certain policy ideas over a substantial debate (Hogan et al., 2016a). Foundations differ from more traditional research organisations, such as universities, in being more willing to blur boundaries between research and advocacy (DeBray-Pelot, Lubienski, & Scott, 2007). For instance, the studies conducted and funded by new philanthropies tend to be based on the pre-existing epistemic positions of these organisations. Foundations hire staff, consultants or research organisations that hold similar epistemic and political positions as them. This practice produces what Hogan, Sellar and Lingard (2016a) call a "new policy genre" that over-simplifies complicated policy issues:

> This new genre reflects new kinds of interactions between governments and non-state actors such as edu-businesses and consultancy firms. The hallmark of this genre is a simplification of policy problems and the articulation of straightforward policy solutions, somewhat akin to a reductive "what works" approach. This commercialisation must be understood in the context of comparison becoming a central element of new modes of state governance. (p. 244)

An interviewee from Lemann Foundation describes how the organisation has been working for the advocacy of a new standard curriculum in Brazil with the MNLS, producing evidence to support the policy solution advocated:

> We started producing research here in Brazil *about the need* of having learning standards for Brazilian students ... This is what we try to do, the focus of our advocacy is making sure that people can make *decisions based on evidence*, having subsidies to make the best choices. So this is what we do, we share information. (Interview, Lemann Foundation, 2016, added emphasis)

With a clear agenda, studies are carried out to "demonstrate the need" of a policy solution, which is introduced as "evidence" to decision-makers and the general public. As this interviewee illustrates, policy entrepreneurship involves not only advocating for certain policy solutions, but perhaps most importantly, the participation in the selection of what consists a problem and defining their solutions. In this case, it concerns studying why a curriculum is needed, and then disseminating the information that, in the first place, seemed from a specific worldview. Entrepreneurs "are responsible not only for prompting important people to pay attention, but also for coupling solutions to problems and for coupling both problems and solutions to politics" (Kingdon, 2013, p. 20). To be sure, they not only "defend ideas", but actively participate in the framing of policy problems and solutions, connecting policy ideas to each other and to politics. At the same time other solutions are debunked or excluded from consideration.

This evidence is used, cited and corroborated by other foundations, creating the "echo chamber effect" (Goldie et al., 2014), with an unfunded perception of consensus. New philanthropists work to "collect, package and promote, but not necessarily produce, research evidence aligned with the agendas of their funders" (Lubienski et al., 2016, p. 7). This work can be referred to as "knowledge mobilisation", which involves the "intentional efforts to increase the use of research evidence [...] in policy and practice at multiple levels of the education sector" (Cooper, 2014, p. 29). It entails the production of research and studies, or support to like-minded organisations, to frame policy debates. The reports produced are used to create the discursive basis and justifications for their positions, proposals and activities. Carrying out such "studies" is fundamental to the systematisation of the "new" policy ideas that are put forward and to frame them in ways that can be regarded as or claim to be "evidence".

In this dynamic, policy solutions may exist before the very policy problem they claim to address (Kingdom, 2013). For example, the Ayrton

Senna Institute had a "full-time schools"[3] project before collaborating with the city of Rio de Janeiro in 2014 to bring a "policy solution" to the city, which was supported by the company Procter & Gamble (Interview, Ayrton Senna Institute, 2016). After this partnership, the project became established as a "tried and tested education policy solution" of the Ayrton Senna Institute, and it can be adopted through a PPP by any local and regional authority. About this policy solution, an interviewee from the Institute said, "Is there a demand? If there is not, there will be" (Interview, Ayrton Senna Institute, 2016). In this example, the Institute had already planned, formulated and tested a policy solution which was not yet "required" or "need", but was likely to be as the increase of full-time schools was established as a goal in the 2014 National Plan of Education. To confirm the efficacy of the solution, the Institute claims in its website that "in the first school to pilot this proposal, the learning improvement has been 10 times superior than the average of the Brazilian student in the past decade. If all schools in Brazil had the same result, we would go up 30 positions in PISA" (Ayrton Senna Institute website)

Second, the selection and use of evidence in policymaking is also permeated by power relations, not all "evidence" is perceived as equally valid, as Verger et al. (2016) explain:

> The *selection* of particular policy solutions by decision-makers is another key moment in education policy reform. It implies the identification of the most suitable interpretations of what the existing problems are, as well as the most complementary policy solutions. When it comes to selecting policy solutions and matching them to these perceived problems, more and more governments aim to base their decisions on scientific evidence, especially in moments of crisis and uncertainty. Scientific evidence helps policy-makers to "make sense of the world and stabilize structures of action" (Jessop 2015). *However, not all types of evidence – nor all sources of evidence – are equally perceived and considered by policy-makers*, with some international actors enjoying a privileged position when it comes to, on the one hand, constructing social problems and their causes – what Jessop (2015) calls a global *aetiology* – and, on the other, guiding countries in dealing with the complexity of educational change. (Verger, Fontdevila, & Zancajo, 2017, p. 760)

3   In Brazil most schools are part-time. There is a long-standing popular demand to offer full-time schools to all students, which became part of the National Plan of Education in 2014 and should be implemented by 2024.

Working with universities

Foundations also develop a close relationship to universities, especially Lemann Foundation and Ayrton Senna, to work with prestigious researchers who can produce robust and persuasive reports. The first has partnerships with Harvard University, MIT, the Teachers College – Columbia University, Stanford University, University of Illinois, University of Southern California and Oxford University (and formerly Yale and UCLA); and the second with Insper, in Brazil, and the University of Ghent, in Belgium. Such relationships, in themselves, give credibility to the work of the foundations and to their publications (and are a source of income to the providers). Ayrton Senna Institute has also created a network of education researchers, the *Rede Nacional de Ciencia pela Educação*[4], or the National Network of Science for Education.[5] The network connects eighty-eight research groups in Brazil, and aims to bring together researchers and practitioners to create collaborations that may support innovation and "evidence-based" policies. Also participating in research spaces, including academic ones, TPE has been presenting papers in conferences and seminars, publishing papers in journals and conference proceedings, and partaking in different studies, including policy analysis work for the government[6].

New philanthropies can claim expertise by associating their policy efforts with recognised "experts", which may include researchers or experienced educators and practitioners. To justify their policy choices, foundations claim that an "expert" has designed their policy solutions and education projects. For instance, the large project *Conviva* alleges to have been created in response to the findings of a research project conducted by the higher education institution *Fundação Getulio Vargas* (FGV). The research

---

4 <https://www.institutoayrtonsenna.org.br/pt-br/como-atuamos/rede-nacional-de-ciencia-para-educacao.html>.

5 <www.institutoayrtonsenna.org.br/content/institutoayrtonsenna/pt-br/Atuacao/rede-nacional-de-ciencia-para-educacao.html>.

6 see complete list in <https://www.todospelaeducacao.org.br/biblioteca/conteudo-tpe/>.

investigated the policy support needed by municipal governments and found that secretaries of education required training in education management. Thus, an online platform was created with support of several foundations (including Natura Institute, Lemann Foundation, Ayrton Senna Institute and others). It offers training to local secretaries of education, with several types of content, including readings, tutorials and video classes that address the diagnosed needs (Interview, Natura Institute, 2016). Natura Institute, the manager of the platform, claims to "have one stream of work which is about content", with which "we gather a series of *specialists* in the specific team and then these people build this content, content that we construct. These *specialists* are usually former secretaries of education" (Interview, Natura Institute, 2016, added emphasis). Thus, in *Conviva*, "experts" participate in the creation of the content, or the "solutions", besides partaking in the identification of municipal policy problems in this platform.

Lemann Foundation also employs the trope of the "experts" in the narrative of how its initiatives are developed. The foundation has an annual seminar with Stanford University, in which researchers from the university present their studies and discuss the foundation's topics of interest. In 2016 the seminar concerned Brazilian national learning standards, and in this event there was "a round table of *specialists* from Stanford University that did a critical reading of the first version of the document" (Interview, Lemann Foundation, 2016, added emphasis).

The "expert" is invoked to explain the creation process of a foundation's initiative, in an idealised narrative, or to allegedly demonstrate the rigour of such a solution. "Experts" are also said to evaluate the foundations initiatives, to legitimise foundations' projects. Natura Institute has a department completely dedicated to evaluating its projects, which is run by an "evaluation expert" (Interview, Natura Institute, 2016). In these examples, the "experts" are not named, nor are their affiliations or official credentials mentioned and made known in interviews. Nonetheless, foundations are still able to claim expertise through the employment of the imagery of "experts".

In the process of "specialists" taking charge of the creation, development and evaluation of policy solutions, new philanthropies engage with policy as a technical matter, in which decisions are made based on technical evidence. Political discussions, positions, debates and dialogues are not considered in the processes and narratives, ignoring the political aspects involved in policy and governance.

The research effort undertaken by or for foundations is also fundamental to the maintenance of policy networks. Studies fulfil a role of providing or articulating meanings and discourses for the network, as "the work of practising policy networks is always constituted by a duality of material strategies [...] and the ideological work of framing how policy is imagined and contested. These research and advocacy organisations thus serve as the meaning-making and framing arms of the policy networks cultivated by philanthropic foundations" (Ferrare & Apple, 2017, p. 26). Policy ideas, concerning policy issues and solutions, are shared in and through the policy network, framing how policies are imagined and framed, opening the way for certain policies and actors, while also excluding others as "once a particular problem comes to capture the attention of important people, some whole classes of approaches come into favour and others fall from grace" (Kingdon, 2013, p. 115).

Working with the press and disseminating ideas

Knowledge mobilisation involves the sharing of the produced knowledge. Foundations have increasingly been portrayed in the media as "thought leaders" amid public debates, making use of this space to mobilise public opinion around education matters and working to steer the agenda around education. Education reform advocates turn to communication channels, including the press, to reach the general public and make the case for particular solutions – making use of available evidence and framing stories in a tactical way (Goldie et al., 2014; Lubienski et al., 2016). There are three main types of interaction between new philanthropies and the press in Brazil: writing for the press, training journalists and the ownership of media vehicles, like magazines.

First, new philanthropists have a growing presence in the press as columnists in newspapers and magazines or by being invited to comment on policy issues. With a growing status of "experts", they occupy a central role in public debates about education. From TPE, Priscila Cruz is the writer of a weekly column in *UOL Educação*, from the large newspaper *Folha*. Viviane Senna (Ayrton Senna Institute) and Ricardo Henriques (Unibanco Institute) are often interviewed in major newspapers to discuss education policy issues. Similarly, the foundations' research efforts are often released in the press as well. Foundations even count "media hits" in their annual reports as part of their "impact". TPE proudly reported 12 published articles in press, 2000 press clippings, 600 interview requests and 100 journalists trained on "how to cover education in the press" in 2015. Similarly, Unibanco Institute reported 609 mentions in press, with 131 in the national press and 189 specifically mentioning with Ricardo Henriques, the Institute's Executive Superintendent in that year. Arguably, this is beneficial for these organisations not only for the construction of the "expert" image, but also for marketing purposes within the logics of philanthrocapitalism (Bishop & Green, 2010; McAlister & Ferrell, 2002). Except for TPE, the other four institutes carry with them the names of the funding companies or families.

A second dynamic built with the press concerns the instructing and training of journalists to "properly cover education issues". TPE is the main example of this, with an axis of action named "Mobilisation and Communication". The organisation has been promoting courses to train journalists, which have been attended by more than 2000 journalists (Martins, 2013; 2016). Besides this, the organisation also compiles news and suggests information sources and experts for interviews for journalists (Martins, 2013).

A third relationship built between foundations and the press in Brazil concerns the ownership of communication vehicles. The Lemann Foundation and the Ayrton Senna Institute are owners and publishers of education magazines. Lemann Foundation became the proprietor of two "non-profit" magazines in education, *Nova Escola* and *Gestão Escolar*. These are the two largest magazines for teachers and educators in the country, with more than 120,000 magazines sold per volume, 45,000 subscribers and 2.5 million website access per month (*Nova Escola* website). Besides being a major vehicle of communication, influence and discourse sharing with teachers and head teachers, these magazines are also a space for the commodification of education. In spite of being "non-profit", companies can purchase advertisement space in the magazine, including the so-called "branded content". In this option, publicity is done through a "practical and informative content" (*Nova Escola* website), where the brand is displayed as the sponsor. Here, the selling of education products and services can be masked as "practical" and "informative" content, and as technical support for teachers.

The work of knowledge mobilisation, both the publication of "research" studies and their coverage in the press, has been very important for foundations to gain credibility, be seen as legitimate by the public and thus become an "authoritative voice" in education policy (Ball, 1993). Relatedly, the press can be used to put pressure on governments, as is made clear by a Lemann Foundation representative in saying: "with the press as well, in a last case, if we truly believe in a cause and the Ministry of Education and the government do not abide by it, then going to the press is always a good opportunity" (Interview, Lemann Foundation, 2016). By working with the press, new philanthropy is able to draw from their studies and perform public communication to build up an image of themselves as education experts, in spite of having no official position in the decision-making process, or possessing more traditional "expertise" like education practitioners or universities. The claim of expertise is used as a discursive device to portray new philanthropy as an "authoritative voice" in the "politics of truth". This allows otherwise unlikely actors to partake in policymaking, such as a beauty products company, a billionaire businessman, a socialite, a conglomerate of for-profit companies and others. "These experts are enacting particular forms of 'techno-politics' (Mitchell, 2002) that link knowledge and expertise to political power in diverse and distinctive forms" (Larner & Laurie, 2010, p. 223) (see Chapter 5, with an example of MNLS's use of "experts" in meetings).

Sharing ideas in many venues

Successful policy entrepreneurs disseminate their policy ideas in many venues, and build up political connections and negotiating skills to gain support to such ideas, including from people that participate in decision-making processes (Kingdon, 2013). So entrepreneurs present their policy ideas in a plethora of ways and spaces to reach different audiences (Kindgon, 2013). This involves networking, in which the entrepreneur is connected not only to specialists or policymakers, but also the general public or particular working groups or organisations – like teachers, principals, teacher organisations, local government, etc. In networking, entrepreneurs aim at convincing others about their ideas while also understanding how different groups interpret certain issues and learning ways to reframe their proposals to different audiences (Capella, 2016).

New philanthropists share new policy ideas, backed by the "evidence" produced by foundations and their partners, with a variety of stakeholders involved in the policy field. Many venues, channels and spaces can be used, including introducing a bill, holding congressional hearings, with speeches, issuing studies, reports and other papers, personal conversations, public events and informal meetings. Time, money, effort and prestige are invested in pushing one's agenda forward, as "policy entrepreneurs do not leave consideration of their proposals to accident. Instead, they push for consideration in many ways and in many forums" (Kingdon, 2013, p. 201). As relevant as considering foundations' legitimacy gained through research, and their network and social capital invested in brokering policies, Kingdon stresses a basic, yet key, aspect in policy entrepreneurs' work, which is "sheer tenacity" in advocating for a policy:

> many potentially influential people might have expertise and political skill, but sheer tenacity pays off. Most of these people spend a great deal of time giving talks, writing position papers, sending letters to important people, drafting bills, testifying before congressional committees and executive branch commissions, and having lunch, all with the aim of pushing their ideas in whatever way and forum might further the cause. (Kingdon, 2013, p. 181)

These foundations seem to be everywhere, in every seminar, every meeting, every public audition, bill voting, press release and so on, as mentioned, there is a certain "ubiquity" in their work. Lemann Foundation, both in its individual work and representing the MNLS, deliberately aims at reaching different groups and actors to gain support for its agenda:

> They do a bunch of meetings, a lot of conversation to help solving the main difficulties, exchange ideas, talk with the Movement. But also talk with deputies, talk with the writing team and talk with everyone that is important in this debate. [...] So sometimes, no, not sometimes, we always include in this discussion the states and municipalities as well. We promote meetings with secretaries of education, municipal and state based ... It depends a lot, it usually is with everyone that is important for that discussion, everyone that has some importance in decision-making over that matter. (Interview, Lemann Foundation, 2016)

Talking to "everyone that matters" includes specific decision-makers. Lemann Foundation has an employee in Brasília, the capital of Brazil, who is part of the "government relations" team within the foundation. He stays in Brasília "creating dialogue with the congress and other actors" (Interview, Lemann Foundation, 2016). A member of the foundation's governance board described his work as "lobbying": "We hired someone 'super', who is in Brasilia now, only doing lobby. But it is lobby for this kind of thing, you know? It is someone who has in his diary talking to people that have power, or that participate in the process of eventually having connectivity" (Interview, Lemann Foundation, 2016). Strategically, this "government relations" employee targets specific people to present short proposals based on Lemann Foundation research efforts:

> We work very closely so that when he arrives to the room of a deputy, or the president of a company, something like that, he always arrive with something ready, a "one-page" with the main facts of what we ... our claims and suggestions, matching the profile of the person he is going to talk to. (Interview, Lemann Foundation, 2016)

This person has also been carefully selected, with the profile and professional experience of a "boundary spanner": "He is really cool because he is someone who came from the public sector ... he was in the government of Aécio with Falconi to improve the public management in different areas. Then he applied for a Lemann scholarship and went to Stanford for his masters" (Interview, Lemman Foundation, 2016).

As the example of Lemann Foundation makes clear, the policy entrepreneur's work is not limited to framing and sharing ideas. Instead, "besides operating in the context of ideas, entrepreneurs pay attention to institutional arrangements that may restrict or incentivise decisions concerning the policy at stake" (Capella, 2016, p. 499). Thus, entrepreneurs pursue reform projects in other policy contexts like policy writing and enactment, as "they coordinate networks involving groups of people and organisations needed to guarantee change. Thus, entrepreneurs are not atomised individuals, on the contrary, they are, and must be, inserted in networks" (Capella, 2016, p. 499). Some aspects of this work are analysed in this chapter, but a further in-depth discussion of networks can be found in Chapter 5, as well as an in-depth discussion of working with decision-makers in the government can be found in Chapter 6.

Widespread action is essential to the success of policy entrepreneurship. Without the establishment of an extensive agreement, policies are less likely to be accepted when an opportunity, or policy window, happens. Hence, in addition to starting discussions of their proposals, they push their ideas in many different forums. These entrepreneurs attempt to "soften up" both policy communities, which tend to be inertia-bound and resistant to major changes, and larger publics, getting them used to new ideas and building acceptance for their proposals (Kingdon, 2013, p. 128).

Mobilising resources: Leveraging limited funds and investing different capitals

To maintain the efforts of knowledge production and sharing, creating networks, disseminating policy ideas, entrepreneurs need persistence and a disposition of investing great amounts of resources. Investments of time, money, energy and reputation are required, and entrepreneurs are willing to invest different kinds of resources to push their policy ideas forward (Capella, 2016), as "persistence implies a willingness to invest large and sometimes remarkable quantities of one's resources" (Kindgon, 2013, p. 181).

Within the logics of new philanthropy, policy entrepreneurship offers a better "return of investment" than "traditional" philanthropy with local education projects. New philanthropists may opt to invest in policy efforts "because advocacy grants could influence government spending" (Reckhow & Snyder, 2014, p. 2). The former chief executive of GIFE articulates how foundations use their private investments in a way to steer public investments, which are much larger:

> It is pointless trying to do what the state does by complementing it, because it [the state] comes in with 100 and you with 001. So it is more interesting that you guide your investment in a way that these 100 billion have more efficacy. (Interview, GIFE, 2016)

Hence, working with the government and with policy is construed as a strategy to leverage philanthropy's limited funding. Instead of executing local projects, which are fully funded and operated by the foundation, new philanthropists see the public budget as an opportunity of leveraging their own investment and reaching results of a larger scale. In this context, a central argument revolves around the fact that philanthropy's budget is much smaller, they must steer the federal ministry money.

The leveraging of private investments rests on the prospect of steering public investments towards the policies new philanthropists see as desirable, namely, the corporate reform of education (see Chapter 1). Drawing from a corporate view of public management, foundations aim to "teach" governments "good practices": "From the public manager we have a single goal: encourage and disseminate good practices of public management" (Interview, Natura Institute, 2016). Foundations are interested in disseminating corporate practices in education policy, with principles of effectiveness, performativity, economic development and competitiveness, so new philanthropy:

> treats giving to public schooling as a "social investment" that, like venture capital, must begin with a business plan, involve quantitative measurement of efficacy, be replicable to be "brought to scale," and ideally will "leverage" public spending in ways compatible with the strategic donor. Grants are referred to as "investments," donors are called "investors," impact is renamed "social return," evaluation becomes "performance measurement," grant-reviewing turns into "due diligence," the grant list is renamed an "investment portfolio," charter networks are referred to as "franchises," to name but some of the remodelling of giving on investment and particularly on venture capital models. (Saltman, 2010, p. 64)

Complementarily, a member of the governance board of Lemann Foundation claims that, although challenging, working with governments is interesting not only for its "leverage" potential, but is a "necessary evil" to deal with structural problems that cannot be solved by philanthropy itself:

> The area of policy is one that, well, it depends a lot on the government. But it is something we judged essential to put effort in because of its potential of *leverage*, right? … So we think that in the area of policy we face these challenges of execution from the government, but these are things that if they work, they are very *multiplicative*, because it ends up being adopted in the entire country. If you spend "1" the result is "100". So that was a criterion we used to choose where we would put our effort, our money. (Interview, Lemann Foundation, 2016)

After having started its philanthropic work through local projects, Lemann Foundation changed its working logics because "soon it became very clear for the foundation that there were structural obstacles to improve education, which could only be solved through changes in the federal policy. Then they decided to create an education policy team" (Interview, Lemann Foundation, 2016). Thus, Lemann Foundation created a department with a similar structure and size of previous ones, and later added a "sub team" of "governmental relations, with someone who stays in Brasilia building up dialogues with congressman and other actors" (Interview, Lemann Foundation, 2016). The foundation now has a group that works full-time on policy entrepreneurship, commissioning or carrying out studies, publishing, having meetings with different organisations, speaking in government hearings and so on.

Consequently, working with policy can be an instrument for foundations; a means to develop an education and social project, as an interviewee from Natura Institute, argues "we have the understanding that the education issue will never be resolved without the state, so working with public policy is indispensable for us *to attain what we want*". The work of new philanthropists brings about both a set of new policy contents and new methods of policy. They labour to establish an agenda of education reform conceived within the models and logics of business (Saltman, 2010), in doing so, they also rework the policy arena they partake in. They are "new players to the field of social and education policy, repopulating and reworking existing policy networks, and giving legitimacy to the role of business in the solution of social problems" (Olmedo, 2016, p. 49). In this reworking, "strategically, philanthropy has provided a 'Trojan horse' for modernizing moves that opened the 'policy door' to new actors and new ideas and sensibilities" (Ball & Junemann, 2012, p. 32).

New philanthropists can also invest social and network capital. To execute the work, Lemann Foundation has hired people who had previously worked in the public sector, in order "to know how governments work and do not work" (Interview, Lemann Foundation, 2016). These employees are boundary-spanners who bring to the foundation invaluable information and network capital, which "comprises access to communication technologies, transport and the social and technical skills of coordinating and networking more generally" (Larsen et al., 2008, p. 656) (see Chapter 5 for a fuller discussion on network capital).

Similarly, the narrative of the creation of TPE is an example of how new philanthropists can make use of their social capital and gain access to decision-makers. One main founder of the movement retells how quickly the TPE was acknowledged by the Ministry of Education as an important group in Brazilian education. According to him, some colleagues decided to mobilise to become an active voice in education policy in Brazil after a political scandal was made public through the press, which involved the president at the time, Luis Inácio Lula da Silva. Within ten days, the document "Ten causes and 23 commitments to education" was created by bringing together proposals and ideas from "recognised authorities", such as the Four Pillars of UNESCO. Two days later, the group had a meeting with the Minister of Education, Fernando Haddad, to pitch their project shortly before a UNESCO social event. Immediately after their private meeting, the following happened: "At the microphone, when he was going to speak about UNESCO, Fernando Haddad said 'Now I want to announce to you something interesting, unrelated to today's topic. I have the impression today the biggest commitment in the Brazilian history is being made, regarding education'" (Interview, FEAC, 2016). The group had the social and network capital that enabled them to quickly, directly and personally reach the Minister of Education, and have a private meeting with him to present policy ideas (see Chapter 5 for an in-depth discussion of the use of meetings for policy entrepreneurship in policy networks).

In sum, to reiterate, foundations frame policy ideas making use of research in an instrumental way. This is especially relevant to build the image of the specialist and create a "claim to hearing" (Kingdon, 2013) and an "authoritative voice" (Ball, 1993). Policy ideas are shared persistently in many ways and venues, including more indirect ways, such as the press, and also approaching decision-makers and policymakers directly. To sustain this widespread labour, investments of different types are mobilised.

The Mobilisation for the National Learning Standards: Framing curriculum policy ideas

The Mobilisation for the National Learning Standards (MNLS) describes itself as an "advocacy movement" with a diverse membership that sees a standard curriculum as "a crucial step to promote educational equity and align the elements of the educational system in Brazil" (MNLS website). For the Mobilisation, creating a core curriculum will work as "a dorsal spine for the learning rights of each student, for teacher training, for teaching materials and external assessments" (MNLS website). Concisely, in their principles they claim the learning standards must be focused on essential knowledge, skills and values; be clear and objective; be underpinned by "research evidence"; and be mandatory for all schools in the country. On the other hand, they claim the curriculum should have diversity, respect the autonomy of the federal entities to build their curricula and that the learning standards should be formulated in a collaboration between federal, state and municipal governments (MNLS website).

The MNLS has been engaged in shaping discourses around the curriculum, working with policymakers and media, promoting events and funding advocacy studies.[7] At the same time, education organisations, such

---

7   See MNLS website <http://movimentopelabase.org.br/referencias/>.

as teacher unions, including the National Confederation of Education Workers,[8] universities and local authorities have been taking part in the debate as well. The opposing groups often criticise the MNLS and its policy ideas around the learning standards, arguing the MNLS's agenda leads to a narrow and impoverished school experience. They also argue these new Learning Standards, with the format defended by the MNLS, support the use of market solutions to education problems through the private provision of teaching materials, teacher training and assessment.

The MNLS consists of a network of individuals and organisations, a discourse community focused on the need for education reform. The group is made up of policy entrepreneurs, traveling technocrats and "thought leaders" offering solutions to education policy "problems". The members, in various ways, claim a certain expertise and they are enacting particular forms of what Mitchell (2002) calls "techno-politics" that link expert knowledge to political power in diverse and distinctive forms (Larner & Laurie, 2010, p. 223). Its intersecting and overlapping relations and interactions are now part of the education reform process in Brazil. Nonetheless, this is a policy network that is *under construction*; "always in the process of being made ... never finished; never closed" (Massey, 2005, p. 9). The MNLS's network draws on a variety of direct interpersonal social relations and high levels of interpersonal trust and is animated by various kinds of *meetingness* (Urry, 2003). Conferences, workshops, discussion groups are occasions for the reiteration, reinvigoration, and re-affirmation of discourse and allegiances, a shared language is borrowed/developed to re-name the social.

The MNLS consists of both people and institutions. The "institutional supporters" of the movement include new philanthropy organisations (family or corporate), research organisations and education civil

---

8 Confederação Nacional dos Trabalhadores da Educação (CNTE in Portuguese), IE's representative in Brazil. It has recently held seminars about privatisation, marketisation and the national curriculum. They also have concluded two research projects about privatisation, focusing on the National Congress board on education, and education funding. This proposed study would complement well these two research efforts and strengthen not only the work of IE but also CNTE. (see <http://www.sinprodf.org.br/educadores-contra-a-privatizacao>).

servants associations. The Mobilisation's decisions are taken in group meetings, where all members can voice opinions. Lemann Foundation, Natura Institute and the bank Itau BBA fund it, and Lemann Foundation is also the "executive secretariat", with the task of carrying out the decisions taken by the group. The institutional supporters are presented in Table 4.

Table 4. Mobilisation for the National Learning Standards institutional supporters

Type of institution	Names
Research Association or Organisation	ABAVE: Brazilian Association of Education Assessment CENPEC: Centre of Studies and Research in Education, Culture and Community Action, run by Maria Alice Setubal, member of the family owner of the conglomerate bank Itaú-Unibanco
Family Philanthropy	Lemann Foundation: Swiss-Brazilian investor Jorge Paulo Lemann Roberto Marinho Foundation: the newspaper Globo Ayrton Senna Institute: the deceased racer Ayrton Senna Inspirare Institute: the Gradin family, civil construction company Odebrecht
Corporate Philanthropy	Natura Institute: the cosmetic products company Natura Unibanco Institute: the conglomerate bank Itau-Unibanco
Education civil servants associations	CONSED: Council of State Secretariats of Education UNDIME: National Union of Municipal Directors of Education
Corporate advocacy coalition	Todos pela Educação: organisation with companies that advocates for education reform
NGO	Educational Community CEDAC

The Mobilisation was created in 2013, and "had at first the goal of bringing the theme of the national base into the agenda of education in Brazil" (Interview, Lemann Foundation, 2016). As a policy entrepreneur, the group started its work by labouring to bring attention to the policy idea of a standardised curriculum, and create support to it:

> So in 2013 we brought together a group of specialists, institutions, public managers and started to feel how this debate would go here, if it would go forwards, if people were interested in discussing it. For our surprise they were really interested, they really believed this theme had a great potential, as a structural reform of education, with great potential to make a difference and this group started to work together. (Interview, Lemann Foundation, 2016)

As mentioned, policy entrepreneurs frame existing social conditions in a way they become a policy problem that demands government action (Kingdon, 2013). Policy problems and solutions, then, are not understood to be a "given", or a "fact", but instead "policy discourses and technologies mobilise truth claims and constitute rather than reflect social reality" (Ball, 2015, p. 307). This framing depends both on the entrepreneur's interests and worldview, but also political contexts. Amid many interpretative possibilities, the entrepreneur strategically elaborates a point of view that will facilitate the support for certain ideas (Capella, 2016). Even if the solution pre-exists the problem, or they are not directly connected, it is up to the entrepreneur to argue and create new understandings of the problem/solution to favour his own view, in this case an agenda of reforming education with corporate values and purposes (see Chapter 1).

In this case, the MNLS is focused on reforming education, and believe a systemic and wide reform can be started and promoted by a standard curriculum. The MNLS was able to formulate a "powerful supporting idea", one that is hard to refute (Baumgartner et al., 2009), by framing the curriculum as a policy solution to social and education inequality. The members argue the learning standards would be a tool to ensure all children's "right to learn" through the country, regardless of one's social situation or the city and state they are from. This is an example of how "powerful supporting ideas" are "generally connected to core political values which can be communicated directly and simply through image and rhetoric. The best are such things as progress, participation, patriotism, independence from foreign domination, fairness, economic growth - things no one taken seriously in the political system can contest" (Baumgartner et al., 2009, p. 7). Opposing a policy, in this case a standardised curriculum, is made "unthinkable", rending resistance untenable or easily dismissed. As Macedo (2017) puts it:

> I have been working with the understanding that the political articulations for the definition of a learning standard are responsible not only for the proposition of a national curriculum, but for creating its need as well. In an even deeper level, the naturalisation of such a need lies on and supports the creation of an understanding of a curriculum, restricting the multiplicity of the term in the national and international literature. Such literature register that there are no conclusive studies concerning the impact of national curricula, rather over the quality of education or the reduction of inequality and growth of social justice. (Macedo, 2017, p. 510)

The Mobilisation then became engaged in activities to "defend ideas" (Capella, 2016), advocating with "sheer tenacity" (Kingdon, 2013), or labouring to speak to a wide-range of audiences, in many different spaces:

> At first as I said, putting the topic in the agenda. So speaking about it in different ways, in the press, in events, in meetings with the government, with congressman, with all kinds of "interlocutors". Second, we started to produce research here in Brazil about the need of a common curricular base for Brazilian students, what this learning standard would be like, what were the main concerns, what teachers thought about it, comparing the existing curricula in the states to see what we already have here. (Interview, Lemann Foundation, 2016)

The MNLS has worked to reach a wide-range of groups and stakeholders, making use of a variety of strategies, tools and spaces (press, events, private meetings), and producing research with "specialists" to create a legitimate "evidence-based" case for its policy ideas. The group has invested considerable resources and effort in producing "studies" of various kinds. In its website, over fifty reports and studies are made available, most of these are not produced by Lemann Foundation itself. Instead, they are contracted out to other institutions. Namely, ACARA and the Curriculum Foundation have written the majority of reports, but some national organisations and members of the MNLS have collaborated to the "research portfolio" as well, such as CENPEC, which produced a report comparing the curricula existing in Brazilian states.

In MNLS, as a network, resources and knowledge are shared, in such a way that a report produced by one member of movement becomes a "material" to be used by the entire group: "CENPEC is a member of the movement, so it is one of the studies the movement offers. […] As these organisations are also dedicated to research in the area of education, we end up gathering it all in the movement" (Interview, Lemann Foundation, 2016). Similarly, MNLS's members are organised in working groups, which are created according to identified needs. There is, for example, the working group of "knowledge production", which produces studies and reports regarding curricula: "There is a subgroup of people who are interested in the topic, who created a group that produces knowledge about the theme. So they do research, check with ACARA the high school formats in the world, discuss with MEC, create political arrangements and so on" (Interview, Lemann Foundation, 2016). The MNLS then is not a single policy entrepreneur, it is a *policy network entrepreneur*, in which resources are shared, and each member contributes with something, each institution or person contributes with their own strengths and expertise.

The produced studies and reports are described as "policy inputs" (*"insumos"*) by the MNLS interviewees, documents that are used to reach, gain the attention of and influence policymakers. One representative of Lemann Foundation shows how he wished they were the ones writing the curriculum, and regrets they are not. Instead, the adopted strategy is to produce materials that may influence or steer decision-makers:

> I am a producer of education policy, so it is a proper work of advocacy. We try, but sadly it is not us who are writing the Learning Standards, but we try to produce inputs to help the ones who have the pen in their hands. It is about having influence over people with these inputs we produce. (Interview, Lemann Foundation, 2016)

In this sense, the use of the word "input" is telling about the foundation's view of policy. Coming from the field of economics, the term "input" refers to the products that enter the production line of goods or services. The MNLS sees its reports as an element that enters the "production line" of policies, which together with other inputs will make up the final product, demonstrating a technical view of the policymaking process, rather than political.

An example of an "input" provided by the MNLS to MEC is the "Curriculum Writing Guide". MEC recruited "subject specialists" to discuss, formulate and write the learning standards documents. However, according to a Lemann Foundation staff member, writing a curriculum is a "sophisticated skill in itself", which involves not only knowing the content and creating a teaching order, but also – and specially – writing it clearly through learning goals. Allegedly, this skill was not "available in Brazil", thus with support of ACARA and the Curriculum Foundation the MNLS created a guide: "ACARA and other partners produced a guide of how to elaborate curricula, a guide of thirty pages with tips and examples, very useful, very accessible, any person can read and understand 'oh, I see now, this is how a curriculum has to be organised and this is how you write a learning goal'" (Interview, Lemann Foundation, 2016).

Although the complete version of guide is not available at the MNLS's website, there is a two-page long version titled "Reference Guide for the Writing of Learning Goals". The document describes simplistically and rigidly how a learning goal should be elaborated, including a list of verbs that should be completely avoided for being "hard to measure". In this situation, through the creation and provision of a "curriculum writing guide" from MNLS to MEC, the two organisations entered into a cooperative relationship, in which MNLS's "inputs" – which carry with them MNLS's view of education and curriculum – were directly used by MEC to frame and instruct the curriculum writing team. Differently from a traditional understanding of "advocacy", the "inputs" are not used as an external tool by MNLS, as an agent who tries to influence internal decision-makers. Instead, the movement is able to participate in the process of framing and conceptualising the curriculum and curriculum making. Not only the material was disseminated to the writing team, but through the creation of such "expertise", made official by the studies created and the network capital brought to bear, MCNB "trained" the writers of the curriculum.

Such internal access and participation raises questions regarding accountability. In spite of a short-version of the guide being publicly available, the complete document is not, like many other "inputs": "Other inputs depend on the strategy of 'influence' and how receptive the ministry and other agencies are. Sometimes it is better not to advertise we are doing this work, you know?" (Interview, Lemann Foundation, 2016). Thus, whether or not documents and reports are made publically available depend on a political agreement between the actors, MNLS and the Ministry of Education. In other words, weather the parts see it as beneficial advertising the collaboration or not, depending on the material and context at stake.

MNLS has shown "sheer tenacity" (Kingdon, 2013) in policy entrepreneurship labour. The Mobilisation has promoted countless events, including seminars and small meetings with deputies, representatives of MEC, of state and municipal secretaries, the writing team of the curriculum and so on. The group has also invested in public communications, with email lists, YouTube videos, Twitter and Facebook posts:

> Yes, we mobilise whoever wants to help in the cause. Sometimes there is this direct dialogue with MEC, sometimes the writers of the Learning Standards, which are scholars that work full-time in public universities, so they are not part of the permanent team of MEC, so we have relationships with them too and other stakeholders, such as the teachers' union and the press - in a last case, in case the government does not abide (*acatar*), going to the press is always an option. (Interview, Lemann Foundation, 2016)

The group creates relationships with many actors around the learning standards – the Ministry of Education, university scholars that are participating in the process, teacher unions and the press. Such relationships build a network that is far-reaching and diverse, but also fragile, ever changing and temporary. The reach of the network is important for gaining legitimacy and is fundamental not only for framing problems and solutions, but also for bringing about change and disseminating a policy epistemology – the "how" of policy and policy knowledge (Capella, 2016). Maintaining such networks, however, demands a lot of labour. Lemann Foundation has a small team solely focused on network building – which is also employed in MNLS (see next chapter). The team has one manager and two coordinators – one focused on technical aspects and input production, and the other focused on communication and articulation, which is reported as having "the same importance as the technical side" (Interview, Lemann Foundation, 2016). Thus, Lemann Foundation's institutional governance of "policy advocacy" reflects the two key aspects in policy entrepreneurship: framing policy ideas (with support of "evidence"), and disseminating such ideas through communication and networks (for a fuller discussion on how policy ideas are defended through networking, especially events and meetings, see the next chapter).

Global policy entrepreneurship: MNLS's international consultancies and benchmarking

In its effort to frame and disseminate policy ideas, the MNLS has drawn upon educational reforms undertaken in other countries, including the United States, Canada, England, Chile and Australia. Many of the materials produced by the group have an international character, either by deriving from institutions from other countries through consulting services or by comparing education reforms and curricula in different countries in search for "best-practices", which is referred to as "benchmarking". Namely, the Australian agency ACARA and the English organisation Curriculum Foundation have been MNLS's official international consultants, which were hired to write commissioned studies. ACARA has provided, for example, the guide on how to write a curriculum, presented in the previous section. There are fourteen documents in MNLS's website written by ACARA, about the Australian and the Brazilian curricula and many videos on YouTube. Representatives of ACARA have been to Brazil numerous times with different goals and have attended numerous meetings, events, and seminars with representatives of Lemann Foundation, the MNLS, the Ministry of Education, the National Council of Education, the congress and the senate, and the writing team of the Learning Standards:

> Only this year ACARA came to Brazil twice. ... And they come and do a bunch of meetings, a lot of talks to help solving the main difficulties, exchange ideas, talk with the Mobilisation. But also talk with deputies, talk with the writing team and talk with everyone that is important in this debate. (Interview, Lemann Foundation, 2016)

Policy pipelines (McCann & Ward, 2012), are built through events, meetings and the production of reports, through which policies "travel". Consultants make distant places close by creating such policy pipelines. Policies are made mobile with reports, presentations and seminar talks, and "the production of such artifacts involves work of 'lifting out' knowledge from elsewhere and skillfully 'folding' it into the municipal decision-making process" (Hurl, 2017, p. 186).

The Australian example has become especially important for MNLS. This country has adopted a standardised curriculum and claims to be a "policy model" (Lingard & McGregor, 2014) and is referred to by MNLS as a "case of success" that faced similar challenges as Brazil due to being organised in a federal system. As an interviewee from Lemann Foundation describes:

> It has been gaining space, we believe it is a very interesting reference indeed. They also created a curriculum by competences, so we believe an inspiration in this direction will favour a more modern curriculum. I believe they understand our difficulties, they have gone through similar challenges, and really I think the Ministry has identified itself with the Australian Curriculum, as a reference. We are happy because it is a good reference, which brought results. (Interview, Lemann Foundation, 2016)

However, the selection of MNLS's "international influences" (MNLS website) is not made solely based on their "curriculum models", but also previous connections the Mobilisation had with "experts" from such countries. Regarding the USA, Lemann Foundation had previous partnerships with influential universities in the country, including Stanford, Harvard, Columbia, MIT and UCLA. Similarly, England is included in the "cases list" due to Lemann Foundation's previous relationships with Oxford University. Regarding Chile, the University of Chile participates in an annual teacher-training programme in Stanford, which facilitates connections with Lemann Foundation. Thus, "it was kind of natural that we reached these people" (Interview, Lemann Foundation, 2016). This illustrates how:

> Models, in this sense, do not simply designate place-specific processes of innovation or sites of creative invention, as the diffusionist paradigm might have it; *they connote networks of policymaking sites, linked by overlapping ideological orientations, shared aspirations, and at least partly congruent political projects*. (Peck & Theodore, 2010, p. 171, added emphasis)

The policy models pointed to by MNLS are not selected in any simple way. Instead of being chosen due to their "success" or "innovation", several aspects are engaged in this selection. These can include personal or institutional connections that have little to do with curriculum matters (and perhaps education itself) – shared interests, ideological affinities and so on. Concerning the Australian "case", MNLS was especially interested and had "overlapping ideological orientations" with ACARA due to its standard curriculum, which can be easily measured and centrally managed.

These policy models are "creatures of dominant interests, traveling from centres of authority along politically constructed and ideologically lubricated channels" (Peck & Theodore, 2010, p. 170). The creation of models involves two somewhat contradictory processes. On the one hand, policies are detached from their contexts and simplified in idealised abstractions; they are "externally projected as widely generalizable, if not wholly immutable and universal" (Peck & Theodore, 2010, p. 170). Hence, they have an "expectation of comparable results, despite obvious differences in institutional arrangements and political alignments between the places of policy innovation and the zones of policy emulation" (Peck & Theodore, 2010, p. 170). On the other, they are symbolically and politically grounded in one place to evoke credibility and desirability, because "models that (appear to) come from somewhere travel with the license of pragmatic credibility, and models that emanate from the 'right' places invoke positive associations of (preferred forms of) best practice" (Peck & Theodore, 2010, p. 170) – they are "what works". Thus, policy models came from specific places, ones with "an ideologically palatable origin story" (Peck & Theodore, 2010) and "the reason why many models achieve mobility in the first place is that they have, in some way or another, been ideologically anointed or sanctioned. There is a pre-constituted market for lessons from Barcelona or Vancouver, locations that are consonant with prevailing policy fixes" (Peck & Theodore, 2010, p. 171).

In this sense, although there are global trends of searching for silver-bullet solutions (Ball & Olmedo, 2011, p. 85), a development perspective that understands that policies from "the right places" (Peck & Theodore, 2010) need to be imported by "developing countries" sustains this policy mobility dynamic. In spite of changing international relations, there are persistent

> global governance discourses, which effectively enframe and organize the evolving normative consensus, [that] continue to bear the imprint of what Sheppard and

> Leitner call a "developmentalist socio-spatial imaginary," which preemptively legitimizes first-world expertise and which combines a stageist teleology with an essentially neoliberal vision of competitive leveling. (Peck & Theodore, 2010, p. 171)

What is striking is that "these global development discourses are today less likely to be enforced by the blunt instruments of structural adjustment" but "increasingly, they travel in the form of favoured models of development and socio-technical fixes" (Peck & Theodore, 2010). These models do not "always originate from organizations like the World Bank, but instead are selectively harvested from the fields of decentralized governance, refined into development models and (best) practices, and purposefully re-circulated through global networks" (Peck & Theodore, 2010, p. 172).

Indeed, some interviewees treated policy mobility as a developmental duty: "Anyone that comes to Brazil after being in Europe, sees quite quickly: Brazil's biggest need is education" (Interview, Bosch Foundation, 2016). A global mobility of education policy is framed as a "need", and policy mobility is embraced as a duty to ensure development. The "need" of "importing" from other countries in order to develop/adopt/adapt certain policy solutions was made clear by a representative of Lemann Foundation, while explaining why MNLS hired ACARA for a series of services, including creating a guide and a training workshop on how to write curricula:

> That is what was missing in Brazil, because the country does not have experience in developing documents of this kind. So that is why we searched abroad and ACARA and other partners produced a guide on how to elaborate a curriculum. It is a thirty page-long guide with tips, examples and so on, very useful, anyone can read and understand "oh, I see now, this is how a curriculum has to be organised and this is how you write a learning goal". So we outsourced this work, because there was no expertise here in Brazil. We later translated to Portuguese and distributed it to MEC. (Interview, Lemann Foundation, 2016)

In this quote, the underestimation of Brazilian teachers, educators, researchers, scholars, policymakers and other types of professionals that would be well suited for the job is striking. There is a contrast between the ones who were not considered in the process, like local practitioners, with ACARA, one that can be branded as an international expert, in spite of national criticisms towards current curriculum and assessment education policies in Australia (Lingard & Sellar, 2014). The "successes" travel, the criticisms do not. Global power relations, informed by colonial views, are at stake here, which claim certain knowledge is not present in the entire country of Brazil, but "legitimizes first-world expertise" (Peck & Theodore, 2010).

In this global arena, ACARA, as the model creator, is also interested in the creation of this "policy pipeline" (Cook & Ward, 2012). The organisation aims to position itself as a global leader and example in education (ACARA Annual Report 2016). Thus, it must be able to enrol followers, because "a model can only become a model, needless to say, if it has followers, but it will not enrol followers unless it holds the promise of extralocal salience. Models that travel therefore reveal at least as much about 'demand-side' needs, imperatives, and anxieties as they do about supply-side inventiveness" (Peck & Theodore, 2010, p. 172). In this case, it seems Brazil was successfully enrolled as a follower. This is, in part, a manifestation of the concomitant state restructuring and new modes of governing in Australia, wherein state agencies are increasingly expected to be partly self-funded. In a globalised context, in which policies are cross-scalar and not limited to national boundaries, state reforms in one location can relate to and have effects to governing reforms elsewhere (see Chapter 6 for a discussion on *global heterarchies*).

The framing of the curriculum policy problems and solutions advocated and undertaken by MNLS is not nationally bounded. Instead, it has been developed in and through global policy networks, through which information, discourses and resources flow. Indeed, the adoption of certain "policy models" reinforces and stabilises the framing of policy problems and solutions, as "substantially, models perform 'formatting' functions (cf. Mitchell, 2002), in that they effectively crystallize not only a preferred bundle of practices and conventions, they also stitch together particular readings of policy problems with putative solutions" (Peck & Theodore, 2010, p. 170). Similarly, the dissemination and communication of MNLS has also been influenced by these international connections, as they provide legitimacy to MNLS and leverage in negotiating and convincing other stakeholders (Kingdon, 2013).

Final remarks. Framing education policy with vast resources

New philanthropy has been investing high volumes of resources, including money, connections and time, in framing, defending and disseminating education policy ideas. To make it possible, new philanthropists have been assembling the impression of being "experts" to create a claim of being heard, and having an "authoritative voice". Part of this effort involves sharing ideas in many spaces, such as the press, events, public hearings and others, working with "sheer tenacity" (Kingdon, 2013). Knowledge mobilisation is especially important in this context, done through published studies and the dissemination of ideas in the press, in events, meetings and networking. In this process, policy problems and solutions are framed, according to the foundations' corporate views of education and education reform interests.

The Mobilisation for the National Learning Standards has been a particularly successful policy entrepreneur. Having framed the need of a new curriculum as a solution to social and educational inequality and an opportunity for a wide reform of the Brazilian education, the MNLS created a "powerful support idea" (Baumgartner & Jones, 2009), one that is attached to widely held social values, such as social equality, making the policy solution unlikely to be dismissed. This framing has not been done within national borders. Instead, it has been framed within global policy networks, through which hegemonic discourses and ideas and resources flow. A consultancy service from the Australian agency ACARA has been especially relevant, making possible the mobility of a particular standardised curriculum "policy model". All of this has made possible to produce what Tarlau and Moeller (2020) call "philanthropising consent".

The operation of these policy entrepreneurial activities requires considerable volumes of capitals of different sorts. With its corporate connections, new philanthropy is able to mobilise vast financial, social and network capitals that are not available to other policy actors, such as grassroots movements. At the same time, in creating a claim to being heard, new philanthropy has created a safe space for corporate actors to disseminate their policy ideas, including institutions and individuals. Having less resistance than for profit companies, "strategically, philanthropy has provided a 'Trojan horse' for modernizing moves that opened the 'policy door' to new actors and new ideas and sensibilities" (Ball & Junemann, 2012, p. 32). This "raises serious concerns regarding the disproportionate power of super wealthy individuals and their related philanthropic organizations relative to public education policy and the democratic decision-making process" (Au & Ferrare, 2014, p. 19). New philanthropy, with its vast and intense policy entrepreneurial efforts "is able to carry its reform agenda and ideology forward into fully realized education policy through sheer force of material and symbolic sponsorship, but with little public accountability" (Au & Ferrare, 2014, p. 19). So further research is required to better understand the flow of investments, material and symbolic, within new philanthropy. In Brazil, unlike some countries such as the USA, foundations are not required to publicly account for their financial investments. Some organisations, including Lemann Foundation, refuse to publicise the amounts and sources of their funding.

CHAPTER 4

Working to collaborate in and through networks

> The goal of the programme was to create an understanding of and consensus around the importance of improving education among Brazil's new political leadership at the national and state levels. In closed-door sessions, Brazilian senators, congressmen, governors, and education leaders discussed the country's pressing educational issues and strategised how to affect change.
>
> World Yale News, 2016

Meetings, seminars, conference calls, email lists, shared ventures and projects and so much more: the list of efforts invested in networking is vast. To reach large-scale impact and affect change in education, new philanthropists work in and through networks, which involve formal and informal relationships, material and discursive, with strong and weak ties. New philanthropists know well how to network, this is a soft skill they inherit from the business world, and they use it skilfully in education policy to multiply and maximise their efficacy and efficiency in participating in the education governance and promoting policy changes. Formal and more stable partnerships can be created to gather strength in the political arena, in large coalitions such as the MNLS, Todos pela Educação and GIFE. Sometimes a project brings foundations together, such as Conviva (see below). These partnerships allow the sharing of labour, investments and knowledge. Foundations also use networks as a means to create capillarity, creating connections with people in different places and contexts. This can be done through fellowship schemes, such Lemann Fellows with former scholarship holders that keep in touch, or online platforms, like the ones organised by Ayrton Senna Institute and Natura Institute.

Whilst doing all these activities, policy networks join up diverse actors in many ways and involve both pragmatic social relations and the constitution of moral and epistemic communities (Junemann et al., 2018). The maintenance and activation of these networks require "chains of on-going effort" (Fenwick, 2011), which involve continuous communication and moments of *meetingness* (Urry, 2003). Thus, foundations invest resources in initiating and maintaining interactions both virtually and face-to-face, with frequent meetings through seminars, conferences and social events, that become key sites, or network nodes, for policymaking. They are "sites of knowledge exchange" and "sites of persuasion" (McCann, 2008), where relationships are built or strengthened, and policy discourses are shared. Thus, it becomes fundamental that policy analysis pays attention to the "wheres" of policy (Ball et al., 2017).

A fundamental trait of networks is the exchange of resources, as "the work of these groups is based predominantly on forms of group exchange involving people, materials, resources, histories, and struggles" (McFarlane, 2009, p. 566). Different types of resources are exchanged in the coordination of networks. Namely, money, connections and labour are continuously exchanged in fluid networks. So among the diverse field of studies of policy networks, with its different theoretical basis and possible uses (to describe, explain, manage, interpret), the literature shares a concept of policy networks, in which, at minimum, authors agree they are characterised by interdependence and coordination (Enroth, 2011). First, interdependence is "commonly construed as mutual resource dependence, meaning simply that the actors in a network are believed to be dependent on each other's resources – whatever resources – in order to realise their objectives" (Bevir, 2008, p. 114). However, network actors do not interact and collaborate solely on the need of resources. In addition, there is a need to reach common understandings on policy issues, or to pool resources to implement a policy (Enroth, 2011). Thus, second, coordination "occurs whenever two or more policy actors pursue a common outcome and work together to produce it", which is "both a driving force of governance and one of its goals" (Bevir, 2008, p. 56).

This chapter explores *how* philanthropies labour to animate policy networks, with attention to the interdependence and coordination of these actors. Within this, I carefully look at the relevance of events for global education policy networks. First, the chapter offers a general overview of the pragmatic and mundane activities carried out for the construction of network relationships, analysing how on-going chains of effort are used to activate and coordinate policy networks. To offer a glimpse of how much happens in a single event, one seminar is closely examined – with an exploration of its relevance for the policy debates at the time, for the mobilisation of MNLS and the connection of global networks.

New philanthropy and education networks: Resource sharing and labour to coordinate

The companies Procter and Gamble (P&G) and CODIN (Company of Industrial Development of the State of Rio de Janeiro) have funded a project of the Ayrton Senna Institute and the Secretary of Education of Rio de Janeiro since 2013. When local authorities approached the institute, the former already had a "policy solution" to create an "innovative curriculum model" for "full-time" schools (Interview, Ayrton Senna Institute, 2016). The programme also included technologies of "management, training, follow up and evaluation" (Ayrton Senna Institute Website), and was first adopted by the city in a single pilot school. Now, this initiative has been implemented in thirty-five schools and is considered a public policy of the Rio de Janeiro municipality (Interview, Ayrton Senna Institute, 2016). As for the Ayrton Senna Institute, it has rolled out the project to the state of Santa Catarina and included the "policy solution" in its "portfolio" of technologies (see Chapter 6). This PPP project that has grown into a multi-sited reform was made possible by the private funding offered by for-profit companies – including the multinational P&G. Here, the sharing of financial resources was fundamental in developing this "policy solution", and illustrate how interdependence is a fundamental aspect of networks.

This funding model is not an exception, many public-private partnerships bring together foundations and secretaries of education, which draw on financial support from businesses. In a previous reform effort in the state of Minas Gerais, for-profit and not-for-profit organisations came together to fund a project of the Ayrton Senna Institute with a consultancy by McKinsey (Interview, Ayrton Senna Institute, 2016).

The flow of funding from companies to foundations and public secretaries of education is done in exchange of other benefits, such as marketing, as an interviewee explains:

> There is a lot of people who want to fund a project, who see that the Institute has good relationships... and people like to link their brand to the name of the Institute. In Minas Gerais, our project was funded by the Fundação Brava, that brought 5 or 6 partners to fund the coming of McKinsey there, including Lemann Foundation, Camargo Correa and others. (Interview, Ayrton Senna Institute, 2016)

A complex network is created with an interdependence of money, expertise, reputation and work deriving out of for-profit and not-for profit organisations wishing to fund Ayrton Senna's projects in an attempt of benefiting from its public image. Here, simply being connected to the Ayrton Senna Institute becomes a good to be exchanged. Connections themselves are turned into "resources" that are shared in networks, in what can be understood as "network capital" (Urry, 2007). Urry (2007) defines network capital as "the capacity to engender and sustain social relations with those people who are not necessarily proximate and which generates emotional, financial and practical benefit" (p. 197). Differently from social capital, "network capital is not to be viewed as an attribute of individual subjects ... [It] is a product of the relationality of individuals with others and with the affordances of the 'environment' (Urry, 2007, p. 198).

Network capital depends on the active participation in networks, one that changes and is changed by the "environment". With a high volume of network capital, Lemann Foundation benefits from the shared connections of Jorge Paulo Lemann's companies, such as Ambev, to reach its policy entrepreneurship goals, including lobbying purposes. Lemann Foundation and other foundations like it are able to "span boundaries" (Williams, 2002) and "tend to have high network capital because they are proficient at creating inter and intra-organizational social connections, including between the public and the private sector. Here *power becomes a case of who you know, not what you know* (Elliot & Urry, 2010)" (Hogan et al., 2015, p. 46, added emphasis). As one member of this foundation's governance body, explains:

> It is like "we need lobbying" - then "well, talk to that person in Ambev", which is the person in Ambev responsible for I don't know what... So there goes Denis, talk to someone in Ambev who is *the* man in that area... [it is like that] in any area, ok? So the foundation benefits because he (Jorge Paulo Lemann) does a lot of brain-picking in the companies of the group. (Interview, Lemann Foundation, 2016)

There is a double blurring of public and private boundaries in sharing financial and network capitals. First, there is a blurring regarding funding, with money flows between private organisations, not-for-profit philanthropy and government institutions. Second, there is a blurring concerning people, with connections that are shared between for-profit and not-for-profit organisations. This enables foundations and companies to have access to people and spaces not possible otherwise.

Foundations develop high volumes of network capital in crossing and erasing boundaries between public and private, and are an example of how network capital is unevenly distributed. The distribution of network capital, or the "position in a network – and ultimately power" (Hogan et al., 2015a, p. 45) depends on *mobilities*. Here, it is understood that "mobilities are not necessarily about travel, but rather the movement of people, ideas, objects and information, what Appadurai (1996) referred to as 'flows'" (Hogan et al., 2015, p. 45). To perform such mobilities, certain resources and competences are needed. Particularly, network capital "requires the physical supports for networking—the infrastructure that enables mobility and connectivity—as well the embodied competencies of individuals and groups to gain advantage from these supports to different degrees" (Hogan et al., 2015, p. 45). New philanthropies can span boundaries and use their easy access to the required tools for mobilities: both the physical support – with movements of people and ideas through trips, events, meetings and technologies of communication (and the required financial support) – and the embodied competences to use them – with the corporate practices and values of networking and building relationships. In doing so, new philanthropists work as boundary spanners, "movers and shakers" (Williams, 2002) – someone (or something) "who has the ability to connect and ensure cooperation within and across different networks by sharing common goals and combining resources" (Ball, 2017, p. 33). They bring "unlikely partners together" break "through red tape", and see "things in a different way" (Williams, 2002, p. 109).

Coordinating networks: Formal and informal efforts

Foundations employ formal and informal efforts to coordinate networks. The first includes initiatives that deliberately enrol members, like groups, movements or mobilisations, coalitions and platforms. The second involves on-going efforts of meeting and talking, face-to-face or virtually, to strengthen ties and discourses in epistemic communities (Ball & Junemann, 2011), which are encapsulated by the idea of "meetingness" (Urry, 2003). This effort of maintaining networks is fundamental, as networks are more unstable than we tend to imagine them, as

> despite some unfortunate metaphorical baggage of networks as self-contained linear pipelines or reified engineered linkages, networks can be envisioned as far more ephemeral and rhizomatic in nature. Networks are simply webs that grow through connections. The connections can be thick and thin, rigid and limp, close and distant, dyadic and multiple, material and immaterial. And the connections have spaces between them. (Fenwick, 2011, p. 119)

Formal efforts to coordinate networks

In a rather deliberate attempt to organise and coordinate policy communities, foundations try to create formal groups to bring together specific (and strategically valuable) actors, people with similar pre-occupations or interests. Examples include networks of researchers, educators, teachers, or scholarship fellows. These formal groups require some kind of "enrolment" or official affiliation, and create new spaces for collaboration and exchange. A lot of labour is invested in growing and managing these communities (which are named by the members as "networks"), to create and strengthen connections between people that would not meet or collaborate otherwise. Thus, these groups have email lists, annual meetings, seminars and workshops, online platforms and virtual seminars provided and organised by the supporting foundation to "animate" networks. In Table 5 there are some examples.

Table 5. New philanthropies' initiatives of formal coordination of networks

Institution	Groups	Enrolled actors
Lemann Foundation	Lemann Fellows Talentos da Educação Rede de Cientistas Conselho de Classe	Former scholarship grantees that studied in universities abroad Educators with "innovative" projects Education researchers Teachers from public schools
Natura Institute	Conviva Escola Digital Rede de Apoio a Educacao	Municipal secretaries of education Teachers and students Municipal secretaries of education
Ayrton Senna Institute	Rede Nacional de Ciencia para a Educacao Gestores em Rede	Education researchers Head teachers

Lemann Foundation has a department solely dedicated to managing these groups, with a member of staff, a "network manager", with the responsibility of activating and coordinating Lemann Foundation's groups. He describes how the foundation "understands it is necessary to have a number of social leaders with large-scale social impact work". Thus, the foundation creates, organises and animates different communities to recruit and enlist people, which ultimately enlarge the organisation's reach (and network capital) (Interview, Lemann Foundation, 2016). He says:

> My area takes care of these networks. There's the Lemann Fellows network, [and] there's the *Talentos da Educação* network. We have scholarships for students [to go]

abroad, but we [also] bring good people in the education field and encourage those people who want to do social impact on an even larger scale. So we seek these people with this profile, but also look for those who have the potential to develop something, to develop something on a larger scale, greater impact, and we offer a lot of support, and training accordingly. (Interview, Lemann Foundation, 2016)

He continued to describe how the Lemann Foundation labours to manage these groups and animate networks. The group "Talents of Education" (*Talentos da Educação*) brings together fifty-eight people, and offers "scholarships to subsidize courses, as well as an 'immersion' with high level speakers, well qualified" (Interview, Lemann Foundation, 2016). The "high level" training might include international speakers, like scholars from Yale.

Moderating and stimulating connections between members, the group is another effort undertaken by the foundation. Indeed, this is promoted as one of the benefits of participating in these groups, having access to a network of people in different professional fields, as the interviewee puts it "if they need support, articulation of something, we try to help, even within the *Talentos'* network itself" (Interview, Lemann Foundation, 2016). In other words, being a member of these groups represents having access to greater network capital. Network members can help each other, drawing from the shared resources of the network, and eventually have greater participation in policymaking together. At the same time, the foundation's network capital is also enlarged, since the members open access to new spaces.

The management of these groups is challenging: as when members change employment and occupations, the networks change as well. In this fluid context, Lemann Foundation maintains an effort to map and monitor its own networks and connections. Besides organising annual meetings of the groups, this Lemann Foundation staff member keeps track of people's employment affiliations and work activities, animates virtual communications and guides possibly beneficial contacts within the network, as reported from one member:

One day in Lemann I received an email asking who were the most influential people in education that I knew by telephone or email. They were doing a network mapping of influence in education. [...] In the *Imersão*, of the *Estudar* [Foundation],

I am there in the list of people to talk in the events of *Imersão*. (Interview, member of Lemann Foundation network Telentos da Educação, 2016)

With all these efforts of network coordination, Lemann Foundation operates as an active and reflexive node in wide and far-reaching networks. It occupies a broker position that joins up and articulates different parts of a disparate network.

This formal coordination of networks is also made clear in Natura Institute's work in mapping the interests, investments and programmes of different foundations in an attempt to create partnerships, straightening relationships and create efficiency in the network. Working from the assumption that the complexity of networks needs to be managed and contained, Natura Institute has an effort of building up partnerships to foster efficiency and efficacy in networks:

> The Natura Institute is an institute highly recognized for working with partnerships. I particularly believe the third sector has a huge waste of energy, because it has a lot of duplicated work, people who do something and find out two years later that someone else was doing the same thing. So there's a lot that is wasted energy. [...] there was an idea, many people have this idea, this idea is not mine, but many people already had this idea "Come on, let's try to find some way to articulate all this", via GIFE for example. The truth is, nobody ever got it. So what the Institute Natura tries to do… we try to be this hub. (Interview, Natura Institute, 2016)

In a deliberate and planned way, Natura Institute has been mapping the activities and efforts the organisation has in common with other foundations. In the quote below there are details of mundane and pragmatic actions put in place to coordinate networks:

> So, for example, now we are in a round of meetings with institutes, the last thing we did was with the Ayrton Senna Institute. What we did is: we went through everything we do, they went through everything they do and we found synergies and next steps. And we're doing this with all the institutes so that we can get a mapping and so on and know what - not all, the main ones - what each one does, for us to be able to find synergy. This is daily, then when some opportunity happens we make a partnership and try to be an articulator. In this full-time school thing, we participate in the Centre of Reference, that belongs to the Aprendiz, Itau Social, SM Foundation and others ... we participate with the institute Sonho Grande, Itau BBA, of a group which discusses full-time school, right? I'm going to welcome someone from the

Ayrton Senna Institute to talk about this subject. We work a little as a proactive hub in which we seek these partnerships. (Interview, Natura Institute, 2016)

A series of smaller tasks need to be put in place for the maintenance of formal efforts of coordination, "chains of on-going effort" (Fenwick, 2009, p. 104), with a series of processes, bodies of governance, meetings, emails, online platforms, annual conferences and so on. These depend on the "infrastructure" and a lot of labour that is invested as "network participants need to act jointly in order to realise shared objectives" (Enroth, 2011, p. 27), with a series of mundane activities to coordinate, align and activate the network, which costs money and demands investments (see Chapter 4). For the coordination of the *Conviva* project, for example:

> We have a few rituals of governance. So we have this ADE that is the presidents of the institutes and foundations. They participate in a strategic meeting twice a year, about Conviva. Then afterwards we have another group, another space which is the COMEX, the executive committee with people of each institute and foundation that take care of Conviva. They meet three times a year. We also have the working groups for the project. So, for example, there is a group that regards communication, then the institutes and foundations that want to participate come and say "I want to participate in communication group". Then we have this group that will meet to make decisions concerning the daily routine of the project.
>
> The Natura Institute leads this project, so here we have a team that is paid by the Conviva, each one of the funders comes in with a part, you know? And this money pays for the execution of the project. We have a team here that runs the project, but this team does nothing that goes against the decisions made by the governance. (Interview, Natura Institute, 2016)

The interviewee describes in detail how a lot of labour is invested in a strategic approach (which might be uncommon), as in having meetings, organising working groups, emailing participants, enacting the decisions made and so on. In this context, this labour is divided amongst the participants. Similarly, financial resources are needed to maintain this network operating, to pay for the employees, meetings, communication activities and so on. The labour and cost of maintaining this coordination infrastructure might be high, but generates returns in that foundations can create large-scale projects, with national reach, and achieve impacts on education politics, policies and discourses. The project Conviva is an example this large-scale effect. Led by Natura Institute, it is supported by many organisations, including UNDIME, Itau Social, Lemann Foundation, Maria Souto Vidigal Foundation, Roberto Marinho Foundation, SM Foundation, Telefonica-Vivo Foundation, Victor Civita Foundation, C&A Institute, Itau BBA and Todos Pela Educação. In 2016, there were about 5200 cities that subscribed (about 93 per cent of Brazilian municipalities), about 1,700 cities use the platform frequently and 1,200 attended the face-to-face training meeting (2016 Annual Report Natura Institute). *Conviva*, it is claimed by a senior representative of the Natura Institute was created to unite efforts in a large education project, as the interviewee reports:

> *Conviva* came about precisely from this desire to be able to articulate foundations and institutes in some way. As we could not do something with all the institutes, we choose to work with the main ones, the largest ones, with some classification they did at the time. Then they tried to identify a topic in which everyone is more or less interested. […] So it was a group that met informally, without a specific project, but seeking to find something to do together. […] They hired the FGV to do research and understand how we could help municipalities in this management issue and such. And then something came up out of this research and the plan was designed, so *Conviva* begun to be planned. The project was put together among all those partners that are from the governance group. And so there was some designing of the project, there was a process of "sewing" to understand what each municipality, every institute, wanted and such… The project was designed with an efficient governance to get everyone involved in some way. (Interview, Natura Institute, 2016)

Informal efforts

The creation, use and maintenance of networks can be, to an extent, a deliberate and planned strategy. In other situations, temporary or informal partnerships and relationships are created, which are also fundamental for the maintenance of networks. Thus, part of the coordination of networks revolves around official groups and representations, such as the MNLS. Other efforts are more informal and continuous, with "chains of on-going effort", a myriad of activities that activate relationships in a network. A portion of such effort is done in spaces of "meetingness", or "moments of *meetingness* when network members from a range of backgrounds come together, where stories are told, visions are shared, arguments are reiterated, new relations and commitments are made, partnerships are forged" (Ball, 2017, p. 37). It is also where "a form of 'buzz' (is) generated by the co-presence of policymakers and practitioners from a range of different contexts" (Cook and Ward, 2012, p. 150).

In more informal ways of coordination, foundations use meetings and events as a tool, and a fundamental one in their operation. These are spaces deliberately crafted as opportunities and possibilities for policy conversations that involve the articulation and reiteration of carefully selected values. Seminars, for example, are planned to gather specifically chosen people: selected "specialists", who will articulate and reinforce the funder's beliefs, and provide a value-added to legitimacy. They bring together "everyone that is important in this debate" (quote from Lemann Foundation interview) – bearing in mind the crafted exclusivity of who and what is important – or the policymakers and supporters needed to advance the organiser's agenda. These seminars usually present the results of the studies mentioned earlier (Chapter 4). In these spaces, discourses are shared, policy solutions are presented and public/private partnerships are created or maintained.

Meetings are central to networks, and are "necessary to 'form' and to 'cement' weak ties at least for another stretch of time" (Urry, 2003, p. 231). By "meeting" Urry (2003) refers to "both the highly formalized with 'agendas', structure and timetables and the informal to where the specific space and time are planned in advance to where they are negotiated en route" (p. 232). In what follows there are examples of small meetings – such as a local breakfast social event organised by a venture philanthropy agency in the state of São Paulo – Brazil, and two large seminars – the GIFE Congress and the Unibanco Seminar.

Most large foundations have their own seminar series, usually an annual and biannual meeting that gathers representatives from government, new philanthropy, business and research. For example, Lemann Foundation organises an annual conference with Stanford, in which all Lemann Fellows (research students funded by Lemann Foundation) present the results of their studies to an audience with representatives from diverse organisations. Another example is the seminar series organised by the Unibanco Institute, named "Quality of Education". The 2015 seminar gathered many representatives of the advocacy group MNLS and the Ministry of Education in a pivotal moment of debate about the creation of a standard curriculum in Brazil, which will be analysed in depth in the next section. These events also "announced" the standing and authority of foundations and key actors as, what are called in the lexicon of new philanthropy, "thought leaders" (see Table 6).

Table 6. Examples of new philanthropies events

Institution	Events
Todos Pela Educação	Yearly seminar
Lemann Foundation	Yearly seminars with Stanford Lemann Centre and Transformar One-off events, like "Excellence with Equity" Lemann Dialogue series[a]
Ayrton Senna Institute	Edulab 21 Seminars to connect "experts" and policymakers, such as Desafios do Ensino Médio, Fórum Internacional de Políticas Públicas (with MEC and OECD)
Unibanco Institute	International Seminar Series "Pathways for the quality of public education"

[a] <http://www.fundacaolemann.org.br/lemann-dialogue/>.

These spaces of meetingness have both discursive and relational aspects. First, meetings are spaces for framing and sharing policy ideas. These are spaces attentively crafted for policymaking that involve carefully selected values, speakers and attendees. A representative from Lemann Foundation describes events as the following: "It is about working in the same way as the advocacy, we bring subsidies for the discussion, we promote exchanges, meetings, talking..." (Interview, Lemann Foundation, 2016).

In a small breakfast of corporate investors to discuss venture philanthropic investments there was a poignant example of how discourses can be shared and reinforced in events. In a nice-looking room, inside a prestigious hotel in one central avenue of a large Brazilian city, about thirty corporate people gathered to have breakfast together. With a large table with breads, cheeses, fruits, juices and coffee, there were a few round tables and a little stage put up at the front of the room. Everyone was dressed in formal business clothes – men in suits and women with stiletto shoes. A new Venture Philanthropy company promoted the event, which was a space for networking and promoting their services. This organisation does management of social investment, just as venture capital managers would do. They search for investment opportunities, they classify them, create a portfolio to offer to buyers, and manage investments.

Here, a businessman from the audience shared bluntly his beliefs, using the space to articulate his ideas, which was received with claps from the audience:

> Lets bring liberalism to Brazil, lets teach the children and teenagers that being a liberal is not a bad thing, nothing to be ashamed of. That having a small state is not a bad thing, that having private organisations in public services is not a bad thing.

He continued.

> I am sure our goal here today is this one, to occupy this vacuum that is created in this fantastic country Brazil, and seize this opportunity to bring these "collaborators" [employees] to our side, and society as whole to our side. And show them that we are the ones creating wealth, but not our wealth, a wealth we want to share with society to eliminate exactly what he mentioned, the social injustices, inequalities. That is why we need to educate the young to be less individualists, to believe in this liberal model, but respecting values [...] Now is the moment. (Field work notes, 2016)

At the same time, meetings and events have a relational aspect and purpose. Meetings combine social and discursive aspects in the coordination of networks. Besides sharing discourses, it is also evident that the social aspect of this meeting over breakfast was no less important. In this case, guests came for a rich breakfast with abundant food, and used that space to "talk and touch" (Santori et al., 2015), fostering trust in a policy network. Events reinforce weak relationships that are fundamental for the maintenance of networks of governance.

In a different context, a very large conference, the same two aspects, discursive and relational, are clear. GIFE organises biannual conferences that bring together representatives from the largest foundations in the country, as well as representatives from business and public organisations. In 2016 the event was held in a prestigious hotel in São Paulo, with more than 800[1] people attending the event. Its three-day long programme was packed with about 100 presentations about different sectors, issues and trends in corporate philanthropy in Brazil, in Latin America and the world. The presentations were heavily attended, which required a somewhat expensive ticket of BRL 1000.00 (about £200), the cost of which was often financed by institutions.

As usual, in between talks and round tables there was plenty of time for coffee breaks and socialising. Indeed, the conference had a lounge dedicated for this purpose, which was decorated with sofas and stands of the main funders: Lemann Foundation, Unibanco Institute, Itau Educacional Foundation, Bradesco Foundation and C&A Institute. People chatted while walking between the displays. One could hear conversations that ranged from personal issues to comments on the talks attended in the conference.

Figure 3. GIFE 2016 Conference – social lounge

1 <https://gife.org.br/congresso-gife-2016-reune-mais-de-800-pessoas-em-sao-paulo-para-debater-o-sentido-publico-do-investimento-social-privado/>.

Thus, networks are "held in place" with effort and labour. However, it is not only work, but as Marsh and Smith (2002) put it, "networks involve the institutionalization of beliefs, values, cultures and particular forms of behaviour" (p. 6). These are made up not simply of pragmatic relations, but also constitute "moral and epistemic communities" (Ball, 2017). These spaces can strengthen discourses and belief systems in networks, "holding them in place", as they are "united by not only a corporate vision for education but a view of knowledge, curriculum, and culture" (Saltman, 2010, p. 6). Beliefs are fundamental, and they constitute epistemic communities in networks.

Policy networks are not just a set of connections between sites, but also represent a history of effort and various forms of materiality and performance (Ball, 2017). So these network are "always *under construction*" (Ball, 2017); "always in the process of being made ... never finished; never closed" (Massey, 2005, p. 9). As an example of how much effort, work and history of relations is present in a single event, in what follows there is an in-depth analysis of a single event, the seminar of Unibanco Institute of 2015.

MNLS's network creation and coordination: The use of meetings

The Mobilisation for the National Learning Standards has been frequently promoting meetings, seminars and events since its creation. This meetingness has created a privileged access to spaces of policy-making, but these efforts and engagement with policy remain mainly opaque and informal. In this section I discuss how MNLS has been using meetings strategically by analysing its creation through a series of seminars. Second, I explore how the MNLS was well represented at the Unibanco Institute Seminar "*Gestão Escolar*", which was held amid debates over the needs and purposes of a standardised national curriculum in Brazil.

Seminars for the creation of the MNLS

MNLS used meetings and seminars as strategic spaces for policymaking since its creation. As examples of how meetings and events are used to activate networks, three fundamental seminars are highlighted in the creation of MNLS (in a long series of events), organised by Lemann Foundation. The first was held in April 2013 at Yale University, in New Haven, USA, which is referred to by interviewees and on websites as the "creation moment" of MNLS. Titled "Leading Educational Reforms: Empowering Brazil for the 21st Century", the event gathered thirty-five participants, including members of Brazil's National Congress, state and municipal secretaries of education, officials from foundations and civil society organisations, and representatives of other stakeholders in Brazil's education system (Yale News). The Brazilian group heard talks from Yale faculty, school administrators, policymakers and advocates who had been part to the development and promotion of the common core curriculum in the United States. According to the Yale News website, "during their time in New Haven, the participants discussed education reform in Brazil and developed an action plan they could implement upon returning home".

In October 2013 there was a "follow-up" event in Campinas, São Paulo, Brazil. This time, the conference focus was specifically on the development of common core curriculum standards. The conference participants were given "insider perspectives on the development of the Common Core State Standards in the U.S. by Susan Pimentel and Michael Cohen" (Yale School of Medicine News). Pimentel was the main author of the Common Core for literacy and the vice chair of the National Assessment Governing Board that advises on the National Assessment of Educational Progress (NAEP), the U.S. national report card, and Michael Cohen shared strategic lessons from the Common Core State Standards Initiative (Yale School of Medicine News). Complementarily, on the very next day, another seminar was held in São Paulo, organised by CONSED and supported Lemann Foundations, held at Insper (higher education institution) with the scholar Michael Young, from England, as the main speaker.

In March 2015, another seminar was held at Yale, again organised by Lemann Foundation. Titled "Leading Educational Reforms: Opportunities and Challenges Ahead", this second seminar, referred to in Yale website as a "leadership programme for Brazilian leaders", had forty-five Brazilian public officials, as well as Lemann Foundation leadership and staff in a four-day seminar with lectures and workshops by "international education experts". At this moment:

> the goal of the programme was to create an understanding of and consensus around the importance of improving education among Brazil's new political leadership at the national and state levels. In closed-door sessions, Brazilian senators, congressmen, governors, and education leaders discussed the country's pressing educational issues and strategised how to affect change. (World Yale News)

This series of events brought together a set of representatives from new philanthropy and academia with bureaucrats and politicians from federal, state and municipal levels. Lemann Foundation invited all of the attendees. In the quote below, from a representative from Lemann Foundation, meetings are described as one way in which the foundation does its policy "work", and how it targets the actors they want to build a relationship with:

> MNLS surfaced in 2013[2] with the goal of bringing the national common base to the public agenda in Brazil. Since we started this process [with MNLS] we have organised many meetings. Twice already we have taken a group of about 50 people for a week-long immersion at Yale University. Back in 2013 that was how we started, we took a group of people to Yale to discuss curriculum, and there the Movement was created. Then last year [2015] we did it with people that were starting their mandates in January, state secretariats, federal deputies, state deputies, governors... These events are very common, [we do] many meetings, many talks to solve the main difficulties, exchange ideas, talk with the MNLS, but also talk with deputies, with the curriculum writing team, *talk with everyone that is important in this debate*. (Interview, Lemann Foundation, 2016, added emphasis)

---

2   in spite of claiming to have been funded in 2013, MNLS only shows public activities on the second half of 2015. The website of the movement was created in June 2015, it is possible to find a list of members from October 2015, which was dramatically enlarged after the second seminar at the end of October. There are no mentions in mass media about the group either.

These events are sites that support the creation, evolution and maintenance of an unstable and expanding policy network, within and through which new philanthropy and the state can interact. As noted, network relations are established and "held in place" by "chains of on-going effort" (Fenwick, 2009) – meetings, events, conversations, visits, funding, alliances, etc. These are some of "the chains, circuits, networks, webs, and translations in and through which policy and its associated discourses and ideologies are made mobile and mutable" (McCann & Ward, 2012, p. 43). MNLS seeks to "teach" decision-makers about the importance of a standard curriculum, and clearly points towards the model of the USA Common Core. This series of events was aimed both at gathering support from different actors in different spaces and creating a shared belief in and commitment to the need for a national curriculum. Part of this ideological labour relied on the authority invoked by Yale University. This "teaching" of decision-makers demands the creation of "models" (see Chapter 4), and the persuasion of the audience these provide examples to be followed, as Cook and Ward (2012) put it: "Their place on the stage relies on their ability (and that of the organizers) to situate them within widely accepted and acknowledged successful examples" (Cook & Ward, 2012, p. 140).

Further, the social aspect of such events, and trips, should not be neglected. They propel conversations and the building of personal relationships and trust, which are essential for the coherence of networks. These are not simply pragmatic relations but also constitute moral and epistemic communities. Over time, members of this "community" have come to know each other well, they work together and share the values which inform their choices and commitments; and they generate and share persuasive arguments that can be used in more hostile contexts (Grek, 2013, p. 56).

MNLS in the Unibanco Seminar: One event as a case

In this section I look at one specific network of actors within the space of an event, a seminar called "Paths for the Quality of Public Education: School Management", which took place in São Paulo, Brazil in September 2015.

In June 2015 there had been an on-going debate about "what", "how" and "who" should decide on teaching and learning in Brazil (Galian, 2014). This seminar, organised by a group of Brazilian new philanthropists and companies illustrates very well the use of events to promote the meeting of international representatives from government, business and philanthropy to discuss education policy. The data regards one seminar on education and the policy relations represented at this event.

The seminar entitled "Paths for the Quality of Public Education: School Management" was organised by the Instituto Unibanco[3] and the newspaper Folha,[4] with the support of Insper[5] – that is, a big national bank and a large national newspaper, supported by a higher education institution that was created and is directed by new philanthropists in Brazil. The organisers were able to employ their financial and social capitals in the organisation of this event: the former, to fund the seminar, and the latter to invite (and fund) high-profile speakers and policymakers, and ensure intense media coverage.

This event was chosen as a focus of analysis for three reasons: the relevance of the organising institutions, the size and importance of the event and the presence of international speakers, the latter was strategically framed by the organisers as being the comparative aspect of the seminar. According to the official website, the seminar aimed at "promoting the dialogue between the Brazilian experience of school management and international cases that reached relevant improvements in student learning results". It is an interesting example of "meetingness" in education policymaking, within a large event that promoted the encounter of national and international actors from government, business and new philanthropy. It illustrates the changing nature of face-to-face meetings, which are "less concerned with traditional (one-way) presentations of information and passive learning and more with building and sustaining

---

3   Created in 1982, this institute is part of the social investment of the bank Itau-Unibanco, which works mainly with secondary school.
4   Brazilian newspaper, the second in circulation in the country.
5   Non-profit private institution of Higher Education and research. Co-created by Lemann, Sicupira and Telles, in its councils there are relevant new philanthropists.

networks and exchanging social goods" (Urry, 2007, p. 165). All of this is done in highly produced ways, with marketing and design that make events look polished and professional.

The main "international" speakers were Barry McGaw, from Australia, Michael Wilshaw and Anthony McNamara, from England, and Mary Jean Gallagher, from Canada. Each of these speakers brought a "symbolic association with specific locations [that] evokes a grounded form of authenticity, implies feasibility, and signals an ideologically palatable origin story" (Peck & Theodore, 2010, p. 170). They are "embodied policy mobilities" (Ball, 2016; Larner & Laurie, 2010), or "travelling technocrats are embodied actors who knowingly create careers for themselves through and against broader political-economic processes and national imaginaries" (Larner & Laurie, 2010, p. 219). All of them later became "consultants" with their own companies, as "now our 'experts' 'develop' economies and 'experts' elsewhere" (Cowen, 2009, p. 21). Some further information about the speakers is presented in Table 7.

Among the Brazilian speakers, there were representatives from the Ministry of Education (MEC), state and municipal secretariats of education, multilateral organisations, universities and foundations. Two national "cases" were highlighted at the seminar programme: Sobral (and its state Ceará) and the state of Goiás. The first case is increasingly used by new philanthropists in Brazil as a "policy story" (Ball, 2016) or a compelling argument for education reform. The second case, Goiás has been discussing the privatisation of school management drawing on the models of the American Charter School and English Academies programme. At the event, the Education Secretary of Goiás announced a new educational reform in this direction. The state representatives, speakers and attendees, are a receptive audience to the possibilities of further reform and are willing receivers or emulators. The seminar speakers are presented in Table 7.

Table 7. Unibanco Institute 2015 Seminar – List of Speakers

Name	Affiliation at the time of the event / some key information
Mary Jean Gallagher	- Vice minister of Education from the province of Ontario - Gallagher became recognised for improving the test results of literacy and numeracy, and graduation rates of Ontario school students. In 2015 she left the Ministry and became an "educational consultant and speaker" of "improvement and system implementation" at MJ Gallagher and Associates.
Barry McGaw	- Melbourne University, former president of the Australian Curriculum, Assessment and Reporting Authority (ACARA). - McGaw was Director of Education at OECD between 1998 and 2005. Worked at the University of Melbourne between 2006 and 2014, and is now Honorary Professorial Associate. Was chair of ACARA's board between 2008 and 2015. Now is Managing Director of the McGaw Group Pty Ltd.
Michael Wilshaw	- Chief of Inspections at OFSTED (UK) - Wilshaw was chief inspector at OFSTED between 2012 and 2016. Before that, Wilshaw was a teacher at the Mossbourne Community Academy. Since 2017 he works an education consultant at Sir Michael Wilshaw Educational Services Limited.
Anthony McNamara	- International Associate in National College for Teaching and Leadership (NCTL), UK - McNamara works as a "consultant on school leadership" at McNamara Education Consultancy after eighteen years as a secondary head teacher. One "expertise" of his is to "support school leadership in Brazil". Has been to the country numerous times by invitation of the British Council, Senac, CONSED and Unibanco Institute.
Renato Janine	- Minister of Education – MEC - Before and after his work as Minister, Janine worked as Professor of Philosophy at the University of São Paulo.
Manuel Palácios	Secretary of Basic Education – MEC

Table 7. Continued

Name	Affiliation at the time of the event / some key information
Claudia Costin	- Senior Director for Global Education – World Bank - Prior to the World Bank, Costin was the Secretary of Education in Rio de Janeiro between 2009 and 2014, when high-stakes tests were implemented, which faced a strong opposition by teachers. After the World Bank, she opened an education policy consultancy firm. Afterwards she became the director of *Centro de Excelência e Inovação em Políticas Educacionais* (CEIPE, or Centre of Excellence and Innovation in Education Policy), a think tank created by FGV (private higher education institution) in partnership with Harvard and the Brookings Institute.
Francisco Soares	President of the Anísio Teixeira National Institute of Educational Research and Studies (INEP)
Julio Cesar C. Alexandre	Secretary of Education – Sobral Municipal Secretariat of Education
Mauricio H. Maia	Secretary of Education – Ceará State Secretariat of Education
Raquel Teixeira	Secretary of Education – Goiás State Secretariat of Education
Ricardo Henriques	Executive Superintendent of Unibanco Institute
Pedro Malan	- Vice-President of Unibanco Institute Council - Engineer and economist, has a PhD in Economy by Berkley and has taught at PUC Rio de Janeiro (private higher education institution). Was Minister during the Fernando Henrique Cardoso government.
Ricardo Paes de Barros	Professor at Insper, Cátedra Instituto Ayrton Senna

The seminar speakers were "followed" digitally, with the intention of identifying previous relations and connections, other places they had "visited", projects executed and so on. The policy network graph below represents the connections between speakers prior to the seminar, and can represent co-presence in previous events (as speakers), financial investments and partnerships in projects. The following discussion does not aim to offer an exhaustive account of all the people and relations represented at this event, but rather it is a purposeful selection. I focus on two aspects of this network: Firstly, although not made known in the seminar programme, many of the MNLS supporters (institutional or individual) were at this seminar. This is an example of how events are spaces for policy influence and dialogue, and how this can be done with little accountability and transparency. Second, there is a discussion of the series of events that "joined up" the seminar speakers, and an account of their previous meetings, focusing on the international speakers, as "embodied" policy mobilities (Larner & Laurie, 2010).

The graph in Figure 4 illustrates how the MNLS was well represented at this seminar. Placed centrally in the network, it joins up all communities: foundation's staff members, the Australian representatives Barry McGaw and ACARA, as well as other research organisations, the English representatives from OFSTED and the British Council, and the Canadian, together with the Sobral and Ceará, representatives. Although in the seminar's programme the name of MNLS never appeared, through social network analysis it became clear the Mobilisation was a fundamental influence in it, with considerable representation amongst the organisation and speakers. At a moment in which the debates around the curriculum were heated, members of the MNLS and state representatives could "talk and touch" (Santori et al., 2015), and share and shape policy discourses.

Collaborate in and through networks 143

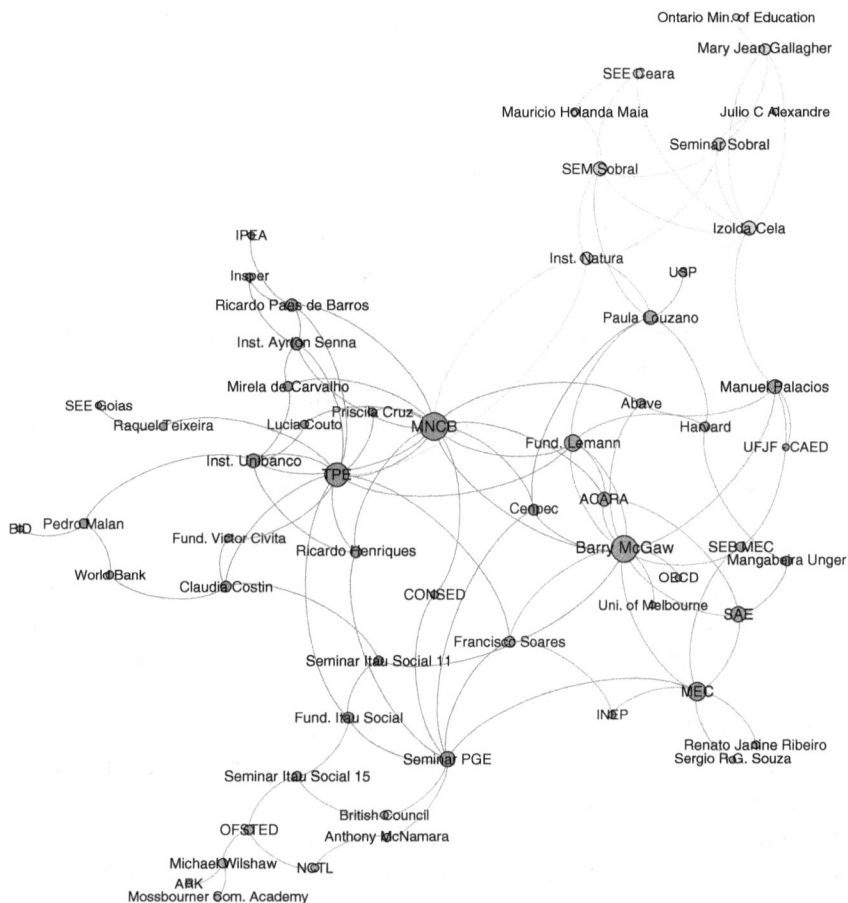

Figure 4. Connections between speakers prior to the Unibanco Institute 2015 seminar

Problematically, the work of MNLS in this space and context remains "unannounced", their presence and labour are neither transparent nor accountable to citizens. Its action around policy, or advocacy as members refer to it, is different from more traditional policy advocacy strategies, which often operate openly and publically through manifestos, strikes and street manifestations. In this example and others, new philanthropists can organise such events by applying their economic, social and network capitals, and invite relevant policymakers under the safeguarding of offering a formative event, where international specialists "gather to share best policy practices".

Although the event was about school management, most of the speakers were related to or part of an advocacy group concerned with curriculum policies. They were direct supporters, MNLS project consultants, or had worked for institutions that support it (like TPE and Itau BBA). When asked about this representation from MNLS at the seminar, a project manager from Lemann Foundation replied:

> Unibanco Institute is a member of the Mobilisation. So if it is going to do a seminar of education that will discuss curriculum, it will make use of the Mobilisation's network. I think it is one of the differences of the Mobilisation, that we really created a body with many tentacles, in a good way. So if one is doing an event, it will ask the others who is the best speaker to invite, and in the end the members of the Mobilisation are all in the same events. (Interview, Lemann Foundation, 2016)

As MNLS has organised itself as a network with many powerful foundations as members, it is able to populate and steer events, and in doing so, reach more people and disseminate policies and discourses. A small group of foundations can, together, arrange events with policymakers and choose speakers who support their policy agenda, within their epistemic community. So, as the interviewee puts it, it is always the same group of people that populate these policy events, shaping discourses and delimiting what is thinkable and unthinkable. By not being announced in the programme and news, MNLS's presence and labour are neither transparent nor accountable. In a way, this is a "double event", with a formal and public agenda, which can be "spectacular" sometimes, with a display of wealth and power, and a behind-the-scenes event, with meetings discussions and relationships that benefit the organisers themselves.

Events like this resemble the meetingness promoted in other areas, including the academic field and other social organisations, like workers' unions and grass roots movements. Researchers and activists are used to attending conferences and seminars to share ideas and network. However, what is new and striking here is the hyperagency of new philanthropies expressed in the power to organise events and steer agendas with a small number of people, and the reach of these events to policymakers. So first, in contrast to academic conferences organised by universities, research associations or grass roots movements (all with a number of members that can participate in decision-making), new philanthropies (with a reduced number of members, specially with decision-making power) can mobilise large amounts of capital to organise and promote these events and frame them according to their agendas. Second, new philanthropies can bring together state, market and philanthropy in these events with unique efficacy, in ways that scholars and education professionals usually are not able to. In this regard, new philanthropies can also bring together global travelling technocrats, in ways that assemble legitimacy to their policy entrepreneurship.

Global networks: Many meetings assembling an international policy network

The Unibanco seminar was one among many other events that together were used to create and maintain policy relations and incite a climate for change in relation to a national learning standard. Most of the speakers at this seminar had already presented together in previous events, demonstrating how "sites in translocal assemblages have more depth than the notion of 'node' or 'point' suggests – as connoted by network – in terms of their *histories, the labour required to produce them*" (McFarlane, 2009, p. 561, added emphasis). Prior to the Unibanco seminar, the key international speakers Mary Gallagher, Barry McGaw and Anthony McNamara had each previously been to Brazil at other events or meetings with Brazilian institutions and individuals also present at this seminar. The previous contacts between speakers illustrate the role and importance of meetings and the dense connection among seminar speakers, as represented in the network graph.

In June 2015, about two months before the Seminar, Sobral's Municipal Government promoted an event focused on "Education Management and Curriculum Reformulation", where Mary Jean Gallagher was the keynote speaker. At that moment, Gallagher presented Ontario's education reform at the event that aimed at promoting an exchange of education experiences between Sobral and Ontario, focusing on "education management and curriculum reformulation". In the same week she had meetings with the State Secretary of Education, the state university and signed a collaboration agreement between Sobral and Ontario. The event was organised by the municipal and state governments together with Natura Institute, also a member of MNLS.

Natura Institute has a longstanding relation with Sobral. Since 2013 the institute has been supporting education reforms in the city and aims to make Sobral a "showcase" of educational policies for Brazil (Natura's website). In 2014, Natura Institute, *Instituto de Co-responsabilidade* and Sobral's Secretary of Education implemented "full-time"[6] schools in the city. After supporting this reform in the city, Natura Institute started to invest in a curricular reform in the city of Sobral. Later in the same year, Sobral's mayor attended a business meeting in São Paulo, with Natura Institute and the Brazilian multinational company Votorantim to discuss a curriculum reform. Not long after, in May 2015, Paula Lozano, a consultant from Lemann Foundation was hired by Natura Institute and presented a "diagnostic study" together with a proposal for a new curriculum for Sobral.[7] A month later, Gallagher visited the state of Ceará where she attended a seminar, had a meeting with a state university and with Izolda Cela (also a speaker at the Unibanco seminar), the State Secretary of Education.

Thus, Mary Jean Gallagher was part of an education reform effort of Sobral, supported by Natura Institute. Natura Institute has been working on issues of curriculum reform in Sobral since 2014, which is used as a case, or a "policy story" by the MNLS. Hence, here there is a concatenation of activities that exploit a policy window (Kingdon, 2013), created by the receptiveness of state governments, to piloting new education policies, with the more general goal of constructing a policy story that will inform and support advocacy at the national level. The director of the Natura Institute described their intention in an interview:

6   Full-time schools are the ones where children spend the entire day in school, differently from what happens in the majority of Brazilian schools, where children spend either the morning or afternoon.
7   This is not publically available at the present time.

In Sobral we are helping them to reconsider their curriculum. So to do that, the first step is to know what exists "out there" (outside Brazil). Then the work Ontario did concerning curriculum was relevant, so we brought here a person from there to talk to them. [...] And every benchmarking that was done, for this project in Sobral, was made available to MNLS, for the specialists to study. So we try to link one thing to the other, we never do anything isolated. (Interview, Natura Institute, 2016)

Anthony McNamara, another international speaker at the Unibanco seminar, had spoken at a large seminar organised by CONSED with support of new philanthropy, including Itau Social, CENPEC and Natura Institute in 2014. The event had speakers from the Brazilian Ministry of Education, INEP, Unibanco Institute and CEDAC. Following this event, a group of thirty Brazilian head teachers undertook a two-week long course in England with McNamara at the NCTL.

Most importantly, Barry McGaw had been visiting Brazil since 2011, when he spoke at a seminar organised by Itau Social, where Claudia Costin was also a speaker. In 2013 he presented a lecture at the ABAVE biannual meeting and offered an interview to CENPEC (interviewed by Paula Lozano). McGaw also visited Brazil in July 2015, less than two months before the seminar, to attend meetings with the Brazilian Ministry of Education – including Renato Janine, Manuel Palácios and Francisco Soares, who were also speakers at the Unibanco seminar. After attending meetings in Brasília (the capital of Brazil), McGaw went to São Paulo for meetings with new philanthropy institutions and Lemann Foundation.

In sum, Gallagher had met state and municipal representatives at a seminar, funded by Natura Institute. McNamara had also met new philanthropists and state representatives in another seminar organised by CENPEC and Itaú. McGaw had also met federal representatives in an official government visit, and then new philanthropists from MNLS in another seminar. In all of these situations, these people were "traveling technocrats", "experts [that] are increasingly moving between private, public and third sector organisations, and between local, national and international institutions, reshaping these accordingly" (Larner & Laurie, 2010, p. 219). They were welcomed as "experts", providing "advice", and their meeting with public authorities was made possible by foundations, who mediated, organized and, most importantly, funded their traveling. As Hurl (2017) puts it, consultants make distant places close, and can perform the "work of 'lifting out' knowledge from elsewhere and skilfully 'folding' it into the municipal decision-making process" (p. 186) (as discussed in Chapter 4 concerning the use of "experts" and "expertise").

This sequence of meetings clearly illustrates that "networks have a history" that meetings "join-up" networks, and that events are spaces where "the past, the present and possible futures co-exist" (McCann & Ward, 2012). There might be, and there are likely to be, other spaces, virtual or face-to-face, where these actors maintain such relationships. However, these events are the traceable, though scattered, fragments of opaque and fast-changing policy relations.

Final remarks: Meetings as cornerstones of global education policy networks

Recently, researchers have set out to "understand and explain how neoliberalism gets done in practice" (Au & Ferrare, 2015; Ball & Junemann 2015, 2012; Olmedo, 2014, among others). That is to "unpack the mechanisms by which neoliberal discourses and rationalities take shape and transform our everyday lives and experiences" (Olmedo, 2014, p. 576). The labour for the coordination of networks described in this chapter, especially meetingness, is an example of how new philanthropies' actually "do" globalisation and neoliberalism.

Foundations share resources in networks in ways that make them interdependent, but also enable them to collaborate towards large-scale goals. To do so, formal and informal efforts are executed to coordinate networks, including commissions, work groups, online networks, annual meetings, conferences, seminars, phone calls and so on. In this context, *meetingness* is fundamental for the maintenance of relationships and networks (Urry, 2003).

Taking one seminar as the focal point, it becomes possible to see how policymakers use events as an opportunity to reiterate, recontextualise and disseminate global policy discourses, or "education solutions" as they refer to them. "Thought leaders" and "policy entrepreneurs" from different countries, like Canada, United Kingdom, Australia and Brazil, meet in these events with traditional policy actors and new philanthropy actors to discuss education problems, policies, partnerships and investments and to mediate and translate transposable policy models. These are "sociologically complex actors [...] whose identities and professional trajectories are often bound up with the policy positions and fixes they espouse" (Peck & Theodore, 2010, p. 210). They are "travelling technocrats" (Larner & Laurie, 2010), who connect knowledge and politics. In this sense, the choice of invited speakers makes evident the policy models the organisers aim to promote. The policy entrepreneurs bring with them "models that emanate from the 'right' places invoke positive associations of (preferred forms of) best practices [...] they connote networks of policymaking sites, linked by overlapping ideological orientations" (Larner & Laurie, 2010, p. 171).

Invitation to such events is also a reflection of the embodied network capital, that is "the real and potential social relations that mobilities afford" (Urry, 2007, p. 196) as well as an opportunity for a further reshaping and re-investment and enhancement of this capital. All three international speakers of the analysed event, Mary Jean Gallagher (Canada), Barry McGaw (Australia) and Anthony McNamara (England), had been in Brazil two months before the Unibanco Institute seminar, fostering relations with Brazilian actors also present in the event. In this sense, although the international speakers are presented as representatives of "international best cases", they are also products of previous networked relations that depend of different kinds of capitals, including financial and network capital.

Therefore, policy networks have a history. As McCann and Ward (2012) put it, these events are "relational sites where the past, present and potential future of a policy can co-exist. Past 'successes', current 'problems' and future 'scenarios' are discussed comparatively" (p. 48). I would argue that not only the past, present and possible futures of a policy co-exist in events, but also the past, present and future of policy networks themselves. In events, actors bring to bear the relationships they have built over time, they engage with network members building new relations and have the possibility of initiating or being recruited to new policy endeavours.

Thus, policy networks depend on people's labour. This labour might involve traveling to sites of policy, meeting over conference calls, or investing time and money in maintaining social relationships, formal and informal, as well as, more publically, writing reports and blogs, giving newspaper interviews and speaking at public events. Having access to many parts of this network labour is challenging to researchers, as a great deal of this labour is opaque, not publically visible. Nonetheless, "following policy" is a productive research tool. By following policy it was possible to identify some aspects of the labour involved in the global mobility of curriculum policies, such as network members co-attending previous events, having meetings with state policymakers and presenting their policy "solutions" to different audiences. By following actors it was possible to identify previously unknown relations between actors and institutions, such as between MNLS and ACARA, and their development over time and the flows of discourse and policy models through them. These relations, the interactions that take place among them, and the spaces of policy in which they are enacted, are part of a reconstruction of the mix between bureaucracy, markets and networks that constitutes educational governance and concomitantly the reform.

CHAPTER 5

Working to change structures and institutionalise a reform agenda

> "It is really very close, the people here [from the institute] of this project in Rio are... almost-secretariat, the relationship is really very close"
> Interview, Ayrton Senna Institute, 2016

Diverse public-private relationships are constantly created and ended, a series of services and products are offered by different foundations, and the same institutions play different roles at different points in time and space. Foundations can participate in education governance in a series of spaces, from schools' classrooms to closed doors meetings with secretaries of education. With very intimate relationships, it is difficult, if not impossible sometimes, to say where the line between public and private is. All of this is part of the *heterarchisation* of the state. Foundations and public authorities mobilise material, social and temporal conditions in heterarchies is complex ways, involving on-going negotiations, commitments and compromises (Jessop, 2011). In this chapter I analyse the work of foundations within *heterarchical* structures of governance, and it illustrates the complexity in practice, exploring the labour invested in heterarchies and how heterarchical relationships are being organised in the Brazilian education.

In what follows is an attempt to make sense of how heterarchies work in practice in one setting, to give flesh to the concept. However, order has not been inscribed in this account for the sake of order, there is a deliberate effort of not over-simplifying things that are persistently complex and difficult to track down and exhaust. Thus, the variety and amount of work done by foundations and of different possible relationships between public and private actors can seem overwhelming and confusing.

The following sections explore the new actors (institutional and individual people), new roles of public sector organisations and foundations, new blurring of public and private, new policy spaces and new channels of policy mobility – all of which are created and create, maintain and expand heterarchies. I consider how foundations in Brazil have been enrolled in the processes of heterarchical governance in different states of the country, co-writing policy with governments, providing advice and consultancy, entering into partnerships, taking on the responsibility for enacting projects and programmes, with a series of different relationships that vary in format and intensity. Heterarchies here are similar to "networks as a form", as Knox et al. (2006) put it, as a "descriptor of empirically identifiable social forms" (p. 135). Second, I look at some of the ways in which MNLS has built a profoundly intertwined network with the Ministry of Education, with the effect of creating new spaces of policymaking. Finally, I discuss how Lemann Foundation made possible an international triad between MEC, ACARA and MNLS, building global policy pipelines for policy mobility between Australia and Brazil. Together, these sections illustrate how heterarchies work in practice by discussing how foundations and governments collaborate in many ways in governance through many partnerships, how individuals connect public and private sectors, how new policymaking spaces are created and finally how global heterarchies make policy mobility possible. The chapter concludes with a reflection on how heterarchies work in practice.

Several types of relationships are built between foundations and secretariats of education in new heterarchical structures of labour sharing and interdependence between public and private actors. Different activities are executed by new philanthropies, offered as "services" to public secretaries of education in collaborative regimes. The analysis here presented does not attempt to be exhaustive, but to display the complexity of the labour sharing in heterarchies, as well as how foundations operate different kinds of tasks. Analysing, understanding and categorising such arrangements is challenging not only due to the complexities of public governance, but also the complex and instable institutional governance of private organisations.

By this I mean that some foundations do not have a clear "portfolio" of activities. They are fluid and mutant, they adapt to demands, agendas and opportunities that arise, being agile in their work and responding to new contexts.

Nonetheless, the services executed by new philanthropy can be divided between those that affect teaching situations, and the ones that affect the management of education systems, which indirectly affect the school organisation and the pedagogical practices in schools. Adrião et al. (2012) conducted a thorough study of the PPPs carried out in the municipalities of São Paulo and describe these partnerships as having direct and indirect effect over education. Foundations then promote programmes that can directly affect or seek to affect pedagogical practices, or aim to shift the management of education systems. Drawing on this distinction, the activities executed by foundations are here separated between those aimed at pedagogy and those aimed at policy and management. In the first case, philanthropy "bypasses" the state and affects pedagogy directly, with activities such as teacher-training courses. In the second, philanthropy disrupts structures with activities such as support in policymaking through pre-fabricated policies and consultancy-like services, and clearly becomes part of the weave of governance networks. The latter is specially explored here due to a lack of literature around it and its relevance for heterarchical governance, and promotion of interdependence of public and private actors.

However, the two types of programme, towards pedagogy and policymaking, are not clear-cut. They meet and blur in different moments and situations. Both types show a messy and uneven institutionalisation of heterarchies, in which responsibilities over public education are reframe and rebalanced. As Ball and Olmedo (2011) describe:

> The processes involved here both act "on" and act "against" the state and state sector education. Put succinctly, entrenched problems of educational development and educational quality and access are now being addressed by the involvement of social enterprises and edu-businesses in the delivery of educational services, both privately and on behalf of the state. (p. 88)

Programmes aiming at pedagogy

Some of the efforts and programmes of foundations aim at contributing and steering pedagogical aspects of schooling and learning. These revolve mainly around the provision of teaching and learning materials (books, online content, long-distance learning courses, apps…) and teacher-training courses, which are usually associated to the teaching materials and related pedagogical techniques. Below there is a table with examples of programmes run by foundations. This is not an exhaustive list, as programmes are often created and extinguished, and there might be smaller programmes run in specific places that are not clearly accounted for in institutional websites. The programmes in Table 8 were presented and highlighted in the foundation's websites and annual reports.

Foundations produce teaching products and services that do not depend on official partnerships with public education authorities. These are aimed at and adopted by teachers and/or students. In spite of seeming somewhat independently run by private organisations, these initiatives are operated in the shadow of the state (Börzel & Risse, 2005). These materials respond to and fit within national plans, bills and policies, and do claim to aim at fulfilling policy goals. At the same time, they interfere in and influence how education is done and thought about, creating new discourses and sensibilities (Ball & Olmedo, 2011).

Lemann Foundation is specially interested in *blended learning*, the use of technology in education and how technology can make learning "teacher-proof" (or "ensure" students learning rights in spite of their school context). So the foundation has put considerable effort into creating digital teaching/learning content and tools, that can be both autonomously adopted by teachers, or implemented within a partnership in a public education system. Khan Academy is an example, taken from the USA to Brazil by the Lemann Foundation with support of Natura Institute. The foundation translated the educational videos to Portuguese, which can be watched by students at home, in schools and be employed by teachers as a teaching material. YouTube Edu is a similar example, which is organised in partnership with Google and has video classes that can be watched by students and used by

Table 8. Examples of new philanthropies' initiatives aiming at pedagogy

Org.	Programme	Description
Fundação Lemann	YouTube Edu	YouTube Edu is done in a partnership between Fundação Lemann and Google. It brings together educational content of YouTube, with a selection done by Lemann Foundation. It includes classes by school disciplines.
	Khan Academy	Khan Academy is a learning platform for mathematics, created in 2006 by Salman Khan. It offers video classes and more than 30000 free activities. It is able to recognise the student's progress and skills that must be practiced. Teachers have access to the students' work and grades. Since 2014 it has been translated into Portuguese by Lemann Foundation, which also offers training for teachers in public schools.
	Geekie	Personalisation of studies, it offers tools that can be adequate to each student needs. Geekie games: tests, plan of studies, ENEM simulate and Geekie Lab: hybrid teaching with credentials of MEC.
	Programme	Brings together free tools to learn and teach coding. It includes teaching plans and a course for teachers.
	Eduqmais	EduqMais is a mobile text message service to stimulate the participation of families in students' school lives. The content includes motivational texts and also covers activities to be done at home to support the development of socio-emotional skills.
	Edu app	Connected to YouTube Edu, it is an app with video classes and activities.
	Google lesson plans	Digital lesson plans that are based on the National Learning Standards and can be downloaded into teachers' mobile phones. The project received funding from both Google and Lemann Foundation, and is run by the magazine Nova Escola (run by Lemann Foundation, see Chapter 4).

(continued)

Table 8. Continued

Org.	Programme	Description
Natura Institute	Trilhas	Trilhas is a project for literacy teaching, with teacher training and teaching materials. The kit includes teacher guides, recommendation of literature books, language games and activities. It aims to work towards the goal of having all children able to read by 8 years of age (following the Plano de Metas Compromisso Todos pela Educação e Pacto Nacional pela Alfabetização na Idade Certa). It has two formats: printed and online.
Ayrton Senna Institute	Letramento em programação	Learn coding, with teacher training and teaching material – implemented in only four cities.
	Formula da Vitoria	Teaching material of Portuguese and Mathematics for underperforming students. The material is built based on textual genres to create interest from students. There are pedagogical projects to be used. In mathematics there are activities based on solving problems to support reflection and interest. It is used on the school extra hours, before or after regular classes. The material includes homework, group activities, and monthly follow up by the teacher.
	Se liga	Teaching material for literacy, every teaching room has at least 30 children literature books. Each student should read these books through the year. There are metrics adopted: school days, teacher and students' attendance, observations by the mediators, teacher meetings for planning, fulfilling of homework by students.
Unibanco Institute	Estudar vale a pena	A programme of voluntary work, done in partnership with secretaries of education, to promote the reflection of students about their life plans, decision-making and consequences. With a material with games, the first stage involves talking about wishes and dreams to build life projects that should include concluding studies. The second stage includes wider discussions and concrete steps. 6281 volunteers, more than 60000 students have participated in 327 schools.

teachers. *Programaê* and *Geekie* work in similar lines, with instructions to support the teaching and learning of coding, and provide customisable exercises for students. Eduapp is a phone text service that aims to get parents more involved in their children's studies and school life, with advice and activities that can be done at home to promote this participation.

Not related to technology, but still in the realm of pedagogical content, Natura Institute offers the teaching material *Trilhas*, focused on literacy, which can be employed by teachers in classrooms and adopted together with a teacher-training course. Natura Institute says *Trilhas* has been "adopted as public policy", inasmuch as in 2012 the material was distributed to 72051 schools "amongst the municipalities considered priority by MEC's policy" (*Trilhas* website). Staff from local authorities, head teachers and teachers have been trained to use the material.

Many of these teaching materials have related teacher-training courses. Some courses simply aim to instruct teachers on how to use the material effectively. Lemann Foundation programmes are offered on individual and partnership formats. In the first case, schools and teachers can go through distance learning courses, and then use the free teaching material available in the foundation's website. In the second, Lemann Foundation created a "package" named "Innovation in Schools" (*Inovação nas Escolas*), in which teachers are trained to incorporate technology in their teaching practice, specially the tools promoted by the foundation such as Khan Academy and YouTube Edu. Ayrton Senna's programme "Coding Literacy" (*Letramento em Programação*) is also focused on technology. This small initiative, implemented in four cities, includes the teaching material for developing coding skills, as well as five modules for teachers that should be developed with both online and face-to-face activities.

However, there are also teacher-training courses that aim at more profound pedagogical changes, not just the implementation of certain teaching materials. Lemann Foundation created in 2011 the course "Classroom Management" (*Gestão de Sala de Aula*), together with Elos Educacional and supported by the World Bank. It was formulated with basis on the book "Teach Like a Champion: 49 techniques that put students on the path to college", written by the North American author Doug Lemov. The book was translated to Portuguese by Lemann Foundation ("*Aula Nota 10: 49*

Técnicas para Ser um Professor Campeão de Audiência"). It aims to "promote a school culture of high expectations of learning and efficient and democratic management, with focus on the pedagogical work to guarantee all students learn" (*Na Prática* website). This training programme was developed into a series of products that can be purchased. The course is free for teachers, to be taken online with videos, readings, discussion forums and activities. The practical part is executed in classroom, with four teaching plans that must include the teaching techniques explored in the course and be filmed. There is a second version created for "managers" (*gestores*), which aims at head teachers and representatives of Municipal Secretaries of Education. This module is offered in a blended course, with two face-to-face workshops, online activities and the requirement to carry out six pedagogical meetings and classroom observations. Finally, public authorities or private schools can hire this training as a "workshop for teachers", and Elos delivers the face-to-face ones.

Although not directly aimed towards policymaking and management of education systems, these programmes are examples of a new format of sharing of activities and responsibilities, as well as the creation of new discourses, sensibilities and subjectivities in education. These teaching materials promote a certain understanding of teaching, learning and purposes of education. They represent a diversity of heterarchical relationships, with production of pedagogical content and teacher training being shared between public and private actors.

Programmes aiming at policy: Large-scale reform with results-based management

Departing from service delivery and an "influence" or "advocacy" approach to policymaking, foundations invest in being "policy collaborators" (as Denis Mizne, the CEO of Lemann Foundation, puts it), or taking part in planning and enacting policies. In a talk – at the GIFE Conference in São Paulo, Mizne said:

> There has been a movement of greater articulation, to seat together to "qualify the demand". I think it is important to talk about it, because if the idea was not to substitute the state, I also don't think the solution is a city mayor coming, calling the foundations of that city and saying "here is what you should do". It is not like that. That is why it is hard, it is a dialogue. You have your investments, you have your vision, you are representing interests different than the ones represented there. It is not because we want to do good and have a public interest that we all believe in the same strategy, the same way to get there.

He goes on to say:

> …is about sitting down and doing policy together. Maybe because foundations started to gain scale - and in health we have the greatest example, but in education too - more and more we have organisations working with entire states or entire municipalities. Not in the role of service provider, I believe it was a moment we lived, and there still are many organisations (like that) … In this "third wave" we try to build the interventions of the third sector in the logics of public policy. … If you look at the strategic plan of most of organisations in the education sector, one do not position oneself as a substitute of the state, but to *help building policies*. (Denis Mizne, GIFE Congress, São Paulo, 2016, added emphasis)

In Mizne's explanation it is made clear how he considers foundations to be collaborators with public authorities, co-formulating policy. In this relationship the boundary between the state and philanthropy is increasingly blurred, and indeed, the "insider" and "outsider" binary is no longer present. Instead, foundations become part of heterarchical structures of governance, participating in decision-making with state institutions. In Mizne's account we could read a philanthropy shift from "advocacy" to policy entrepreneurship (Kingdon, 2013, see Chapter 4), and from "service delivery" to participation in policymaking in heterarchical structures. Here:

> Bureaucracy is displaced, innovation and creativity are "released" through the participation of business and civil society actors, and inter-related opportunities are created for reform and for profit and for "world making." The elements of a new *policy ecosystem* are outlined here—practices, organizations, infrastructure, and incentives that enable a market in state work. All of this is a reworking, or perhaps even an erasure, of the boundaries of state, economy, and civil society. (Ball, 2017, p. 38)

Foundations conduct projects that fulfil this goal of "helping building policies" described by Mizne, besides the pedagogical services explored before. Echoing the types of private services offered to secretaries of education identified by Adrião et al. (2012), these initiatives affect the management of education systems, especially through what the authors refer to as "private advisory services for education management" (*"assessoria privada para a gestão educacional"*). Amongst the three types of PPPs identified by the authors, this was the least common, but relevant nonetheless. It is understood as

> the modality by which the public administration signs agreements or contracts with private institutions, aiming to: elaborate general guidelines for the functioning of the educational system (a Municipal Education Plan, magistracy status, alternatives of planning and evaluating schools, among others); the training of school administrators and municipal administration staff; the definition of educational strategies and guidelines. (Adrião et al., 2012, p. 537)

As identified by the authors, philanthropic organisations are the main ones executing this type of PPP. The authors identified these institutions as sharing the work principles of corporate management, with a focus on leading actors for the improvement of school achievements, and the introduction of centralised assessment procedures and forms of rewarding achieved goals.

The programmes promoted by new philanthropies described in the following section parallel Adrião et al. (2012) findings. Large foundations, aiming to achieve large-scale "impact", have shifted from service delivery, with local projects addressed to schools, to large-scale projects that aim to change the logics of management employed by secretaries of education. They aim to participate directly in the policymaking process and to make governance and management more "efficient" and based on business-like techniques of management. The changes implemented in the programmes *Jovem de Futuro*, of Unibanco Institute, and *Gestão para a Aprendizagem* and *Formar* of Lemann Foundation, clearly exemplify this shift. Both are programmes that were originally created to offer services to schools in a few cities, and were later transformed into national efforts and adopted as a policy by some states.

These philanthropic programmes of education management are one of the many elements that constitute the heterarchical governance of education in Brazil. In this section I analyse how some philanthropic programmes operate, to explore how heterarchies work in practice. First I briefly describe some programmes of Unibanco Institute and Lemann Foundation to illustrate how foundations are moving from pedagogy-focused initiatives to policy-focused ones, which aim at systematic changes in education governance. These programmes now aim at a "management reform" that is done with "ready-made" solutions that can be customised to secretaries. Foundations create the solutions, with its goals and strategies, and secretaries of education are encouraged/persuaded to incorporate. This process, however, is not linear. Instead, it requires continuous negotiations and customisation. This logic operates within the heterarchical rationality "that is concerned with solving specific coordination problems, on the basis of a commitment to a continuing dialogue to establish the grounds for negotiating consent, resource sharing, and concerted action" (Jessop, 2011, p. 113). Thus, second, I play out how these programmes propel complex sharing of labour and create and animate heterarchical structures of governance. In this scenario, besides the relatively stable "ready-made" solution, foundations have also been offering different services, which resemble "on-demand" and "bespoke" logics.

Shift from service delivery to large-scale reform projects: The programmes of Unibanco Institute and Lemann Foundation

Created in 2006 and operated as a pilot until 2008, the program *Jovem de Futuro* ("Young Talent") of the Unibanco Institute aims to introduce a results-based management process into education. The programme was implemented in a few cities and was certified as a "technology[1] of school

---

[1] Foundations have benefited from a specific federal policy that has been facilitating the expansion of PPPs in the country: since 2008, within the federal policy "Plan

management" in 2009. Later, in 2012, the Ministry of Education and the Unibanco Institute signed a national partnership, which led to the adoption of the programme as the basic policy for High Schools in five states of Brazil (Sandri, 2016). Through partnerships with public secretariats of education, the institute offers "technical assistance, training, instruments and systems to the diverse agents and instances of education" (Unibanco Institute website). States, cities and schools that adopt the programme work towards goals that are established according to a "diagnosis of context and learning results". A plan of action is then agreed upon by a mixed public-private committee, which is implemented, monitored and assessed in a governance structure that involves the entire secretariat, including the secretary of education. A control group is created to produce "impact assessments", but later also receives the programme "actively" (Unibanco Website).

Unibanco Institute developed a method of work named "School Management for Learning Results".[2] It adopts five working principles to improve school management daily routines: participation, high expectations and appreciation, respect to diverse contexts, need to innovate and equity. Thus, it claims that the method reinforces community participation in decision-making, with high expectations of oneself and students (in spite of social conditions), while still taking schools contexts seriously. Protocols are adopted, and claim to make management more efficient as well as open space for innovations that offer learning opportunities for all.

---

of Education Development" (PED), the "Guide of Educational Technologies" has been promoted by the Brazilian Ministry of Education. Within PED, states and municipalities assess the local education, create a local plan of action and adopt suitable "solutions" from the Guide, which lists "educational solutions" created by both the ministry and other institutions from the private sector (Peroni et al., 2013). This guide "can be used by private companies as a type of "seal of approval" advertised in marketing campaigns that assert a certain product has been certified by the Ministry of Education" (Rossi et al., 2013, p. 212). In this context, large foundations such as Ayrton Senna Institute (Comerlatto and Caetano, 2013) and Unibanco Institute (Monteiro, 2013; Rodrigues, 2016) have been expanding their reach in the country after having their programmes recognised as "valid educational solutions".

2   *Gestão Escolar Para Resultados de Aprendizagem.*

This approach revolves around the so-called "Management Circuit",[3] which is inspired by the PDCA method (plan, do, check, act), created by Walter A Shewhard in 1920. The public authority adopting the partnership and Unibanco Institute establish, together, the goals for each school. The schools assess their situation, create a plan and begin its implementation, which is then monitored and assessed. Every three months the entire "circuit" is completed, and is concluded at the "Meeting of Good Practices". School head teachers and the staff of "Support to the Management Circuit" are the fundamental actors for the implementation of the approach. The first leads the process in the school, sharing information, motivating teachers and students and creating solutions for the schools challenges. The second supervises the head teachers and works in the secretariat of education. This programme staff is responsible for connecting public authorities with schools, guiding and monitoring the implementation of the "Management Circuit". Its function is driven by the attainment of goals, as is argued in Unibanco Institute's website as:

> Every time there is an issue in the execution of the circuit and the expected results are not reached, it is up to the professional of support to alert the head teacher and promote discussions to find solutions. […] it must also present to the regional authorities and the secretariat a diagnosis of the conditions and challenges of the education system, besides implementing education policies in the school. (Unibanco Website)

In other words, the *Jovem de Futuro* programme aims to reform managing structures, procedures and discourses by introducing its programme, with its own methods and procedures, into secretaries of education. Part of it involves a clear shift in the work logics of the institute, moving from a pedagogical impact in schools, training teachers and head teachers, to working directly with entire public authorities, entire cities and states – and their public management structures. A manager of the Institute explains:

> So what is the "Jovem de Futuro"? It is a technology of school management focused on results, which also shifts a little the state structure. … The central idea is: we (the Institute) cannot handle anymore - nor do we want to - training school staff directly. Because the knowledge generated in the trainings stayed with us, and we needed to create the conditions and capillarity for the state to have its own trainers. …

---

3   Círculo de Gestão.

So we developed a much more qualified method, with protocols. We created a more elaborated material with protocols that guarantee autonomy, flexibility, but maintains basic qualities for a management work focused on learning results. And then in these states it has become their *Ensino Medio* (high-school) policy. It is not anymore an appendix project in schools and became the public policy of high school for these states. So it gains a new strength and the impact is much greater because we are working on the technical structure of the secretariat from beginning to end. (Interview, Unibanco Institute, 2016)

In another example of a shift from service delivery initiatives to governance programmes, Lemann Foundation has two programmes that aim to affect the public management of education and schools: *Gestão Para a Aprendizagem* (Management for Learning) and *Formar* (Form). *Formar* aims to restructure management "from the secretary to the classroom" (Lemann Foundation 2016 report), and is a telling example of how the goals and strategies of new philanthropy are changing, moving from a concern about service delivery and pedagogical practices to participating in the heterarchical governance of education.

Lemann Foundation created the programme *Gestão para a Aprendizagem* in 2016, which was a derivate from the earlier programme *Gestão de Sala de Aula*, which had been created in 2011 and was focused on classroom and pedagogy (see more in the previous section on pedagogical programmes). This second programme was available to head teachers and aimed to foster "a school culture of planning and classroom observation, with high learning expectations and better use of time, underpinned by classroom management and the important multiplying role of head teachers in the direct work with teachers" (*Na Pratica* website). Compared to the first programme, the second one aspires to change the "school culture" by aiming at head teachers, "school managers" as they are referred to, instead of individual teachers and their teaching practices. It tackles school management and how school leaders can train teachers, enact results-based management and change the school's environment. *Gestão para a Aprendizagem* has two thematic modules and one additional follow up. While the first is mandatory to all participants, with discussions about "strategic management", in the second participants can choose from the themes "pedagogical management and teacher training", "pedagogical management and planning", "people management and school climate", "people management and leadership", "results management"[4] (*Na Prática* website). The programme is presented as a *"consultancy of pedagogical management"* combined with training for schoolteachers, head teachers and staff from the secretary of education (SEED website). The "consultancy" is offered to the leaders of the secretary of education and the technical team that monitors the schools – aiming to develop management guidelines, routines and instruments focused on learning results. The consultancy claims to be based on diagnostics, a formulation and implementation of an action plan and a final evaluation. The technical team of the secretary of education is responsible for monitoring the schools and participating in the training. They are to train the teachers, after having been trained by the Foundation in a blended learning course – online and face-to-face (SEED – SE news)

Later, *Gestão para Aprendizagem* was reformulated in a third programme, *Formar*, in which the foundation "has fully redesigned its work in this area of work" (Lemann Foundation website). In the first half of 2016 nine public systems of education were selected – seven municipal and two state ones; covering a total of 120,000 students in 348 schools. The 2016 report describes it as:

> The objective is to contribute to a more profound, systemic and convergent transformation, which can meet the demands of all involved professionals - from the secretariats to the classrooms - so that they can act aligned for the same goal: to guarantee the learning of each and every one of their students. From this process and objective, in 2016 the Lemann Foundation developed a programme that is focused on training and end-to-end support.

The programme lasts from two to three years and has a wide reach: leaderships of secretaries, the technical teams, the teacher trainers and head teachers. The foundations claim to offer services "from personalized support to identify challenges and design actions with the secretariats of education to training in pedagogical management and specific didactics of

---

4   "gestão pedagógica e formação de professores, gestão pedagógica e planejamento, gestão de pessoas e clima escolar, gestão de pessoas e liderança, gestão de resultados" (Na pratica).

Portuguese and Mathematics for coordinators and directors of schools and trainers of the systems" (Lemann Foundation 2016 report).

These programmes exemplify the aim of large foundation to bring about "systemic" changes in education. They aim to reform education management according to corporate management, with education quality being measured by indicators, with related introduction of centralised assessment procedures and forms of awarding reached goals. Complex heterarchical relationships are put in place for the implementation of these programmes, as will be explored next.

Complex heterarchical labour sharing: Customising "ready-made" solutions and "on-demand" services

The operation of *Jovem de Futuro* programme involves a complex sharing of tasks and roles between all the actors that participate in the education governance: staff from the institute, from the secretariat of education and from the schools. The foundation creates teaching and training materials, provides training for the public servants in the secretariat (and paying for the venue), and hiring a new staff to support the programme in the secretariat (individuals hired by the foundation but work *in* and *for* the secretariat). The secretariat assigns some public servants to the programme, pays for the transportation for the training sessions and is responsible for monitoring the programme. Both are involved in planning goals, selecting the participating schools and following up with developments. The decision regarding the participating schools is made based on quantitative data, especially large-scale test results, analysed by an "intelligence team" and "statisticians" from both parties. This complex sharing of labour can be grasped in the very pragmatic description of the interviewee:

> There is the economic team, the team of content that creates materials, there is a team that thinks about such materials to transform it into something pedagogical that can be used in schools and be replicated. So an entire structure is kept in this new proposal to impact the secretary. …

> The secretariat has priority schools and within its condition they think "well, in my reality today how I can have a differentiated service". This may involve changes in physical structure, or a closer supervision - instead of a fortnight one, in 20 schools for example, or thirty, or fifty - each state established the amount of schools they could provide this differentiated service. And the statistician team of the Institute, with the statisticians of the secretariat, chose the schools according to their results and characteristics of space, place, social as well. (Interview, Unibanco Institute, 2016)

The programme starts as a "ready-made" solution, and is then customised, changed and negotiated with the public partners. In heterarchies mutually beneficial joint projects are identified and participants mobilise the needed conditions to achieve them. Such projects can be redefined when needed. The heterarchy does not require the acceptance of absolute goals from above or on behalf of a specific organisation, but a commitment to the solution of a certain problem and to an on-going dialogue "for negotiating consent, resource sharing, and concerted action" (Jessop, 2011, p. 113). The interviewee goes on to explain this "negotiating consent":

> So it is always done with discernment and adjustments for the project to work according to the state's conditions, right? So there is a team of "intelligence" in the Institute, an internal team that does all the mapping together with the state team regarding the goals, what is possible to reach with the available resources, how much effort must be done to reach what the state hopes to achieve. (Interview, Unibanco Institute, 2016)

This negotiation is also made explicit when the project manager explains how the partnerships need to be constantly remade and closely supervised, especially in moments of political change. As heterarchies temporarily join up actors, in mutually beneficial endeavours that can be renegotiated, without the need of once-and-for-all agreements, these structures are ever changing. They are not static, on the contrary, they are dynamic and complex, involving many institutions and individuals, such as edu-business, foundations, entrepreneurs, consultants, thought leaders, governments, public agencies and so on. This is evident in the evolution and change of the roles and relations of state and foundation actors in the examples above. Nonetheless, in the process of "continuing dialogue to establish the grounds for negotiating consent" (Jessop, 2011, p. 113), it is sometimes the case that consent is revoked and heterarchical structures are disassembled:

> The state of Mato Grosso has left the program. They did not want to continue the project, because it is very influenced as well by the political changes in the secretariat, you know? We have impact, but we are also impacted by the shifts in the states. So last year there was a change in the state government, a lot of people were sacked out, a lot changed, and then we need to renegotiate it all with a new covenant. And in one of these renegotiations, the state secretary of education did not want to stay in. Actually not the secretary, it was the governor that blocked it. The first talk is with the governor, there was a change in the government, we went to redo the covenant and he did not want it. (Interview, Unibanco Institute, 2016)

She continues with another example:

> So today, it was four in the afternoon, I was preparing a training session for Ceará, and the secretary of education of Ceará was sacked. So it was like "Stop everything, wait because we are going to Ceará tomorrow for a meeting", you see? It is at this level, every change you need to do a "re-pact", reintroduce all over again because each one that comes in wants one's own team, undo all done by the previous one to start afresh. (Interview, Unibanco Institute, 2016)

Times of government change are moments of particular vulnerability for heterarchical commitments. Negotiations, promises and compromises are revisited. This highlights how heterarchies "are made of processes (exchanges) and relationships rather than constituting an administrative structure" (Ball & Junemann, 2012, p. 78), and that they "rely on trust and reciprocity, and in some of their aspects they draw upon social relations established elsewhere, in business for example" (Ball & Junemann, 2012, p. 78). When such unstable and uneven relationships and alliances are disturbed, heterarchical collaborations maybe reassessed, and can be abandoned or renegotiated in uneven power relations.

The Lemann Foundation management programmes also involve complex collaborations, in which it is increasingly difficult to separate what is done by the secretariat and what is done by the foundation within partnerships. Tasks are carried out collaboratively, in a way that " 'interests' and 'purposes' become increasingly unclear and difficult to 'trace' and pin down" (Ball & Junemann, 2012, p. 139). The Lemann case exemplifies well the growing complexity of the sharing of labour and responsibilities in the heterarchical education policy regime in Brazil. The first programme, *Gestão de Sala de Aula*, had already established a sharing of responsibilities and tasks between government and philanthropy. Within this programme the training of teachers is planned and carried out by a private partner – Lemann Foundation – while the implementation is shared. While this is done within a heterarchical logic, the foundation does not seem to hold much influence over policy decision-making. The second programme shifts the focus to head teachers, aiming at a larger impact and changing school practices and management values, discourses and practices. Finally, with the third programme the foundation creates and enacts an entire plan of reform "from the secretary to classrooms", indeed touching upon the local authority planning and policymaking. In this programme the foundation operates as a "consultant", with direct participation in decision-making: "Our consultants will work as partners in the formulation of strategic directions for the pedagogic management of secretariats, with support in the formulation and monitoring of the action plans implemented by the secretariat of education" (Raph Gomes, declaration at SEED – SE news). Importantly, the creation and launching of each new programme do not necessarily exclude the previous ones. Instead, they are all kept active, exemplifying the increasing complexity and scope and depth of heterarchies – which do not operate as "once-and-for-all" changes, but insert or build bits and pieces of change, different forms of participation and kinds of relationships, that are uneven across places and spaces of policy.

Besides these ready-made solutions, there are cases in which foundations and governments collaborate to develop new projects. These projects go through negotiations in which both public and private parties bring to bear their interests and epistemes, while also negotiating and conceding in parts. Ayrton Senna Institute has carried out a project with the secretary of Education from Rio de Janeiro, developing what later became Ayrton Senna's programme *Educação Integral*, which is now being implemented in the state of Santa Catarina and being transformed into an educational solution, or a "ready-made" solution. The institute, which has been developing governance reform programmes for a while – namely

Gestão Nota 10, *Educação Integral, Acelera Brasil, Gestão da Política de Alfabetização* and *Se Liga* (Adrião & Peroni, 2010) – made use of a policy window in Rio de Janeiro, in which the local government of Rio de Janeiro aimed to develop a policy regarding full-time schools, following the new federal guidelines. This context brought together the interests of three groups and enabled the planning of a mutually beneficial initiative, the Secretariat of Education of Rio de Janeiro, Ayrton Senna Institute and Procter and Gamble come together for a new project.

> The Institute has a very cool work with the "*educação integral*" (whole education), which goes beyond full-time schooling. It is about an education that contemplates the youth, that puts them in the centre. And then we created a partnership with Rio, which is the large project there in the area of developing a project of "whole education" for Rio. So it is a *public policy* that has been developed together with the State Secretary of Rio. The partnership started from both ends, Rio was interested in a policy of whole education, and then the Institute with an expectation of organising all our policies of young protagonist and social-emotional skills, and then they got in touch… And there was a third-party in this conversation, that was P&G, which wanted to support the development of one of these schools. So the three committed and went on to try out the solution, to see what we could do. (Interview, Ayrton Senna Institute, 2016)

Here the interviewee explains how the partnership was created in a policy window, in which each part had its agenda, interests and expertise. The heterarchical actors identified mutually beneficial projects from a range of possibilities, which were redefined and monitored. To enact them, material, social and temporal conditions were organised. All of this happens without the requirement of agreeing on substantive roles; instead it is based on a procedural rationality that concerns solving specific issues (Jessop, 2011). So in this policy window, these interests converged and enabled the creation of a heterarchical structure, in which "partnerships are a further aspect of the blurring between sectors. In these and other ways 'interests' and 'purposes' become increasingly unclear and difficult to 'trace' and pin down" (Ball & Junemann, 2012, p. 139), including interests of for-profit global companies, such as P&G.

In this case, Ayrton Senna Institute and P&G actively participated not only in the delivery of a service, but indeed in formulating a policy: "Then they [from the secretariat] go on to develop a policy. So every guideline becomes a decree, regarding what is 'whole education' for the state of Rio de Janeiro, and it is all based on what the Institute, P&G and the secretariat designed together. [...] It is really very close, the people [from Ayrton Senna] here of this project in Rio is [pause] *almost secretariat*, the relationship is really very close." (Interview, Ayrton Senna Institute, 2016)

In this account, the planning and design of the project were done together, in a symbiotic environment (Adrião et al., 2012). To explain how this position of "almost secretariat" is operated in practice, the interviewee goes on to describe the practicalities and labour involved, making clear how heterarchies are made of procedures more than structures (Ball & Junemann, 2012):

> Basically, we have the interlocutors in a project. For example, now I entered the training part, we talk with the teams of training and there are levels of interlocution, more or less like the macro governance of a project, but every area has its own interlocutors. The manager of the project talks to the area manager, the technician of the project talks to the technician of the area. We mix, for example, communication channels. For example, long-distance learning, has the channels of the Institute and the channels of the secretariat. ... the secretariat considers as its own project, so people do it together. (Interview, Ayrton Senna Institute, 2016)

Structures of governance are put in place with procedures that align the two hierarchies involved: the institute's and the secretariat's. People with similar positions and tasks are paired up, and collaborate through communications that depend on meetingness (Urry, 2003), with meetings, emails and phone calls. This also creates a sense of ownership, in which both parts feel responsible and merited for the initiative.

These heterarchical procedures and labour, that resemble advisory or consultancy services, may involve different forms of "support", that answer to specific situations and demands in specific secretariats. As an interviewee from Natura Institute puts it, this kind of relationship may be "a support that not always involves a specific knowledge, that is not a consultancy" (Interview, Natura Institute, 2016), but rather pragmatic actions, with great opaqueness of the relationships. For instance, Natura Institute has been supporting the state of Ceará and the city of Sobral in many endeavours. One service provided by the Institute to the secretariat was hiring a new staff to work in the government, collaborating with and supporting civil servants. This person is, himself, the embodiment of the blurriness of public and private, working as a civil servant, paid by the foundation, answering to both – a "heterarchical actor defined by mobility and hybridity" (Ball & Junemann, 2012, p. 139). This type of arrangement is not an exception, as Natura Institute hired two people to work in Ceara's state secretariat of education, and Unibanco Institute hires people to work in the states with their *Jovem de Futuro* programme.

Natura Institute has also worked as a "middle man" for the state of Ceará and the municipality of Sobral, in the context of curriculum reforms in these places. Natura Institute brought the Canadian policy-maker Mrs Mary Jean Gallagher to Ceará, to discuss curriculum making. Concomitantly, Natura Institute hired Paula Lozano and Ilona Becskehazy, consultants with past and present ties with Lemann Foundation, who are named in the second page of the curriculum document as "Coordination and Consultancy". These consultants were included a multi-stakeholder partnership to develop a new local standardised curriculum, one that would became a case for the MNLS (see Chapter 5 for more detail). In these cases, Natura Institute makes possible a flexibility of the contracting out scheme that governments are unable to do. So the heterarchical structures "are a policy device, a way of trying things out, getting things done, changing things and avoiding established public sector lobbies and interests" (Ball & Junemann, 2012, p. 138).

All of these programmes and cases show a move of foundations from the context of practice (school-focused programmes), to the context of influence (advice/consultancy) and to the context of policy writing (partnerships), and thence again to context of practice (municipal and state focused reforms) (Bowe et al., 1992), showing that new philanthropy is active in all policy contexts (Olmedo, 2017). The programmes described are large-scale and aim at structural changes in entire systems of education, bringing about results-based management with ready-made policy solutions that can be customised to suit public partners. They show the longer reach of philanthropy, and a deeper, multi-layered development of heterarchies. They also exemplify a vast diversity of types of relationships that can be involved in such heterarchies, as well as the mundane activities employed

Changing structures and institutionalise a reform agenda   173

to maintain them. These can include hiring new staff for the government, contracting out external consultants, maintaining regular advisory meetings, creating projects from scratch, continued communications, training sessions and so on. Heterarchies are complex, ever changing, ephemeral and "certainly uneven" (Ball & Junemann, 2012). This extensive account of types of activities involved in heterarchical governance gives flesh to this complexity, which is further explored in the MNLS case.

MNLS's heterarchical relationships: Co-affiliations with civil servants

In this section I analyse the network of the Mobilisation for the National Learning Standards and its intense and multi-facetted connections with the Ministry of Education. Differently from the previous section, in which the working of heterarchies was analysed through the work of organisations and public-private partnerships, this section exemplifies even more nuanced and opaque boundary-spanning relationships of individuals. By analysing people's affiliations between the MNLS and other organisations it's possible to see how mobile professionals and the creation of new policymaking spaces are also part of heterarchies. So first I analyse the co-affiliation of the individual supporters of MNLS. Then, aiming to understand how a close relationship was built between MNLS and MEC, I analyse the change of the network, first analysing its composition and then the changes of co-affiliation between MNLS and the National Council of Education. From this, I discuss the work of boundary-spanning professionals, with two relevant examples from this network.

Although being fully funded and maintained by private organisations, MNLS has individual supporters from every level of government (federal, state and municipal as noted above). At the federal level, what is particularly striking is how many members of MNLS hold or have held positions in the National Council of Education (CNE), the Ministry of Education (MEC) and the *Câmara dos Deputados*, the lower congress chamber. By the end of 2016, more than half of MNLS members were working in state institutions. The individual members are fundamental for the functioning of MNLS, both in the decision-making and in advancing their agenda into their diverse contexts and connections. First, according to a representative of Lemann Foundation, "the group of members decides what are the priorities for year, the strategic decisions, and it follows up MNLS developments. The executive secretariat of the movement is in touch with these people every day, literally, exchanging ideas every day, asking for their opinions, for advice and suggestions" (Interview, Lemann Foundation, 2016). Second, the connections the members hold are fundamental for MNLS's "advocacy work". This is made explicit by the same representative of Lemann Foundation in saying:

> Each member of the Mobilisation is an advocacy potential. They are very different people, the Mobilisation is quite plural, so each one of these people has a very different set of "interlocutors". The members are the advocacy of the group because they talk with the most interesting interlocutors for them. There are people with greater dialogue with social movements, there are people with more dialogue with other foundations, some people talk with the government, some people *are* government. So the Mobilisation is an advocacy organism, so it is very interesting that we say the same things, with different colours sometimes, but the principles are the same. Instead of having one advocacy, you have 60. This is very interesting. I believe one of the strengths of the Mobilisation is operating as a bloc. Even if we don't agree with everything, the key messages are always there being repeated for those people that matter (in the debate). (Interview, Lemann Foundation, 2016)

Thus, it is crucial to consider the individual members of MNLS in order to better understand to where, with who and how MNLS's discourses flow. Thus, there is below a co-affiliation network of the individual members of MNLS (for a discussion of what co-affiliations entail, see Chapter 3). Here, the data concerns MNLS individual members and the institutions to which they are affiliated through professional work. To analyse the relationship of MNLS with other organisations, especially state ones, the dual-mode affiliation network (person-by-institution) was converted into a one-mode co-affiliation network (institution-by-institution). It assumes that two institutions that have one or more members in common have a greater chance of ideas being

Changing structures and institutionalise a reform agenda   175

exchanged between them. The graph below was built as an ego network (the network of one institution, MNLS), meaning that all institutions have at least one connection with MNLS (at least one person affiliated to both institutions). The nodes are organised in three circles: in the outer-circle institutions have only one connection to MNLS. In the middle-circle they have two connections. Finally, in the central circle they have three or more (with the exact number presented numerically by the edge).

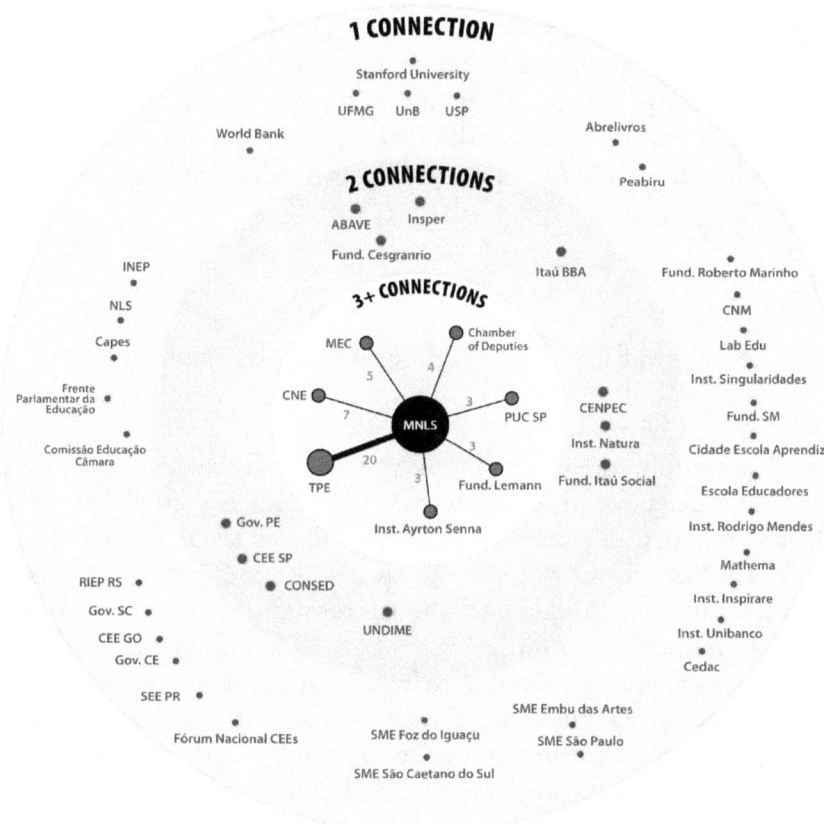

Figure 5. MNLS's co-affiliation ego network (without edges)

The co-affiliation of members between MNLS and fifty-two other institutions is represented in Figure 5. Out of these organisations, seven have more than three connections with MNLS (and are therefore more likely to have a significant exchange of ideas, discourses and/or resources). Todos pela Educação unquestionably has the highest co-affiliation with MNLS (twenty members), elucidating the close relationship between the two movements. Interestingly, among the more connected institutions, there are three federal ones: *Câmara dos Deputados*, MEC and CNE.

To further explore the blurred relation between private and public, new philanthropy and state present in MNLS's network, in what follows there is a discussion of the evolution of this part of the network in a time-span. I also consider the backgrounds and affiliation of some of these members. Some of the questions to be addressed are: How did MNLS build such network? How did they manage to create this close relation with fundamental public institutions, such as MEC and the CNE?

MNLS and MEC/CNE: The network's change in time

To indicate how the composition of MNLS has changed over time, it was tracked for three semesters. The listings here begin from September 2015, the first time MNLS published the names of its supporters. While in effect MNLS was created in 2013, it only began using this name in events and in publishing information about its work (and supporters) in the second semester of 2015. Even in this short period of time, there are considerable changes in the composition of MNLS and an increasing numbers of bureaucrats. Indeed, the amount of change in three semesters is a good example of how these networks are ever changing, unstable and fluid (Ball & Junemann, 2012; Peck & Theodore, 2010; Shiroma, 2013). Figure 6 represents the change in MNLS's composition.

Changing structures and institutionalise a reform agenda

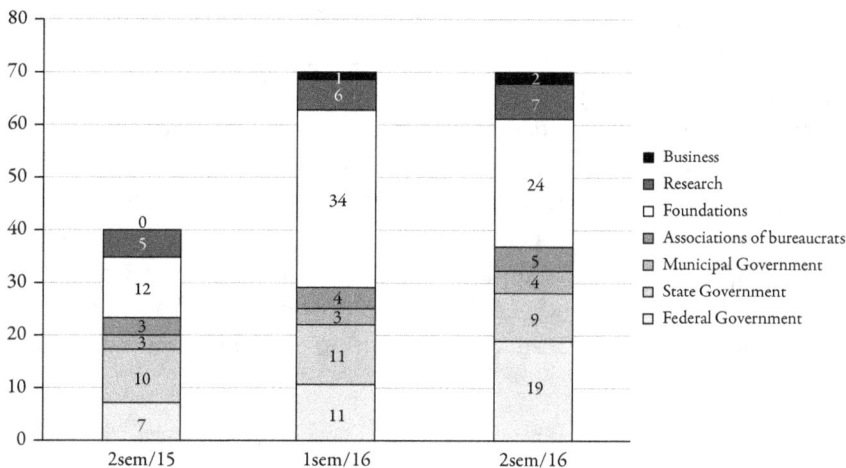

Figure 6. Composition of MNLS's members between 2015 and 2016

Through Figure 6, two changes in the composition of MNLS become visible. The first indicates a growth in the MNLS, evident in the difference between the end of 2015 and the beginning of 2016. In this period, the MNLS grew from forty to seventy members. This growth was mainly reached through the recruitment of foundation representatives: Out of the thirty new members, twenty-four were affiliated to foundations. Regarding bureaucrats, although the overall growth was not as substantial, it is important to stress that by the end of 2015 MNLS recruited four members of the CNE. At this period, MEC had just published the first version of the Learning Standards (September 2015), which created a large public debate about it. MEC, MNLS and local authorities were fomenting discussions through several small seminars and meetings to gather feedback for a second version of the Learning Standards document.

In contrast, the second shift indicates a qualitative change in the MNLS's composition. While in the first semester of 2016 there were twenty-nine members affiliated to state institutions and forty-one to private organisations, in the following semester it changed to thirty-seven members in state institutions and thirty-three in private ones. More importantly, MNLS's composition changed with the addition of members occupying important posts in government (CNE and MEC specially). This shift took place in relation to the controversial change of government when President Dilma Rousseff was impeached and a conservative coalition took over. From only seven members in federal government positions in the first semester of 2015, MNLS reached nineteen by the second half the year.

Below there are three affiliation networks between MNLS, MEC and CNE (and its two chambers, as noted before). Differently from the previous graph, the graphs below are kept as two-mode graphs, with two sets of nodes (institutions and people), to explore how MNLS's co-affiliation with vital federal decision-making institutions have been built over time.

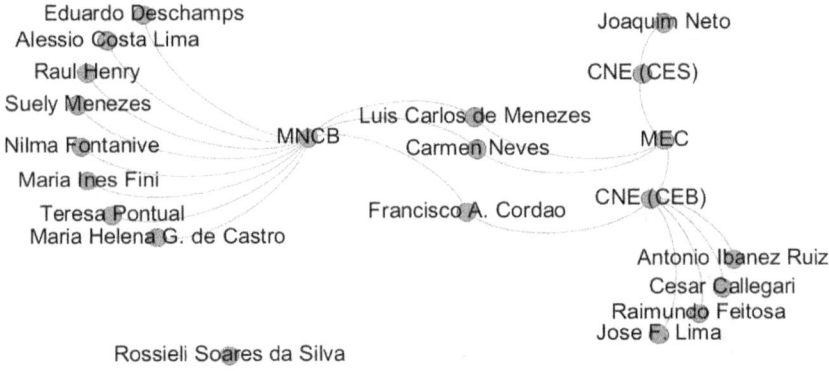

Figure 7. MNLS and MEC – second semester 2015

MNLS had two different directions of interaction with state bureaucracy. First, up to the end of 2015 (see change from Figures 7–9) it was recruiting bureaucrats into the movement, that is people who were on the CNE and then became affiliated to the movement. In interviews, representatives from Lemann Foundation explained (as quoted previously) how Lemann Foundation and MNLS had been investing in relationship-building in Brasilia, Brazil's capital: "We have a person, we hired someone 'super', who is in Brasilia now doing lobby. … He has in his diary talking to people that have power, or that participate in the process of eventually having connectivity" (Interview, Lemann Foundation, 2016).

Changing structures and institutionalise a reform agenda 179

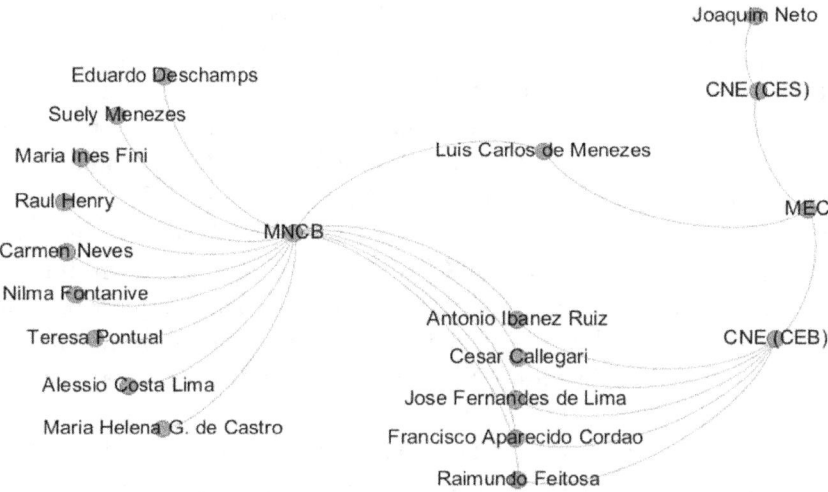

Figure 8. MNLS and MEC – first semester 2016

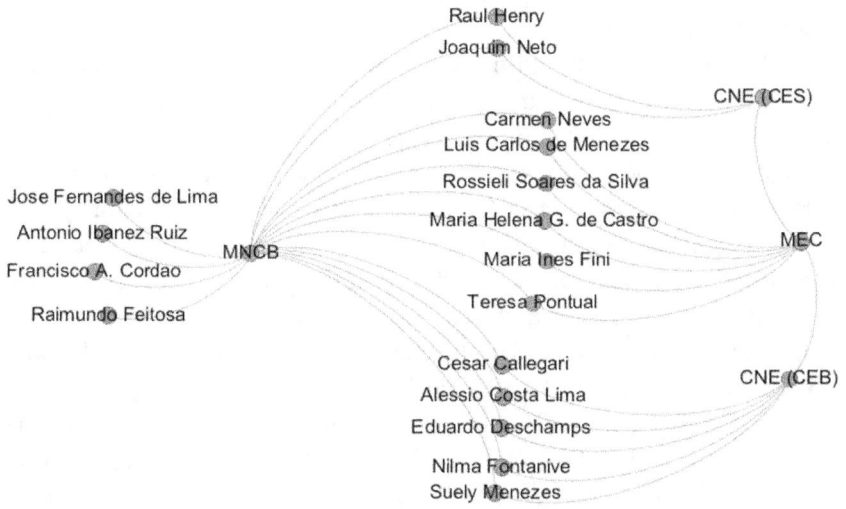

Figure 9. MNLS and MEC – second semester 2016

Second, in a new *policy window* (the change of government and new President), people who were already part of the MNLS were appointed to roles in the bureaucratic structure, indeed to strategic positions in CNE and MEC, both official sites for deliberation and formation of the new national curriculum. In MEC, MNLS members were appointed to the positions of MEC's Executive Secretariat, of the head of the Secretariat of Basic Education (SEB), as well as two out of the three SEB's directorships, and INEP's presidency. In CNE, Michel Temer, at the time interim president, exchanged six out of twelve indications of the former president Dilma Rousseff. In his new name list, there were four names affiliated to private institutions, including Nilma Fontanive and Suely Menezes, members of MNLS.

In both directions of interaction the epistemic relation between the movement and members has been fundamental. Francisco Aparecido Cordão, the first CNE member to join MNLS, was part of the founding team of Todos pela Educação. Similarly, part of the group from CNE that joined MNLS by the end of 2015, Cesar Callegari is in the governance team of Todos pela Educação. In the second shift, Nilma Fontanive, who is part of the technical commission of Todos pela Educação, and Suely Menezes, who is part of the large for-profit higher education chain named Ipiranga, were appointed to the council.

However, the most significant examples of boundary-spanning actors that now are part of MEC are probably Maria Helena Guimarães de Castro and Maria Ines Fini. Both joined MNLS at its early stages, both are now in high-ranking positions in MEC, and both have a long and complex history with education in Brazil, with extensive connections with both public and private sectors. Castro has worked as a professor of political science at the University of Campinas. She has been the president of INEP during the government of Fernando Henrique Cardoso (1995–2001), when large-scale exams were introduced in the country, and in 2002, during the same government, she became the Executive Secretary of MEC (position she holds again now). She has then worked in different states and secretariats, including the secretariat of education in the state of São Paulo, when the state introduced a standard curriculum. She then joined the foundation *Educar para Crescer*, became president of the Fundação Sistema Estadual de Análise de Dados (SEADE, or State System of Data Analysis Foundation), and is part of Todos pela Educação. Maria Ines Fini has also worked at the University of Campinas between 1972 and 1996, where she participated in the creation of the Faculty of Education. Between 1996 and 2002 she worked in INEP with Maria Helena de Castro, where she was a director responsible for two large-scale tests. She also worked in different states and cities in the country and was PISA's director in Brazil. She then became involved in different foundations (FEAC, *Campinas pela Educação*, *Fundação Educare*, Roberto Marinho Foundation) and for-profit high-education institutions (Cesgranrio, SL Mandic). Both are highly connected people in the field of education in Brazil, having operated in different states, with different governments and worked with public and private organisations. Nonetheless, they represent a type of education project, one that values standard teaching, large-scale tests and the participation of private organisations in public education.

To make it clear, as it is common in policy networks, in the MNLS network there is an epistemic connection between members (Santori et al., 2015), one that is often manifested in affiliations, but also transcends them. Network members are bonded together through a shared view of what education should be, what the policy problems in Brazil are and the preferable (and necessary) policy solutions. As one interviewee explains: "These organisations are in the Mobilisation because they truly believe that having learning standards in Brazil can make a lot of difference. So they make this part of their own cause. Then it becomes a natural work to take this with them in whatever task or event they do" (Interview, Lemann Foundation, 2016).

Here the boundary between the state and new philanthropy is increasingly porous, and indeed we might say that MNLS emerges over time as a key site of policy and of state work in its own right. There is also the role of a relatively new kind of hybrid, boundary-spanning actors who manage "within inter-organisational theatres", as Williams (2002, p. 104) puts it, accumulating network capital as they move between sectors. At the same time, new kinds of careers, identities and mobilities are forged within the processes of reform and through the work of such policy networks. These boundary-spanning and mobile policy actors contribute symbolically and substantively to a "power narrative" (McCann, 2008, p. 5) made up of ideas, practices and sensibilities that address the reform of the Brazilian school curriculum. Some we might identify as "movers and shakers" (Williams,

2002) – that is people who have the ability to connect and ensure cooperation within and across different networks by sharing common goals and combining resources. Individual trajectories and histories become embedded in the network, and focused at particular nodal points. These are in effect embodied policy mobilities, people who carry the sensibilities and substance of education reform with them.

The growth and change of MNLS, specially its recruitment of people with decisive positions in MEC, illustrates the creation of new heterarchical policy spaces. Policy is being done by new organisations, new people, in new relationships and new places. Concomitantly, new professionals are made, ones that are "embodied members of epistemic, expert and practice communities. They are sociologically complex actors, located in (shifting) organizational and political fields, whose identities and professional trajectories are often bound up with the policy positions and fixes they espouse" (Peck & Theodore, 2010, p. 170). These opaque relationships raise concerns about democracy and accountability, and these new relationships demand new ways of research and citizen participation in public matters.

Global heterarchies: Heterarchies, policy pipelines and policy mobility between MEC and ACARA

Heterarchies operate on a global scale, connecting public and private, governmental, business and philanthropic actors in different countries, stretching across regions with a complex mix of the public and the private. As Hogan (2015) puts it,

> These relationships function between agencies of the government, business and civil society and extend these, in the case of contemporary education policy, to a global scale. Thus, the concept of heterarchy is able to account for the rescaling of politics and the emergence of new political actors, simultaneously recognising the continuing significance of the state and its bureaucracy and new public/private relations that mediate education policy processes. (Hogan, 2015, p. 385)

One example of the global work of heterarchies concerns the relationship between the Brazilian Ministry of Education and the Australian Ministry of Education, mediated by the Lemann Foundation, working under the auspices of MNLS. Besides managing its national responsibilities, ACARA has been working on different international fronts, specially addressing its fourth purpose regarding "collaboration and leadership". The ACARA's 2015–16 "Corporate Plan" specifies the institution's four purposes in the areas of: curriculum; assessment; data and reporting; and collaboration and leadership. Each purpose is managed with goals and performance criteria. The last includes the aim of "collaborating with international education bodies to ensure ACARA's work and advice to ministers are informed by leading research and better practice, and *provide support services internationally where these align with ACARA's core areas of work*" (ACARA website, added emphasis). For this, ACARA is supposed to create "collaboration with partners (government and non-government school sectors), and national stakeholders and international education bodies".

Hence, ACARA should be able to have "evidence of collaboration through: scheduled meetings of ACARA's key advisory groups; ACARA's attendance at key working groups and peak bodies and evidence of communication with international education bodies" (ACARA Work plan 2015/16). ACARA recognises the importance of meetings and participation in events as a means of networking with influential global actors, exerting meetingness to reinforce network bonds (Urry, 2003).

In these lines, the 2015/2016 Report lists the achievements of having developed the Australia's report for UNESCO,[5] having held a partnership with Ireland and Sweden to develop an online assessment[6] and, most

5   "ACARA developed Australia's report for the United Nations Educational, Scientific and Cultural Organization (UNESCO) 'Network on Education Quality Monitoring the Asia Pacific' comparative study. The project explores practices for assessing transversal competencies, or general capabilities, used by schools and school systems in the Asia-Pacific region. The Australian report includes a description of the national education context and details of school case studies. The Australian material will be synthesised with other participating countries to form the regional report."
6   In 2015–16, ACARA entered into a partnership project with education authorities in Ireland and Sweden to develop and trial innovative online assessment. Data from

importantly, collaborating with Brazil and Saudi Arabia. The organisation reports having discussions with the Kingdom of Saudi Arabia's Public Education and Evaluation Commission to support the country's national curriculum on a fee-for-service basis, and "in 2015, ACARA held meetings with Brazilian government officials and embarked upon work to support Brazil in the development of its national learning standards through a contract with the Lemann Foundation, *acting on behalf of the Brazilian government*" (ACARA report 2015–16, added emphasis).

Thus, amongst the international activities held by ACARA, participating in the development of a new national curriculum on a fee-for-service basis for the Kingdom of Saudi Arabia and the Brazilian government (through Lemann Foundation) are highlighted. Besides attracting new sources of income (Yearly report), these partnerships are portrayed by ACARA as an achievement "built on ACARA's reputation for world-class curriculum, assessment and reporting programmes, including hosting numerous international delegations". And "ACARA's expertise and reputation have also led to international recognition and collaborations across curriculum, assessment and reporting. In 2015–16, ACARA hosted several international delegations, provided advice to support national curriculum work in other countries and attended international forums including the ones held by UNESCO and the Organisation for Economic Co-operation and Development" (2015/16 report). ACARA's international efforts are part of a global reform of education, which encourages a global competition in which the Australian government aims to assert its position as an educational "leader".

The triad: Mediation of Lemann and creation of pipelines

As described in previous chapters, MEC, ACARA and Lemann/MNCN developed an intense and multi-facetted collaboration. ACARA worked with Brazilian authorities, had meetings with government officials, wrote

---

the trial informed a paper for the 2016 International Association for Educational Assessment (IAEA) Conference in Cape Town, South Africa.

analytical reports on preliminary versions of the Learning Standards, and created curriculum guidelines for the writing team, all on a fee-for-service relationship through a contract with the Lemann Foundation, which namely "acted on behalf of the Brazilian government". This relationship is welcomed from all three parts of this triadic relationship. Lemann Foundation and the MNLS have been playing a broker role between the Brazilian and Australian Governments, putting forward a curriculum model within its agenda and understanding of a good curriculum. MEC is proud of drawing upon a model from a "developed" country, and advertises this relationship. Similarly, for ACARA this is both a political and financially lucrative situation.

This triad is a space that has enabled the mobilisation of a hybridised curriculum model drawing on expertise in both Brazil and Australia and interests on both sides, but this was only possible due to the *"heterarchisation"* of both governments involved. The governments were connected and related to each other through aspects of their heterarchical modes of governing and the new practices, tools and goals arising from these. These connections and relations required, on the Brazilian side, a collaboration with private foundations and welcoming Lemann Foundation in different occasions. On the Australian side a shift of government roles that now also involve its agencies, like ACARA, operating as global consultants, collaborating with private entities and offering services for fees. Lemann Foundation (on behalf of MNLS) acts as an intermediary institution. Arguably, none of these arrangements would have been possible in "former" modes of hierarchical government.

The role played by Lemann Foundation has been crucial in manufacturing this triad and enabling the mobility of a curriculum model, specially by building policy pipelines (Cook & Ward, 2014), as for "policy to be moved from one location to another there needs to be some sort of supportive infrastructure ... [which] makes policy mobility more probable, although it is rarely predetermined and there are no guarantees" (Cook & Ward, 2012). Such policy pipelines include fundamental elements for policy mobility, namely "the infrastructure that supports the movement of policies, the representational practices of various 'experts', and the place of conferences as central nodes in the globalizing of urban policies" (Cook & Ward, 2012, p. 142). The reports, videos, press coverage and events, all create the needed "informational infrastructure" that disseminated the discourses about education and curriculum among decision-makers, philanthropists and the general public. They also are "representational practices of 'experts', in which MNLS and ACARA take on the "curriculum expert" position in the policymaking arena (Cook & Ward, 2012). Finally, the numerous conferences funded and organised by MNLS and its members, as explored in the previous chapter, work as "central nodes in globalising of urban policies".

The concept of heterarchies cannot be separated from global networks. Heterarchies are not limited to or within national borders; the policy networks and mobilities that they consist of are international. Indeed, one could argue that policy mobilities are facilitated precisely because of heterarchical governance. In this case, the heterarchy and mobility are in part dependent upon each other: Policy mobility is made possible because of the heterarchical work of the public organisations here involved, and heterarchies are strengthened by the policy pipelines built for and from mobility, through the financial and symbolic capitals invested and exchanged.

In spite of the opaqueness of this triad – or how we cannot fully understand its relationship, contracts, funding, interests – what is striking here is how important the MNLS, with its global partners, is to understanding the formulation of the national learning standards in Brazil. Indeed, as important as other more traditional actors, such as teacher unions and academic researchers. In fact, such organisations have been persistently complaining about not only the curriculum itself, but about how the Ministry of Education has not sufficiently listened to and included them in such process. Instead, this policy network – with corporate, philanthropic and civil servant actors, in partnership with international institutions – seems to have been more successful in partaking and formulating the learning standards.

Final remarks. The heterarchical state in practice

What this chapter has sought to capture is some aspects of how heterarchies operate in practice, and the roles and activities new philanthropy in Brazil has been playing in them. These are parts of general changes in the forms and modalities of the Brazilian state. They are not absolute changes, but rather a set of shifts in the balance or mix between the different elements of government – bureaucracy, markets and networks. This new mix brings new players from business and philanthropy into the work of governance and entangles bureaucratic actors in new sites of policy and new kinds of relations in and with policy. In this chapter I have indicated in particular the formation of new relationships between public authorities and foundations, as well as new kinds of policy actors who operate across and between what were once distinct sectors. They illustrate the changing nature, goals and means of state work, in which new philanthropy (and the MNLS) rises as a new centre of gravity in the topography of education policy in Brazil and its connecting role in global networks.

Within the umbrella concept of heterarchies, there are different types of public-private relationships happening. Namely, I have aimed to illustrate: the creation and offer of pedagogical services and products; the creation and offer of "ready-made" solutions – as well as the customised and advisory-like services; the creation of new policy spaces; and creation of policy pipelines for policy mobility. These heterarchical relationships are negotiated and enacted in an asymmetrical networks, in which there are varying and shifting degrees of autonomy and interdependence between public and private actors. This means the public-private relations might vary from one-off short-termed connections – such as a one-day seminar for teacher training – to deeply interdependent and relatively permanent connections – such as a co-formulation of a policy engendered by a foundation and a secretariat held together by weekly meetings. What this also means is that power is not only unevenly distributed across heterarchies, but also that power relations are constantly shifting. Nonetheless, this is precisely what makes heterarchies – their lack of patterns, hierarchies or set of ordered rules. Instead, their organisation involve horizontal and vertical connections (Ball & Junemann, 2012) in self-regulated and dynamic regimes of interdependence (Jessop, 2011).

The work of foundations do not signal once-and-for-all systemic changes in education policymaking or the education state, rather this is part of a myriad of small moves, experiments and initiatives that may be scaled up, and contribute over time to a more profound system re-engineering. Far from a dramatic "roll-back" or a total "hollowing out" of the state (Holliday, 2000), this newly emerging model of governance implies a "roll-out" of new structures and technologies of governance that redefine the roles and responsibilities of the state but, at the same time, resituate the state strategically in both normative and institutional terms.

These shifts are part of a deeper transformation of the political sphere, a "de-governmentalisation of the state" (Rose, 1996), in such a way that the state no longer acts as the centre of power. Instead, new forms of political organisation – heterarchies – are developing in which governments no longer exert monopolistic control over state work. In this context, "the new heterarchical mode of governance implies a conception of policy that should be seen as the collective efforts of a set of players who compete and form alliances in an ever-increasing networked political arena" (Olmedo, 2014, p. 253). This involves changes both in "who governs" and at the same time "how power is exercised". It occurs through the repopulating and re-working of existing policy networks and the emergence of new networks that give legitimacy to the role of business and/or enterprise and/or philanthropy in the solution of intransigent problems (like the form and content of the school curriculum).

To reiterate, this is a move beyond both bureaucratic and market forms of coordination towards more flexible, asymmetric, heterarchical relationships, within which responsibilities and processes of decision-making are shared by a heterogeneous mix of old and new policy actors, with the effect of re-balancing the governance mix (Ball & Junemann 2012). As Jessop (1998, p. 32) explains:

> the recent expansion of networks at the expense of markets and hierarchies and of governance at the expense of government is not just a pendular swing in some regular succession of dominant modes of policymaking. […] and a corresponding shift in the centre of gravity around which policy cycles move.

Also evident here in the formation and evolution of the MNLS is the construction of what Cook and Ward (2012) call *policy pipelines*. Through transnational policy pipelines extending from USA and Australia to Brazil, mediated by Lemann Foundation and the MNLS, Yale, Australian "consultants" and US policy entrepreneurs, pass both tacit knowledge and knowledge in more codified forms. In such policy pipelines also flows "learning acquired through participation in trans-urban policy pipelines [that] dissipates through the different 'local' clusters of practitioners and policymakers – 'spill-over' " (Cook & Ward, 2012, p. 141) – the idea in this instance of a national curriculum. Thus, we might view MNLS as one small part of a more extensive joined-up policy network, that is a "globally integrated network" (Urry, 2003) of highly interdependent actors and organisations, practices and forms, which are related together in diverse ways in relation to education reform. As Ball (2016) puts it, "these network relations are not outside or over and against the local in any simple sense, they have multiple changing relations to and within 'the local' or in fact different locals" (p. 561), here national, state and municipal. Indeed, "what is local and global is changed/muddied by the relationships and movements traced here" (Ball, 2016, p. 561).

The Brazilian case of education reform is joined up, practically and discursively, in a variety of ways, some described in this account, to a global network of policy ideas and forms of policy. Brazil is at one particular point on a continuum of change that interconnects and replicates a global shift in the form and modalities of the state and concomitant ways of governing differently. The specifics of this account would suggest a clear direction of travel with the work of the state increasingly being done elsewhere by other actors – all of which calls into question the relations between policy, the policy process and democratic politics. This is in some senses a de-politicisation of policy. New unelected and, in many ways, unaccountable voices are having a significant say in determining the methods, contents and purposes of education. MNLS members and its cohorts and partners are in some respects "voting with dollars" (Saltman, 2010). That is to say, financial, reputational and social resources are being deployed to change the landscape of education in Brazil and the experience of education in Brazilian schools.

CHAPTER 6

New philanthropy, education policy networks and issues for a democratic education

With a growing relevance of new philanthropy in education policy-making in Brazil and globally – new philanthropies, both the multinationals (like the Bill and Melinda Gates Foundation and Omidyar Network) and Brazilian ones (like Lemann Foundation, Unibanco Institute, Natura Institute, Ayrton Senna Institute and Todos pela Educação) appear to be committed to a particular and well circumscribed policy set, that relies for the most part on transposing discourses and practices from business into education. Although presented as "non-profit", new philanthropy's work supports education privatisation and marketisation and often aspires to exclude alternatives and challengers. This book has set itself to address the question of how foundations work to participate in the governance of education, becoming influential actors that promote a corporate reform of education.

The answer for the posed question is not simple, and it cannot have been given the complexity of the phenomena and its context. The growing relevance of philanthropy in education governance and policy involves both macro and micro elements, from global shifts to daily mundane activities and strategies. New philanthropy's work and the related education reform project are disseminated and defended with a pervasive approach that includes discursive, relational and institutional aspects. Namely, in shifting structures of governance, new philanthropies invest labour to frame policy ideas, to relate in networks and to institutionalise policy ideas and relationships.

To conclude the book, I try to summarise the findings to respond to the question at hand, sewing back together the many elements explored in the book. The labour modalities of new philanthropy described and analysed in this book – labour to frame policy ideas, to relate and to institutionalise policy ideas and relationships – are deeply intertwined. There are no clear-cut separations between the purposes and practices involved in this work, nor are there stages and spaces that can be traced and pinned down in any simple way. Hence I return to the initial frame of analysis, which is represented below. Each nexus of analysis has developed an analysis of the different forms of labour deployed across the networks' contexts and scales, represented by the vertical arrows in the scheme. Each part of the multi-scalar analysis provided width and depth to the analysis, as well as a *glocal* perspective, which are here represented with the horizontal arrows. To conclude, I try and play out some of the interactions between them, here represented with the circular arrows around the labour modalities (see Figure 10).

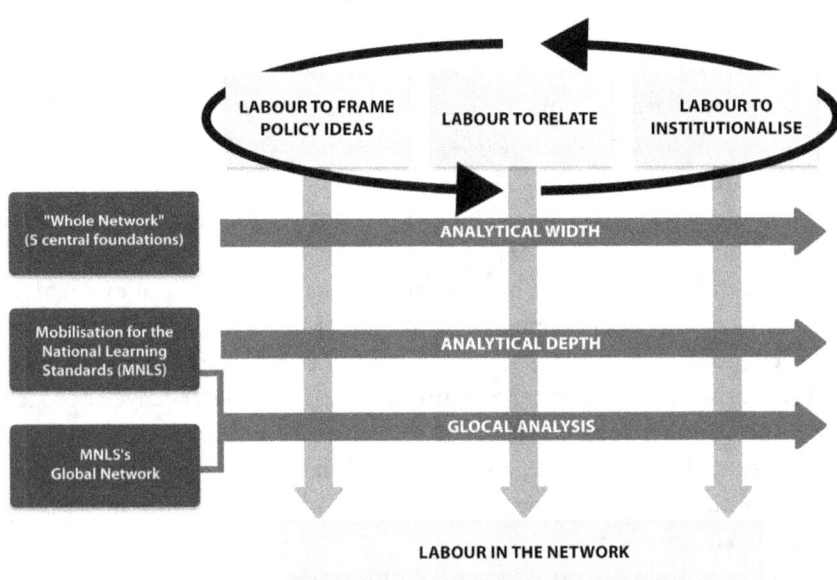

Figure 10. Analytical frame revisited

New philanthropies, in Brazil and elsewhere, distinguish themselves from more traditional charity work by their "strategic" approach to "social investment". They aim to manage their investments, specially money, but also time and social capital, in similar ways as companies manage theirs. New philanthropies aim to find the best "return of investment". Policy entrepreneurship is a way to achieve large-scale changes in education with relatively low cost, given that a relatively "small" budget can steer large amounts of public investment towards the education policy agenda foundations support, usually revolving around a corporate reform of education. At the same time, these new philanthropies disseminate a particular vision and version of policy and education reform that draws primarily upon corporate-inspired practices and discourses, and aim to reform public management according to these. The logics behind this reform work revolve around the idea that "business appears as universally beneficial. After all, it has worked well for them. So business language, values, and ways of seeing should be applied to the public sector" (Saltman, 2010). Policy is treated a technical problem, rather than as a political issue – this is in some sense a de-politisation of the state (Clarke, 2012).

In practice, the policy entrepreneurship of new philanthropists in Brazil involves the organisation, systematisation, framing and articulation of policy ideas through research projects, publications, such as reports and press releases, and articles in the press, meetings, events, etc. More than simply or modestly seeking to convince policymakers, as the idea of "advocacy" infers, these activities are more fundamentally about defining and framing the problems that require government action, and articulating, legitimating and limiting appropriate policy solutions. At the same time, new philanthropies frame themselves as legitimate policy actors, with an "authoritative voice" (Ball, 2012). The MNLS has taken up this "ideological labour" (Ferrare & Apple, 2017) to frame the need of learning standards in Brazil. The Mobilisation's labour involves not only national efforts, but also the building of transnational policy pipelines (McCann & Ward, 2012), enabling the mobility of policy ideas across boundaries. Funding, research, consultants, ideas, all travel more easily (Urry, 2003) in such a way that policy entrepreneurship is no longer conducted within the limits of national borders.

Framing policy problems and solutions requires sharing ideas in many places, and mobilising the financial, social and network resources needed.

This requires an interdependence between network actors, and efforts of co-ordination among them. So different types of capital are shared and flow in networks, including money and social connections. In doing so, new philanthropies can become more effective in their reform efforts, and can mobilise support for policy ideas in many spaces, including in and across the government. Networks are built and animated to gather support to policy ideas, in which not only pragmatic relations are organised, but also epistemic ones, so meetings become especially important as times and places to strengthen relationships and shared beliefs. These relationships, as noted, span national and sector borders, so they are not limited to the Brazilian context, or philanthropy, or education. The MNLS has made use of a series of meetings, small and large, with philanthropists and politicians, in Brazil and elsewhere, especially the USA, to mobilise support for national learning standards in Brazil. Indeed, the Mobilisation claims to have been created in the USA, and draws on-going support from American, Australian and English consultants through meetings in Brazil and elsewhere, and these meetings bring together philanthropists and civil servants from various levels in reform efforts.

Concomitantly, institutional arrangements are reworked within public/private partnerships and the sharing of service delivery and policy formulation. Foundations offer pedagogical services and products, like teaching materials or platforms, which are school-focused and aimed at changing practice at local, institutional and classroom levels. They also offer policy services, with "ready-made" and "custom-made" policy solutions, which include consultancy-like services. In this way, new philanthropists are active in all contexts of policy, in multiple relationships, of different kinds, extending from the context of influence with the "ideological labour" (Ferrare & Apple, 2017), through the context of policy writing with the heterarchical arrangements of policy consultancy, into the context of practice with the pedagogical services, among other possible arrangements.

However, heterarchical relationships are more than institutional partnerships (such as PPPs), and the MNLS is an example of how new careers are being forged, "technocrats may become politicians, scientists may become development experts, academics may become activists, engineers may set up NGOs, and so on" (Larner & Laurie, 2010, p. 219). These are experts that become "travelling technocrats", who are "embodied actors who knowingly create careers for themselves through and against broader political-economic processes and national imaginaries" (Larner & Laurie, 2010, p. 219). They are experts who "are increasingly moving between private, public and third sector organisations, and between local, national and international institutions, reshaping these accordingly" (Larner & Laurie, 2010, p. 219). In doing so, they also become boundary-spanners, people with connections in public and private sectors, and operate in ways that challenge hierarchical government structures and bring about new ways of governing. Members of the MNLS directly and actively participate both in meetings with philanthropists and policymaking in the Ministry of Education. These heterarchical connections also span scales with a strong connections built between the MNLS, MEC and ACARA, which brought to Brazil Australian civil servants that came as "consultants" and "experts".

Institutional partnerships and arrangements, such as PPPs, are clear and tangible examples of the shift from government to governance – they clearly point to a sharing of roles and responsibilities in a network that includes new actors besides public authorities. Nonetheless, all the labour analysed in this book, in all of its modalities, aspects and spheres, are part of a governance shift. The arrangements of the heterarchical governance between government and new philanthropy is made possible because of the discourses, relationships and institutional arrangements that are fostered in and through the analysed labour activities. Foundations can only become relevant actors in education governance by legitimising themselves as authoritative voices of policy (mainly through, but not only, ideological labour), by having sufficient financial and network capital (mainly through, but not only, relational labour), and temporarily stabilising their policy ideas and relationships through projects and partnerships (mainly through, but not only, institutional labour). New philanthropy's participation in education governance depends upon a discourse that frames it as a legitimate governance actor, lots of network capital that gives it access to the right people, and, most importantly, an exorbitant amount of money to maintain all their policy efforts. In all of these mundane activities, epistemic communities are built and connect people across public and private boundaries, which are also part of heterarchies. The "ubiquity" of philanthropy is fundamental for the question addressed here – it is by working in so many fronts, in so many levels, with so many strategies, which depend on a lot of capital, that foundations have become very influential in education policy.

All this labour contributes to a more general process of the *heterarchisation* of the state. This is not a story only about education reform, or individual strategies to influence policy. Instead, there are much larger shifts and issues, specially concerning how the state now works in and through networks, promoting a *heterarchisation* of the state. Some of the efforts involved are not necessarily new, or exclusive to heterarchical forms of governance. Using the media for policy purposes and lobbying activities has long been practiced in contexts of hierarchical governments. Perhaps the novelty here is that new philanthropies are now participating in these spaces. Nonetheless, what I want to argue is that the sheer amount of labour, the ubiquity of foundations, with dispersed and messy work, is exactly what is characteristic of heterarchies. It is the scenario as whole that creates the conditions for the growing participation of new philanthropists in networks of education governance. As some of the analysed efforts are more tangible and more easily categorised into typologies or are more recent and can only be found in heterarchies (such as PPPs), there could be a temptation of deeming these practices as more relevant for the *heterarchisation* of the state, or efficient in pushing reforms by philanthropists. I would say, however, all labour modalities here analysed depend on each other and are fundamental for philanthropy's work in reforming education.

As examples of interactions between the different modalities of labour, the ideological/discursive labour (with research, publications, knowledge mobilisation) together with the relational labour (meetings, events, mobilising support and funding), are part of the creation of epistemic communities. The relational labour of meetings and network coordination facilitates the movement of boundary spanners, who themselves foster new ways of thinking and doing governance. The ideological labour of policy entrepreneurship makes possible the assertion of the authoritative voice of new philanthropy, and frames it as part of necessary, or "needed", policy solutions, thus making it thinkable that companies, businessmen, philanthropists became part of heterarchical governance structures. At the same time, the shift from government to governance creates the context for new philanthropists to participate in policymaking work which then legitimises their voice as authoritative. To reiterate, there are no simple or straightforward relationships and interactions here, and these are far from causal relationships or explanatory models. These are complexly inter-related and interdependent actions and assertions, processes and mobilisation. In Figure 11, there is an attempt to represent and sum up this "interdependence" of labour modalities.

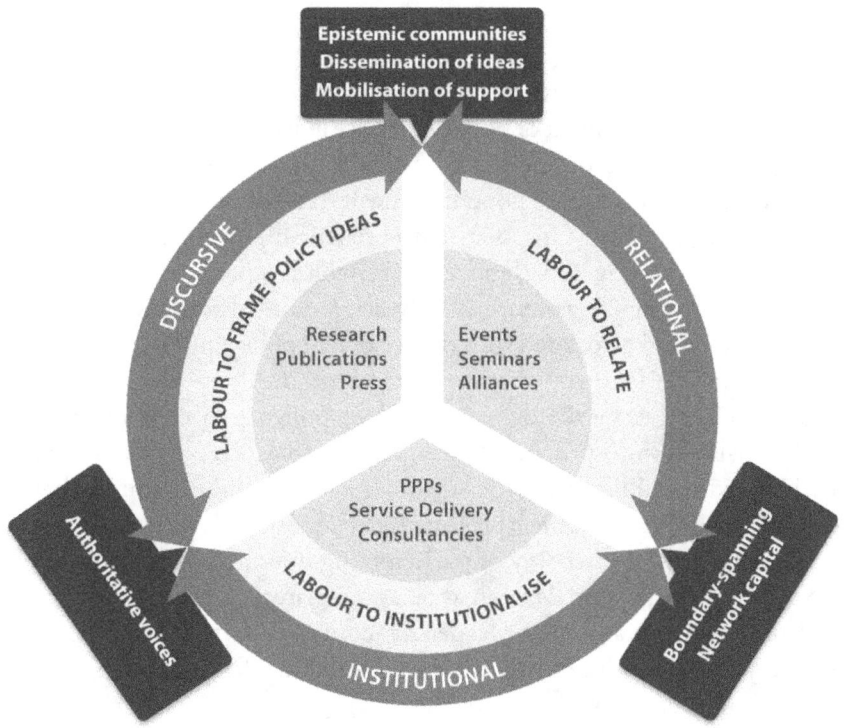

Figure 11. Analytical heuristic revisited

In the process of *heterarchisation*, the work of new philanthropies is not limited to specific spaces, scales or even policy contexts[1] anymore. They

1   Policies move in different contexts and spaces, and can be conceptualised as being developed in three main contexts, which are related in non-linear ways, non-sequential and non-temporal: the context of policy influence, context of text

are now active in all policy contexts and operate in transnational scales. These new actors "have become key political actors not only in delivery activities but also in the conception, advocacy and negotiation of policy processes" (Olmedo, 2014, p. 583). In contrast to previous philanthropic action, which was mainly circumscribed to service delivery, now foundations are also active in the "context of influence" and "context of policy writing" (Bowe et al., 1992), participating in policymaking work of various kinds. Furthermore, the nature of the labour invested by new philanthropists in each of the policy contexts has shifted as well.

First, private organisations, including philanthropic ones, have long been active actors in the context of policy influence in which there are disputes regarding the purposes and meanings of education and agendas, with confessional organisations and grassroots movements (Adrião et al., 2016). However, foundations now invest in policy entrepreneurship (see Chapter 3), with funding and executing studies and research, publishing and collaborating with the press and organising events, all of which are aimed at redirecting policy thinking and thus associated with the context of policy influence.

Second, philanthropy has been present in the context of practice focusing on forms of service delivery, in which policy is enacted, interpreted and translated in to practice. Currently, foundations partake in service delivery with public authorities through PPPs, including the Unibanco Institute and Ayrton Senna's projects *Entre Jovens*, and Acelera (discussed in Chapter 5). Another way of participating in or acting upon this context is supplying materials, such as teaching materials, or more indirectly, running teacher-training and leadership courses. It is in relation to service delivery that PPPs are mostly employed, and it is often the main focus of the research funded by foundations.

What might be regarded as a novelty, in both contexts, is the scale and the boundary-spanning aspect of the invested labour. In the context of influence, new philanthropists aim to frame problems and solutions at national education policy, and can draw from cross-national discourses and networks, while gathering support in both public and private spheres.

---

production and context of practice. Each one has its related arenas, spaces and groups, and involve disputes (Bowe et al., 1992).

A new aspect is the claim of "expertise" (Larner & Laurie, 2010), the creation of an authoritative voice (Ball, 1993) in the field, as well as the instrumental use of research to create the required "evidence" for policymaking (Lubienski et al., 2016). In the context of practice, when enacting policies and providing service delivery, foundations have been engaged in PPPs at the state level, making themselves present across entire educational systems (Peroni & Adrião, 2008). In both contexts, the analytical categories of local-national-international and nation state seem of little, if any, analytical benefit.

Finally, new philanthropies are also active in the context of policy text production, in which is often understood that state actors are the most relevant ones, which can be influenced politically, materially and discursively by social groups. This research supports the understanding that in heterarchical governance, even the activities carried out in this context can be shared in a network of public and private actors. The context of policy text production refers to the context in which discourses, perceived problems and constructed solutions are represented textually, in many formats, including official legal texts, political texts, formal or informal commentaries on such texts, official announcements, videos and others (Bowe et al., 1992; Mainardes, 2006). Such texts are not, necessarily, internally coherent and clear. These texts are not only done in legislative spaces, and the texts are results of struggles for the control of the representations of the policy. New philanthropists and public authorities in Brazil have been developing increasingly complex relationships in heterarchies, in which the division of labour, the interdependency and complexity of services provided are growing. Foundations have been participating in the context of policy writing as consultants, designing policy documents in partnerships with local authorities. In this case, there is yet another methodological and theoretical challenge of studying the work of philanthropy in text production. It is a challenge for researchers to collect data and analyse how texts (bills, speeches, instructions to teachers or schools, programmes…) are produced in practice. Once the policy product is done, one can carry out interviews and content and discourse analysis on the product, but it is challenging to follow ethnographically how the policy texts are formulated, as there is little or no transparency of the related processes.

Throughout all this, global connections are fostered, and the national borders are less and less useful in the analysis of policy. Ideas, resources, labour, meetings, networks, epistemic communities and discourses – all have been globalised. Policy discourses and actors move cross-nationally within and through policy documents, policy advice, seminars, speakers, videoconferences, international seminars, international consultancies and so on. To make sense of current education policies, we need to take "globalisation seriously".

All of these analytical efforts resulted in making evident the complexity of education policy networks in and around Brazil. It is imperative to take this complex, globalised and elaborated governance scheme into account to make some sense of how new philanthropies operate in networks of education governance in the country (and elsewhere). As an example, one cannot begin to understand the current curriculum reform in Brazil and how the MNLS has come to have considerable influence in its formulation without accounting for the complexity of these policy networks. If the MNLS and its members are analysed as atomised actors, we might inaccurately construe the Mobilisation and Lemann Foundation as the lone (and all-powerful) curriculum reformers. However, one organisation, with its labour and resources alone, probably would not have such efficacy. The MNLS needs to be understood as a part of a much larger and longer effort of reform involving the coordinated action of a range of actors, which has involved assembling resources and trust, connecting global partners and so on. This is not to say that the Lemann Foundation could not have achieved some degree of effect working independently and has not been a nodal point, a fundamental funder and coordinator, because it has.

Hence, further research efforts are required, as well as new methods that will advance our understanding of such complex heterarchical structures. To advance this discussion (in Brazil, but also concerning the mobility of curriculum policies), one could "follow back" this curriculum policy to the USA, where MNLS has deep connections, and whose curriculum influenced the Australian curriculum, or England, from where the Curriculum Foundation also provided consulting services to MNLS. Similarly, one could follow the development of the ACARA's consultancy to the Saudi Arabia, and analyse how the same organisation and curriculum were mobilised into different contexts.

However, this does not mean there is a complete and borderless global arena here. Quite the opposite, cross-national networks are very uneven, and only certain places and policies ever get the status of a model, and are mobilised because of it. While there are policy mobilities, there are also policy *immobilities*, policies, people and places that do not move or are "unmoved", so "it is worth tempering talk of policy mobilities with investigation into policy immobilities" to avoid "the danger of privileging and fetishizing mobility" (McCann, 2008, p. 16; see also Sheller and Urry, 2006). In the global education policy field, "mobility and control over mobility both reflect and reinforce power. Mobility is a resource to which not everyone has an equal relationship" (Skeggs, 2004, quoted in Sheller and Urry, 2006, p. 211).

This account of the labour of new philanthropy in networks of education governance in Brazil does not account for the dissident voices. This is in part a result of the method itself, as these voices are not part of these networks, as Ball et al. (2017) put it:

> Also missing from our network and are account are voices of dissent. Now to a great extent that is self evident and self-fulfilling. Such voices are excluded from the epistemic community we explore, because they speak about education differently, but at the same time constitute a network among themselves. These dissident voices question and challenge the shared beliefs of the policy community members, and they are unwelcome and often unheard, or rarely attended to. (Ball et al., 2017, p. 9)

These voices are nonetheless present in other places and spaces, often fighting against and resisting corporate reformers. Dissidents include teachers, students, parents, workers' unions, scholars, journalists, activists, NGOs and other third sector organisations (sometimes funded or related to corporate philanthropists), that are labouring in their own ways to assert alternative education projects, and for the democratic management of education. None of that is reported in this book, and usually is not reported in researches that employ this method.

In similar lines, together with the dissident voices, this book has been limited in its exploration of policy "immobilities". To address this lacking, McCann (2008) argues for some questions that can be addressed in research: "Which policies are not mobilized, why, and who is impacted positively or negatively by this immobility?; how do the subjectivities of experts, class, gender, ethnicity, professional status, etc., influence which policies are, or are not mobilized?" (McCann, 2008, p. 16). These questions require further research.

Final reflections for a democratic education in method and substance

The Brazilian case of education reform is joined up, practically and discursively, in a variety of ways, some described in this book, to a global network of policy ideas and forms of policy. What has been described and analysed here illustrates how the educational system of the country is at one particular point on a continuum of change that interconnects to and emulates a global shift in the form and modalities of the state and ways of governing. This account suggests a clear direction of travel with the work of the state increasingly being done elsewhere by other actors – a polycentric state. All of which calls into question the relations between policy, the policy process and democratic policies and politics.

New unelected and in many ways unaccountable voices are having a significant say in determining the methods, contents and purposes of education. This is, as noted previously, in some senses a de-politicisation of policy (Clarke, 2012). New philanthropists, in spite of arguing that they are working for the improvement of education and the public good, are elected by no one. Their agendas, aims and methods of policy work have no public validation, and cannot be held accountable. As Frumkin (2008) argues, "unlike government, which has elections to set policy directions, and unlike corporations, which have shareholders to whom they must be responsive, philanthropy is able to operate across the boundaries of public and private and to do so with little or no accountability to its many stakeholders" (p. 26).

This means there are issues involving both the methods and the agendas of new philanthropy's participation in governance – the latter has received more attention from scholars that have been trying to evaluate the effects of a corporate reform of education (Ball & Junemann, 2012). However, the "methods", or "*how*" new philanthropists are working in education governance, also require careful scrutiny. New philanthropists have been de-politicising (and re-politicising) policy, in a way in which neither – policy methods and agendas – are publicly discussed, chosen, elected or validated. It becomes challenging, if not sometimes impossible, to assess the role played by private actors within the policy process. There are no means of holding them accountable regarding their investments and results in education.

New philanthropists, including the MNLS and its cohorts and partners, are in some respects "voting with dollars" (Saltman, 2010). That is to say, financial, reputational and social resources are being deployed to change the landscape of education in Brazil and the experience of education in Brazilian schools. New philanthropists are able to mobilise large amounts of capitals and enact what can be referred to as a "hyperagency" (Schervish, 2003). These foundations can do among themselves what it would otherwise take large social groups and movements to achieve. Critique, dialogue and opposition are excluded from the debate about policy in these new arenas, and financial resources become key to achieving policy change. And it is not clear or obvious that the public good is being served, and indeed at least in some respects these "fiscal elites fight to redistribute public priorities and spending in ways that benefit those at the top of the economy. They have more material resources to wage such a battle" (Saltman, 2010, p. 77). This privatising approach to education (of both policy and delivery) becomes even more problematic in contexts of political and economic crisis.

The displacement, silencing and exclusion of other education agendas and social groups must be emphasised. As mentioned before, there is a narrative around philanthropy that frames it as generous and good by default. There is an understanding that given the big and complex problems in society and education, all help is welcome, or that, in the worst case scenario, if philanthropy is not helpful, it is harmless. However, the agenda new philanthropy promotes in education is opposite to the one proposed by critical educators. As it has been reinforced by critical pedagogy for decades, an educational project cannot be politically neutral (Freire, 2018), it either "acts to socialise the learner into the logic of the present system or it becomes the practice of freedom" (Cowden & Ridley, 2019). The global education policy is concerned with increasing literacy and numeracy to promote economic growth. With a general lack of trust on educators, standardised teaching materials and tests are used to achieve this goal. In other words, it is rooted in what Freire termed as a "banking education". Therefore, an education project that aims to support students to "deal critically and creatively with reality and discover how to participate in the transformation of the world" (Freire, 2018, p. 16) is not compatible with new philanthropy's GEP agenda. The conflicts with teachers, unions, critical scholars, exemplifies an active effort of silencing these groups. At the root of this conflict between groups is a conflict of interest. If philanthropies are funded and managed by the elites that benefit from oppressive and unequal social structures, it would be naive to expect them to promote an education that challenges such structures.

However, this discussion about policy contents has been suffocated by new, and excluding, policy methods. As I have argued throughout the book, the struggle with new philanthropy in education is not just a matter of policy agendas (which are supremely important), but also of the methods of policy, the *hows* of governance and policymaking. Democratic, participative and accountable processes and values are important in both aspects. We need schools and curricula that are committed to promoting equality, civic engagement, and fighting any kind of exclusion and discrimination. But this cannot be separated from the means of policy, they are intertwined. A democratic education also needs strong local representative bodies, which work with schools that in turn collaborate with their local communities. In this context, teachers and educators have an active and creative role, central in the entire educational system, and are not silenced or sidelined like in current approached. This is the project of "democratic management" of schools, established by law in Brazil, which has never been fully implemented and is now at great danger (Arelaro, 2017). As Freire enunciates clearly, we cannot expect positive results from an educational program (technical or in political action) that disrespects the particular worldview of people, in spite of whatever good intention (Freire, 2018). Furthermore, "to speak, for instance, about democracy and silence the people is a farce. To talk about humanism and deny humans is a lie" (Freire, 2018).

So there is urgent need make governance more inclusive and transparent. The participation in heterarchical governance cannot be defined by groups (or individuals) possession of capitals (financial, social and network). At the same time, there must be ways to make the policy work of philanthropies both accountable and transparent. In a scenario where foundations have such a decisive role played in policymaking; citizens, researchers, supporters and opposition must be able to verify what and how things are being done. The publication of complete financial reports from foundations would be a step towards greater accountability in the Brazilian governance of education. This would allow citizens and researchers to know the funding figures of and sources that foundations drawn upon in their activities, including what types of tax deductions are given to companies and business people through foundations and social "investments", and trace how these resources have been invested in advocating for what policies.

This depends on a reframing of what are the purposes of education, with a "re-politisation" of the debate and reframing what is considered "quality", as opposed to perspectives that treat education as a simple technical matter. In this sense, Brazilian authors have been pushing for the idea of education of *social* quality (Gadotti, 2010; Paro, 2007, Saviani, 2018), in contrast to the now contested term of "education of quality", which has come to mean a "quality that can be measured by the quantity of information possessed by the students" (Paro, 2007, p. 20). Differently, an education of "social quality" recognises the ethical-political dimension of education, and assumes that schools must work deliberately (and not only diffusely) in the instruction of social values, namely democracy. This implies that "these business ideals and metaphors as applied to public schooling need to be not only dropped but replaced with a recovered public sensibility, a universal value for the public schooling as a crucial part of a democratic public" (Saltman, 2010, p. 78). A democratic education project is needed in means and contents. This means the governance of education policy should be coherent with the educational goals of social inclusion and justice, with policymaking methods that are also democratic.

Bibliography

Adrião, T., Garcia, T., Borghi, R., & Arelaro, L. (2012). As parcerias entre prefeituras paulistas e o setor privado na política educacional: expressão de simbiose? *Educação and Sociedade, 33*(119), 533–549.

Adrião, T., & Peroni, V. (2010). Análise das consequências de parcerias firmadas entre municípios brasileiros e a Fundação Ayrton Senna para a oferta educacional. *Relatório de Pesquisa-CNPq.*

Adrião, T., Peroni, V., & da Costa, M. (2005). *O público e o privado na educação: interfaces entre estado e sociedade.* São Paulo: Editora Xamã.

Adrião, T., Pinto, J. M. de R., Adrião, T., & Pinto, J. M. de R. (2016). Privatização da Educação na América Latina: Estratégias recentes em destaque. *Educação & Sociedade, 37*(134), 11–15.

Antunes, F., & Peroni, V. (2017). Reformas do Estado e políticas públicas: trajetórias de democratização e privatização em educação. Brasil e Portugal, um diálogo entre pesquisas. *Revista Portuguesa de Educação, 30*(1), 181–216.

Apple, M. W. (1993). The politics of official knowledge: Does a national curriculum make sense? *Discourse, 14*(1), 1–16.

Apple, M. W. (2006). *Educating the "right" way: Markets, standards, God, and inequality.* Routledge.

Arelaro, L. R. G. (2007). Formulação e implementação das políticas públicas em educação e as parcerias público-privadas: impasse democrático ou mistificação política? *Educação and Sociedade, 28*(100).

Arelaro, L. R. G. (2017). Reforma do Ensino Médio: O que querem os golpistas. *Retratos Da Escola, 11*(20), 11–17.

Arretche, M. T. (1996). Mitos da descentralização: maior democratização e eficiência das políticas públicas. *Revista Brasileira de Ciências Sociais, 11*(31), 37–49.

Au, W. (2007). High-stakes testing and curricular control: A qualitative metasynthesis. *Educational Researcher, 36*(5), 258–267. <https://doi.org/10.3102/0013189X07306523>

Au, W. (2009). Unequal by design. In *High-stakes testing and the standardization of inequality.* Routledge.

Au, W. (2016). Meritocracy 2.0: High-stakes, standardized testing as a racial project of neoliberal multiculturalism. *Educational Policy, 30*(1), 39–62. <https://doi.org/10.1177/0895904815614916>

Au, W., & Ferrare, J. J. (2014). Sponsors of policy: A network analysis of wealthy elites, their affiliated philanthropies, and charter school reform in Washington State. *Teachers College Record, 116*(08), 1–24.

Au, W., & Ferrare, J. J. (Eds.). (2015). *Mapping corporate education reform: Power and policy networks in the neoliberal state*. Routledge.

Avelar, M., & Ball, S. J. (2019). Mapping new philanthropy and the heterarchical state: The mobilization for the national learning standards in Brazil. *International Journal of Educational Development, 64*, 65–73.

Avelar, M., Nikita, D. P., & Ball, S. J. (2018). Education policy networks and spaces of "meetingness": A network ethnography of a Brazilian seminar. In A. Verger, H. K. Altinyelken, & M. Novelli (Eds.), *Global education policy and international development* (2nd ed.). London: Bloomsbury.

Avelar, M., & Patil, L. (2020). New philanthropy and the disruption of global education. *NORRAG Special Issue (NSI) 04*.

Ball, S. J. (1993). What is policy? Texts, trajectories and toolboxes. *Discourse: Studies in the Cultural Politics of Education, 13*(2), 10–17. <https://doi.org/10.1080/0159630930130203>

Ball, S. J. (2008). New philanthropy, new networks and new governance in education. *Political Studies, 56*(4), 747–765. <https://doi.org/10.1111/j.1467-9248.2008.00722.x194>

Ball, S. J. (2010). New states, new governance and new education policy. In M. W. Apple, S.J. Ball & L. A. Gandin (Eds.), *The Routledge international handbook of the sociology of education* (pp. 155–166). London: Routledge.

Ball, S. J. (2012). *Global Education Inc: New policy networks and the neo-liberal imaginary*. Routledge.

Ball, S. J. (2013). *The education debate* (2nd ed.). Policy Press.

Ball, S. J. (2016). Following policy: Networks, network ethnography and education policy mobilities. *Journal of Education Policy, 31*, 1–18.

Ball, S. J. (2017). Laboring to relate: Neoliberalism, embodied policy, and network dynamics. *Peabody Journal of Education, 92*(1), 29–41.

Ball, S. J., & Junemann, C. (2011). Education policy and philanthropy – the changing landscape of English educational governance. *International Journal of Public Administration, 34*(10), 646–661.

Ball, S. J., & Junemann, C. (2012). *Networks, new governance and education*. Policy Press, University of Bristol.

Ball, S. J. & Junemann, C. (2015). *Pearson and PALF, the mutating giant*. Brussels: Education International.

Ball, S. J., & Junemann, C., & Santori, D. (2017). *Edu. Net: Globalisation and education policy mobility*. Taylor and Francis.

Ball, S. J., & Olmedo, A. (2011). Global social capitalism: Using enterprise to solve the problems of the world. *Citizenship, Social and Economics Education, 10*(2–3), 83–90.

Battilana, J., Leca, B., & Boxenbaum, E. (2009). How actors change institutions: Towards a theory of institutional entrepreneurship. *Academy of Management Annals*, *3*(1), 65–107.

Baumgartner, F. R., Breunig, C., Green-Pedersen, C., Jones, B. D., Mortensen, P. B., Nuytemans, M., & Walgrave, S. (2009). Punctuated equilibrium in comparative perspective. *American Journal of Political Science*, *53*(3), 603–620.

Bevir, M. (2008). *Key concepts in governance*. Sage.

Bevir, M. (2011). Governance as theory, practice, and dilemma. In *The Sage handbook of governance* (pp. 1–16). London: Sage.

Bevir, M., & Rhodes, R. (2003). Decentering British governance: From bureaucracy to networks. *Governance as Social and Political Communication*.

Bevir, M., Rhodes, R. A., & Weller, P. (2003). Traditions of governance: Interpreting the changing role of the public sector. *Public Administration*, *81*(1), 1–17.

Bishop, M. (2006). The business of giving (A survey of wealth and philanthropy). *The Economist*, 378(8466).

Bishop, M., & Green, M. (2010). *Philanthrocapitalism: How giving can save the world*. New York: Bloomsbury.

Bonamino, A., & Sousa, S. Z. (2012). Três gerações de avaliação da educação básica no. *Educação E Pesquisa*, São Paulo, *38*(2), 373–388.

Borgatti, S., & Halgin, D. (2012). Analyzing affiliation networks. In P. Carrington & J. Scott (Eds.), *The Sage handbook of social network analysis*. Sage.

Börzel, T. A. (1998). Organizing Babylon-On the different conceptions of policy networks. *Public Administration*, *76*(2), 253–273.

Börzel, T. A., & Risse, T. (2005). Public-private partnerships: Effective and legitimate tools of international governance. In: E. Grande & L. W. Pauly (Eds.), *Complex sovereignty: Reconstructing political authority in the twenty first century* (pp. 195–216). Toronto: University of Toronto Press.

Bowe, R., Ball, S., & Gold, A. (1992). *Reforming education and changing schools: Case studies in policy sociology*. London/New York: Routledge.

Brakman Reiser, D. (2018). Disruptive Philanthropy: Chan-Zuckerberg, the limited liability company, and the Millionaire next door. *Florida Law Review*, 70, 921.

Brenner, N., & Theodore, N. (2002). Cities and the geographies of "actually existing neoliberalism." *Antipode*, *34*(3), 349–379. <https://doi.org/10.1111/1467-8330.00246>

Bresser Pereira, L. C. B. (1997). A reforma do Estado dos anos 90: lógica e mecanismos de controle. *Lua Nova: Revista de Cultura e Política*, *45*, 49–95.

Bugg-Levine, A., & Emerson, J. (2011). Impact investing: Transforming how we make money while making a difference. *Innovations: Technology, Governance, Globalization*, 6(3), 9–18. <https://doi.org/10.1162/INOV_a_00077>.

Burawoy, M., Blum, J. A., George, S., Thayer, M., Gille, Z., Gowan, T., ... Riain, S. (2000). *Global ethnography: Forces, connections, and imaginations in a postmodern world* (1st ed.). Berkeley: University of California Press.

Burch, P., & Smith, J. M. (2015). Enterprise education policy and embedded layers of corporate influence. In W. Au & J. Ferrare (Eds.), *Mapping corporate education reform: Power and policy networks in the neoliberal state* (pp. 190–207). New York: Routledge.

Caetano, M. R. (2016). O Ensino Médio no Brasil e o Instituto UNIBANCO: um caso de privatização da educação pública e as implicações para o trabalho docente. *Revista Educação e Emancipação*, São Luis, *9*(1), 122–139.

Capella, A. C. N. (2016). A study on the concept of public policy entrepreneur: Ideas, interests, and changes. *Cadernos EBAPE.BR, 14*(SPE), 486–505. <https://doi.org/10.1590/1679-395117178>

Carnoy, M., & Marachi, R. (2020). *Investing for "impact" or investing for profit? Social impact bonds, pay for success, and the next wave of privatisation of social services*. National Education Policy Center.

Clarke, J., & Newman, J. (2009). Elusive publics: Knowledge, power and public service reform. In S. Gerwirtz, et al. (Eds.), *Changing Teacher Profissionalism: International Trends, challenges and ways forward* (pp. 43–53). Routledge.

Clarke, M. (2012). The (absent) politics of neo-liberal education policy. *Critical Studies in Education, 53*(3), 297–310. <https://doi.org/10.1080/17508487.2012.703139>

Comerlatto, L., & Caetano, R. (2013). As parcerias público-privadas na educação brasileira e as decorrências na gestão da educação: o caso do IAS. In *Relações Entre O Público Eo Privado E Implicações Para a Democratização Da Educação: Diálogos Entre Brasil, Argentina, Portugal E Inglaterra*. Brasília: Editora Líber.

Cook, I. R., & Ward, K. (2012). Conferences, informational infrastructures and mobile policies: The process of getting Sweden "BID ready." *European Urban and Regional Studies, 19*(2), 137–152.

Cooper, A. (2014). Knowledge mobilisation in education across Canada: A cross-case analysis of 44 research brokering organisations. *Evidence and Policy: A Journal of Research, Debate and Practice, 10*(1), 29–59. <https://doi.org/10.1332/174426413X662806>

Correa, C. (2013). *Sonho grande: Como Jorge Paulo Lemann, Marcel Telles e Beto Sicupira revolucionaram o capitalismo brasileiro e conquistaram o mundo*. Sextante.

Cowen, R. (2009a). The transfer, translation and transformation of educational processes: And their shape-shifting? *Comparative Education, 45*(3), 315–327. <https://doi.org/10.1080/03050060903184916>

Cowden, S., & Ridley, D. (2019). *The practice of equality: Jacques Rancière and critical pedagogy*. Peter Lang..
Cowen, R. (2009b). Editorial introduction: The national, the international, and the global. In *International handbook of comparative education* (pp. 337–340). Dordrecht: Springer.
Culwell, A. C., & Grant, H. M. (2016). *The giving code: Sillicon Valley nonprofits and philanthropy*. Open Impact.
Cunningham, H. (2016). The multi-layered history of western philanthropy. In *The Routledge companion to philanthropy* (pp. 62–75). Routledge.
Cury, C. R. J. (2008). A educação básica como direito. *Cadernos de Pesquisa, 38*(134), 293–303.
Dale, R., & Robertson, S. (2009). Beyond methodological "ISMS" in comparative education in an era of globalisation. In R. Cowen & A. M. Kazamias (Eds.), *International handbook of comparative education* (pp. 1113–1127). Dordrecht: Springer Netherlands. Retrieved from <https://doi.org/10.1007/978-1-4020-6403-6_69>
Darling-Hammond, L. (2007). Race, inequality and educational accountability: The irony of "No Child Left Behind". *Race Ethnicity and Education, 10*(3), 245–260.
De Carvalho, J. M. (2001). Cidadania no Brasil. *O Longo Caminho, 18*, 18.
De Matos Coelho, M. I. (2008). Vinte anos de avaliação da educação básica no Brasil: aprendizagens e desafios. *Ensaio: Avaliação E Políticas Públicas Em Educação, 16*(59).
De Souza, M. I. S. (1981). *Os empresários e a educação: o IPES e a política educacional após 1964*. Ed. Vozes.
Dean, M. (1999). *Governmentality: Power and rule in modern* society (2nd ed.). Sage.
Dean, M. (2017). Governmentality. In *The Wiley-Blackwell encyclopedia of social theory* (pp. 1–2). Hoboken, NJ: Wiley-Blackwell.
DeBray-Pelot, E. H., Lubienski, C. A., & Scott, J. T. (2007). The institutional landscape of interest group politics and school choice. *Peabody Journal of Education, 82*(2–3), 204–230.
DiMaggio, P. (1988). Interest and agency in institutional theory. . In L. G. Zucker (Ed.), *Institutional patterns and organizations culture and environment* (pp. 3–21). Cambridge, MA: Ballinger.
Edwards, B., & Moschetti, M. (2019). Global education policy, innovation, and social reproduction. In In M. Peters & R. Heraud (Eds.), *Encyclopedia of educational innovation*. Springer.
Edwards, G. (2010). *Mixed-method approaches to social network analysis*. Eprint NCRM/015, National Centre for Research Methods.
Elliot, A., & Urry, J. (2010). *Mobile lives: Self, excess and nature*. Routledge.

Enroth, H. (2011). Policy network theory. In M. Bevir (Ed.), *The Sage handbook of governance* (pp. 19–35). London: Sage.

Evangelista, O., & Leher, R. (2012). Todos pela Educação e o episódio Costin no MEC: a pedagogia do capital em ação na política educacional brasileira. *Trabalho Necessário. Ano, 10*(15), 1–29.

Exley, S., Braun, A., & Ball, S. J. (2011). Global education policy: Networks and flows. *Critical Studies in Education, 52*(3), 213–218. <https://doi.org/10.1080/17508487.2011.604079>.

Fabricant, M., & Fine, M. (2013). *The changing politics of education: Privatization and the dispossessed lives left behind*. Boulder, CO: Paradigm.

Feld, S. L., & Carter, W. C. (1998). When desegregation reduces interracial contact: A class size paradox for weak ties. *American Journal of Sociology, 103*(5), 1165–1186.

Fenwick, T. (2009). Making to measure? Reconsidering assessment in professional continuing education. *Studies in Continuing Education, 31*(3), 229–244. <https://doi.org/10.1080/01580370903271446>.

Fenwick, T. (2011). Reading educational reform with actor network theory: Fluid spaces, otherings, and ambivalences. *Educational Philosophy and Theory, 43*, 114–134. <https://doi.org/10.1111/j.1469-5812.2009.00609.x>

Ferrare, J., & Apple, M. (2017). Practicing policy networks: Using organisational field theory to examine philanthropic involvement in education policy. In J. Lynch, J. Rowlands, T. Gale, & A. Skourdoumbis (Eds.), *Practice theory: Diffractive readings in professional practice and education*. Oxford: Routledge.

Ferrare, J. J., & Reynolds, K. (2016). Has the elite foundation agenda spread beyond the gates? An organizational network analysis of nonmajor philanthropic giving in K–12 education. *American Journal of Education, 123*(1), 137–169.

Fontdevila, C., Verger, A., & Zancajo, A. (2017). Taking advantage of catastrophes: Education privatization reforms in contexts of emergency. In *Private schools and school choice in compulsory education* (pp. 223–244). Springer.

Freire, P. (2018). *Pedagogy of the oppressed*. Bloomsbury.

Freitas, L. C. de. (2004). A avaliação e as reformas dos anos de 1990: novas formas de exclusão, velhas formas de subordinação. *Educação and Sociedade, 25*(86), 131–170.

Freitas, L. C. de. (2012). Os reformadores empresariais da educação: Da desmoralização do magistério à destruição do sistema público de educação. *Educação and Sociedade, 33*(119), 379–404.

Frumkin, P. (2008). *Strategic giving: The art and science of philanthropy*. University of Chicago Press.

Gadotti, M. (2010). Qualidade Na Educação: Uma Nova Abordagem. *Produção de Terceiros Sobre Paulo Freire; Série Livros.*

Galian, C. V. A. (2014). Brazilian curriculum parameters and the development of curricular proposals in Brazil. *Cadernos de Pesquisa, 44*(153), 648–669. <https://doi.org/10.1590/198053142768>

Giridharadas, A. (2018). *Winners take all: The Elite Charade of changing the world*. Knopf.

Goldie, D., Linick, M., Jabbar, H., & Lubienski, C. (2014). Using bibliometric and social media analyses to explore the "echo chamber" hypothesis. *Educational Policy, 28*(2), 281–305.

Gorur, R., Sellar, S., & Steiner-Khamsi, G. (2018). *World yearbook of education 2019: Comparative methodology in the era of big data and global networks*. Routledge.

Grek, S. (2013). Expert moves: International comparative testing and the rise of expertocracy. *Journal of Education Policy, 28*(5), 695–709. <https://doi.org/10.1080/02680939.2012.758825>

Haas, P. M., & Haas, E. B. (1995). Learning to learn: Improving international governance. *Global Governance, 1*(3), 255–285.

Hajer, M., & Laws, D. (2006). Ordering through discourse. In R.Goodin, M. Moran, & M. Rein (Eds.), *The Oxford handbook of public policy* (pp. 251–268). Oxford: Oxford University Press.

Hallinan, M. T., & Sørensen, A. B. (1985). Ability grouping and student friendships. *American Educational Research Journal, 22*(4), 485–499.

Handy, C. (2007). *The new philanthropists: The new generosity*. London: Random House.

Hartnell, C., & Milner, A. (2018). *Philanthropy in Brazil*. Rede de Filantropia pela Justiça Social working paper.

Harvey, D. (2007). Neoliberalism as creative destruction. *The Annals of the American Academy of Political and Social Science, 610*(1), 21–44.

Hogan, A. (2015a). Network ethnography and the cyberflâneur: Evolving policy sociology in education. *International Journal of Qualitative Studies in Education, 29*(3), 1–18.

Hogan, A. (2015b). Boundary spanners, network capital and the rise of edu-businesses: The case of news corporation and its emerging education agenda. *Critical Studies in Education, 56*(3), 301–314.

Hogan, A., Sellar, S., & Lingard, B. (2015). Network restructuring of global edu-business: The case of Pearson's Efficacy Framework. In W. Au & J. Ferrare (Eds.), *Mapping corporate education reform: Power and policy networks in the neoliberal state* (pp. 43–64). New York: Routledge.

Hogan, A., Sellar, S., & Lingard, B. (2016a). Commercialising comparison: Pearson puts the TLC in soft capitalism. *Journal of Education Policy, 31*(3), 243–258.

Hogan, A., Sellar, S., & Lingard, B. (2016b). Corporate social responsibility and neo-social accountability in education: The case of Pearson plc. In A. Verger,

C. Lubienski, G. Steiner-Khansi (Eds.,), *World yearbook of education 2016* (pp. 127–144). Routledge.

Holliday, I. (2000). Is the British state hollowing out? *The Political Quarterly*, *71*(2), 167–176.

Hurl, C. (2017). (Dis)Assembling policy pipelines: Unpacking the work of management consultants at public meetings. *Geographica Helvetica*, *72*(2), 183–195. <https://doi.org/https://doi.org/10.5194/gh-72-183-2017>

Hursh, D. (2000). Neoliberalism and the control of teachers, students, and learning: The rise of standards, standardization, and accountability. *Cultural Logic*, *4*(1), 198.

Hypólito, Á. M. (2008). Estado gerencial, reestruturação educativa e gestão da educação. *Revista Brasileira de Política e Administração Da Educação-Periódico Científico Editado Pela ANPAE*, *24*(1), 63–78.

Hypolito, A. M., & Jorge, T. (2020). OCDE, PISA e Avaliação Em Larga Escala No Brasil. *Sisyphus*, *8*(1), 10–27.

Jessop, B. (1998). The rise of governance and the risks of failure: The case of economic development. *International Social Science Journal*, *50*(155), 29–45.

Jessop, B. (2011). Metagovernance. In M. Bevir (Ed.), *The Sage handbook of governance*. Sage.

Jessop, R. D. (2002). *The future of the capitalist state*. Polity.

Johnson, P. D. (2018). *Global philanthropy report: Perspectives on the global foundation sector*. Harvard Kennedy School, the Hauser Institute for Civil Society at the Center.

Junemann, C., & Ball, S. J. (2013). ARK and the revolution of state education in England. *Education Inquiry*, *4*(3), 423–441.

Junemann, C., Ball, S. J., & Santori, D. (2018). On network(ed) ethnography in the global education policyscape. In *The Wiley handbook of ethnography of education* (pp. 455–477). Wiley Blackwell.

Kingdon, J. W. (1984). *Agendas, alternatives, and public policies*. Boston: Little, Brown.

Kingdon, J. W. (2013). *Agendas, alternatives, and public policies, update edition, with an epilogue on health care: Pearson new international edition* (2nd ed.). Harlow: Pearson.

Knox, H., Savage, M., & Harvey, P. (2006). Social networks and the study of relations: Networks as method, metaphor and form. *Economy and Society*, *35*(1), 113–140.

Krawczyk, N. R., & Vieira, V. L. (2008). *A reforma educacional na América Latina nos anos 1990: uma perspectiva histórico-sociológica*. São Paulo: Ed. Xamã.

Larner, W. (2003). Guest editorial: Neoliberalism? *Environment and Planning D: Society and Space*, *21*(5), 509–512. <https://doi.org/10.1068/d2105ed>

Larner, W., & Laurie, N. (2010). Travelling technocrats, embodied knowledges: Globalising privatisation in telecoms and water. *Geoforum, 41*(2), 218–226. <https://doi.org/10.1016/j.geoforum.2009.11.005>

Larner, W., & Le Heron, R. (2002). The spaces and subjects of a globalising economy: A situated exploration of method. *Environment and Planning D, 20*(6), 753–774.

Larsen, J., Urry, J., & Axhausen, K. (2008). Coordinating face-to-face meetings in mobile network societies. *Information, Communication & Society, 11*(5), 640–658.

Lima, I. G. de. (2016). *As ações do Estado brasileiro na educação básica: uma análise a partir do Sistema de Avaliação da Educação Básica* (PhD thesis). Faculdade de Educação, UFRGS, Porto Alegre.

Lingard, B., & McGregor, G. (2014). Two contrasting Australian Curriculum responses to globalisation: What students should learn or become. *The Curriculum Journal, 25*(1), 90–110.

Lingard, B., & Rawolle, S. (2010). Globalization and the rescaling of education politics and policy. In M. Larsen (Ed.), *New thinking in comparative education. Honouring Robert Cowen* (pp. 33–52). Rotterdam: Sense Publishers.

Lingard, B., & Rawolle, S. (2011). New scalar politics: Implications for education policy. *Comparative Education, 47*(4), 489–502.

Lingard, B., & Sellar, S. (2013). "Catalyst data": Perverse systemic effects of audit and accountability in Australian schooling. *Journal of Education Policy, 28*(5), 634–656.

Lingard, B., Sellar, S., & Savage, G. C. (2014). Re-articulating social justice as equity in schooling policy: The effects of testing and data infrastructures. *British Journal of Sociology of Education, 35*(5), 710–730.

Lipman, P. (2013). *The new political economy of urban education: Neoliberalism, race, and the right to the city*. Taylor and Francis.

Lubienski, C., Brewer, T. J., & La Londe, P. G. (2016). Orchestrating policy ideas: Philanthropies and think tanks in US education policy advocacy networks. *The Australian Educational Researcher, 43*(1), 55–73. <https://doi.org/10.1007/s13384-015-0187-y>

Macedo, E. (2015). Common core for curriculums: Learning rights and development for whom? *Educação & Sociedade, 36*(133), 891–908. <https://doi.org/10.1590/ES0101-73302015155700>

Macedo, E. (2016). In favor of a topological reading of curriculum policies. *Education Policy Analysis Archives, 24*(26). <https://doi.org/10.14507/epaa.24.2075>

Macedo, E. (2017). As demandas conservadoras do Movimento Escola Sem Partido e a Base Nacional Curricular Comum. *Educação & Sociedade, 38*(139), 507–524. <https://doi.org/10.1590/es0101-73302017177445>

Mainardes, J. (2006). Abordagem do ciclo de políticas: uma contribuição para a análise de políticas educacionais. *Educação & Sociedade, 27*(94), 47–69.

Marsh, D., & Smith, M. J. (2001). There is more than one way to do political science: On different ways to study policy networks. *Political Studies, 49*(3), 528–541.

Marsh D., & Smith M. (2002). Understanding policy networks: Towards a dialectical approach. *Political Studies, 48*(1), 4–21. <https://doi.org/10.1111/1467-9248.00247>

Martins, E. M. (2013). *Movimento "todos pela educação": um projeto de nação para a educação brasileira* (Master's dissertation). Faculdade de Educação. Unicamp, Campinas.

Martins, E. M. (2016). *Todos pela educação?–Como os empresários estão determinando a política educacional brasileira*. Rio de Janeiro: Ed. Lamparina.

Martins, E. M. (2019). *Empresariamento Da Educação Básica Na América Latina: Redes Empresariais Prol Educação* (Tese de Doutorado). UNICAMP.

Martins, E. M., & Krawczyk, N. R. (2016). Entrepreneurial influence in Brazilian education policies. In A. Verger, C. Lubienski, & G. Steiner-Khamsi (Eds.), *World yearbook of education 2016: The global education industry* (pp. 78–89). Routledge.

Massey, D. (2005). *For space*. Sage.

McAlister, D. T., & Ferrell, L. (2002). The role of strategic philanthropy in marketing strategy. *European Journal of Marketing, 36*(5/6), 689–705. <https://doi.org/10.1108/03090560210422952>

McCann, E. (2011). Urban policy mobilities and global circuits of knowledge: Toward a research agenda. *Annals of the Association of American Geographers, 101*(1), 107–130.

McCann, E. J. (2008). Expertise, truth, and urban policy mobilities: Global circuits of knowledge in the development of Vancouver, Canada's "four pillar" drug strategy. *Environment and Planning A, 40*(4), 885–904. <https://doi.org/10.1068/a38456200>

McCann, E., & Ward, K. (2012). Assembling urbanism: Following policies and "studying through" the sites and situations of policy making. *Environment and Planning A, 44*(1), 42–51.

McFarland, D. A. (2001). Student resistance: How the formal and informal organization of classrooms facilitate everyday forms of student defiance. *American Journal of Sociology, 107*(3), 612–678.

McFarlane, C. (2009). Translocal assemblages: Space, power and social movements. *Geoforum, 40*(4), 561–567.

McLean, H. (2020). The disruption fantasy: New philanthropy's adventures in education. *NORRAG Special Issue 04*.

Miller, E., & Almon, J. (2009). *Crisis in the Kindergarten: Why children need to play in school*. Alliance for Childhood (NJ3a).
Milner, A. (2018). *The global landscape of philanthropy*. Wings.
Mitchell, T. (2002). *Rule of experts: Egypt, techno-politics, modernity*. University of California Press.
Monteiro, M. (2013). Relação Público-Privada na Educação Básica no Brasil: uma Análise da Proposta do Instituto Unibanco para o Ensino Médio Público. *Redefinições Das Fronteiras Entre O Público E O Privado: Implicações Para a Democratização Da Educação*. Brasília: Liber Livro.
Monteiro, M. (2014). *A formação discursiva neoliberal em escolas públicas estaduais: o Projeto Jovem de Futuro do Instituto Unibanco* (PhD thesis). Faculdade de Educação, UFRGS.
Nichols, S. L., & Berliner, D. C. (2007). *Collateral damage: How high-stakes testing corrupts America's schools*. Harvard Education Press, Cambridge, MA.
OECD, net FWD. (2014). *Venture philanthropy in development: Dynamics, challenges and lessons in the search for greater impact*. Paris: OECD.
Oliveira, R. P. de. (1999). O Direito à Educação na Constituição Federal de 1988 e seu restabelecimento pelo sistema de Justiça. *Revista Brasileira de Educação*, *11*, 61–74.
Oliveira, R. P. de. (2009). The transformation of education into commodity in Brazil. *Educação and Sociedade*, *30*(108), 739–760.
Olmedo, A. (2014). From England with love ... ARK, heterarchies and global "philanthropic governance." *Journal of Education Policy*, *29*(5), 575–597.
Olmedo, A. (2016). Philanthropic governance: Charitable companies, the commercialization of education and that thing called "democracy." In A. Verger, C. Lubienski, & G. Steiner-Khamsi (Eds.), *World yearbook of education 2016: The global education industry* (pp. 44–63). Routledge.
Olmedo, A. (2017). Something old, not much new, and a lot borrowed: Philanthropy, business, and the changing roles of government in global education policy networks. *Oxford Review of Education*, *43*(1), 69–87.
Oxman, A. D., & Fretheim, A. (2009). Can paying for results help to achieve the millennium development goals? Overview of the effectiveness of results-based financing. *Journal of Evidence-Based Medicine*, *2*(2), 70–83.
Oxfam, A. D. (2020). Time to care: Unpaid and underpaid care work and the global inequality crisis. *Oxfam Briefing Paper*.
Ozga, J. (2009). Governing education through data in England: From regulation to self- evaluation. *Journal of Education Policy*, *24*(2), 149–162.
Parker, R. (2007). Networked governance or just networks? Local governance of the knowledge economy in Limerick (Ireland) and Karlskrona (Sweden). *Political Studies*, *55*(1), 113–132.

Paro, V. H. (2007). *Gestão escolar, democracia e qualidade do ensino* (2a ed.). São Paulo: Ed. Intermeios.

Peck, J., & Theodore, N. (2010). Mobilizing policy: Models, methods, and mutations. *Geoforum, 41*(2), 169–174.

Peck, J., & Theodore, N. (2012). Follow the policy: A distended case approach. *Environment and Planning A, 44*(1), 21–30.

Peck, J., & Tickell, A. (2002). Neoliberalizing Space. *Antipode, 34*(3), 380–404.

Peroni, V. M., & Adrião, T. (2008). A relação público/privado e a gestão da educação em tempos de redefinição do papel do Estado. In *Público E Privado Na Educação: Novos Elementos Para O Debate* (pp. 111–127). São Paulo: Xamã.

Peroni, V. M. V. (Ed.). (2013). *Redefinições das fronteiras entre o público e o privado: implicações para a democratização da educação*. Editora Liber Livro.

Peroni, V. M. V., & Comerlatto, L. P. (2017). Parceria público-privada e a gestão da educação: o Programa Gestão Nota 10 do Instituto Ayrton Senna. *Perspectiva, 35*(1), 113–133.

Peroni, V. M. V., de Oliveira Pires, D., Bittencour, J. M. V., Bernardi, L. M., Comerlatto, L. P., & Caetano, M. R. (2013). Relação entre o Público e o Privado na Educação Básica Brasileira: implicações para processos de democratização. *Políticas Educativas, 7*(1), 92–109.

Pires, D. (2013). O histórico da relação público-privada no Brasil: o enfoque jurídico. In V. M. V. Peroni (Eds.), *Redefinições das fronteiras entre o público e o privado: implicações para a democratização da educação* (pp. 159–174). Brasilia: Liber Livro.

Pires, D. O. (2015). *A construção histórica da relação público-privada na promoção do direito à educação no Brasil*. UFRGS PhD Thesis. <https://lume.ufrgs.br/handle/10183/117781>.

Prell, C. (2012). *Social network analysis: History, theory and methodology*. Sage.

Ravitch, D. (2011). *National opportunity to learn summit*. E-priint.

Ravitch, D. (2016). *The death and life of the great American school system: How testing and choice are undermining education*. Basic Books.

Reckhow, S., & Snyder, J. W. (2014). The expanding role of philanthropy in education politics. *Educational Researcher, 43*(4), 186–195.

Rhodes, R. A. (2007). Understanding governance: Ten years on. *Organization Studies, 28*(8), 1243–1264.

Rhodes, R. A. W. (1996). The new governance: Governing without government. *Political Studies, 44*(4), 652–667.

Ribeiro, D. (1995). *O povo brasileiro*. Companhia das Letras. 3a edição (2008).

Riles, A. (2001). *The network inside out*. University of Michigan Press.

Rizvi, F., & Lingard, R. (2010). *Globalizing educational policy*. London: Routledge.

Robertson, S., & Dale, R. (2008). Researching education in a globalising era: Beyond methodological nationalism, methodological statism, methodological educationism and spatial fetishism. In *The production of educational knowledge in the global era* (pp. 17–32). Brill Sense.

Robertson, S., Mundy, K., & Verger, A. (2012). *Public private partnerships in education: New actors and modes of governance in a globalizing world.* Edward Elgar.

Rodrigues, P. de (2016, May 11). *Instituto Unibanco e o projeto jovem do futuro: uma forma de inserção dos empresários nas políticas públicas educacionais para o Ensino Médio* (Master's dissertation). Faculdade de Filosofia, Ciencias e Letras de Ribeirão Preto, Universidade de São Paulo.

Rogers, R. (2011). Why philanthro-policymaking matters. *Society, 48*(5), 376–381.

Rogers, R. (2015). Why the social sciences should take philanthropy seriously. *Society, 52*(6), 533–540.

Rose, N. (1996). The death of the social? Re-figuring the territory of government. *Economy and Society, 25*(3), 327–356.

Rossi, A., Helo, L., & Uczak, L. (2013). Relação público-privada no programa de desenvolvimento da educação: uma análise do plano de ações articuladas. In V. M. V. Peroni (Eds.), *Relações Entre O Público E o Privado E Implicações Para a Democratização Da Educação: Diálogos Entre Brasil, Argentina, Portugal E Inglaterra*. Brasília: Editora Líber.

Rossi, A. J., Bernardi, L. M., & Uczak, L. H. (2017). Relações entre Estado e empresários no PDE/PAR: algumas contradições na política educacional brasileira. *Revista Brasileira de Política E Administração Da Educação-Periódico Científico Editado Pela ANPAE, 33*(2), 355–376.

Roy, A. (2012). Ethnographic circulations: Space–time relations in the worlds of poverty management. *Environment and Planning A, 44*(1), 31–41.

Sabatier, P. A. (1988). An advocacy coalition framework of policy change and the role of policy-oriented learning therein. *Policy Sciences, 21*(2–3), 129–168.

Sabatier, P. A. (1991). Toward better theories of the policy process. *PS: Political Science and Politics, 24*(2), 147–156.

Sahlberg, P. (2011). The fourth way of Finland. *Journal of Educational Change, 12*(2), 173–185.

Sahlberg, P. (2016). The global educational reform movement and its impact on schooling. In *The handbook of global education policy* (pp. 128–144).

Saltman, K. J. (2010). *The gift of education: Public education and venture philanthropy*. Palgrave McMillan.

Saltman, K. J. (2012). *The failure of corporate school reform*. Boulder, CO: Paradigm.

Saltman, K. J. (2018). *The Swindle of innovative educational finance*. University of Minnesota Press.

Sandri, S. (2016). *A relação público-privado no contexto do ensino médio brasileiro: em disputa a formação dos jovens e a gestão da da Escola Pública* (PhD thesis). Setor de Educação, UFPR.

Santori, D., Ball, S. J., & Junemann, C. (2015). mEducation as a site of network governance. In W. Au & J. Ferrare (Eds.), *Mapping corporate education reform: Power and policy networks in the neoliberal state* (pp. 23–42). Routledge.

Saviani, D. (2007). O Plano de Desenvolvimento da Educação: análise do projeto do MEC. *Educação E Sociedade, 28*(100), 1231–1255.

Saviani, D. (2018). *Escola e Democracia*. Autores associados.

Schervish, P. (2003). *Hyperagency and high-tech donors: A new theory of the new philanthropists*. Boston, MA: Boston College, Social Welfare Research Institute.

Schervish, P. G. (2005). Major donors, major motives: The people and purposes behind major gifts. *New Directions for Philanthropic Fundraising, 2005*(47), 59–87.

Schumpeter, J. A. (1983). *The theory of economic development: An inquiry into profits, Capital, credit, interest, and the business cycle*. Transaction Publishers.

Scott, J., & Carrington, P. J. (Eds.). (2011). *Sage handbook of social network analysis*. London: Sage.

Sealander, J. (2003). Curing evils at their source: The arrival of scientific giving. In In L. J. Friedman & M. D. McGarvie (Eds.), *Charity, philanthropy, and civility in American history* (pp. 217–240). Cambridge University Press.

Shamir, R. (2008). The age of responsibilization: On market-embedded morality. *Economy and Society, 37*(1), 1–19.

Sheller, M., & Urry, J. (2006). The new mobilities paradigm. *Environment and Planning A: Economy and Space, 38*(2), 207–226.

Shepsle, K. A. (2006). Rational choice institutionalism. In *The Oxford handbook of political institutions* (pp. 23–38). Oxford University Press.

Shiroma, E. O. (2013). Networks in action: New actors and practices in education policy in Brazil. *Journal of Education Policy, 29*(3), 323–348.

Skelcher, C., Mathur, N., and Smith, M. (2004). *Negotiating the institutional void: Discursive alignments, collaborative institutions and democratic governance*. Political Studies Association Annual Conference, INLOGOV, University of Birmingham.

Srivastava, P. (2016a). Philanthropic engagement in education localised expressions of global flows in India. *Contemporary Education Dialogue, 13*(1), 5–32.

Srivastava, P. (2016b). Questioning the global scaling-up of low-fee private schooling: The nexus between business, philanthropy and PPPs. In A. Verger, C. Lubienski, & G. Steiner-Khamsi (Eds.), *World yearbook of education 2016: The Global Education Industry* (pp. 248–263). New York: Routledge.

Srivastava, P., & Walford, G. (Eds.). (2016). *Non-state actors in education in the Global South*. Oxford Review of Education, Routledge.

Stephenson, K. (2016). Heterarchy. In C. Ansell & J. Torfing (Eds.), *Handbook on theories of governance* (pp. 139–148). Edward Elgar.

Stone, D. (2004). Transfer agents and global networks in the "transnationalization" of policy. *Journal of European Public Policy, 11*(3), 545–566.

Tarlau, R., & Moeller, K. (2020). "Philanthropizing" consent: How a private foundation pushed through national learning standards in Brazil. *Journal of Education Policy, 35*(3), 337–66. <https://doi.org/10.1080/02680939.2018.1560504>.

Urry, J. (2003). Social networks, travel and talk. *British Journal of Sociology, 54*(2), 155–175.

Urry, J. (2007). *Mobilities*. Polity.

Verger, A., Altinyelken, H. K., & Novelli, M. (2018). *Global education policy and international development: New agendas, issues and policies*. Bloomsbury.

Verger, A., Fontdevila, C., & Zancajo, A. (2017). Multiple paths towards education privatization in a globalizing world: A cultural political economy review. *Journal of Education Policy, 32*(6), 757–787.

Verger, A., Lubienski, C., & Steiner-Khamsi, G. (Eds.). (2016). *World yearbook of education 2016: The global education industry*. Routledge.

Wagner, R. E. (1966). Pressure groups and political entrepreneurs: A review article. *Papers on Non-Market Decision Making, 1*(1), 161–170.

Williams, P. (2002). The competent boundary spanner. *Public Administration, 80*(1), 103–124.

New Disciplinary Perspectives on Education

Series Editors
Stephen Cowden is a Social Work educator and researcher with an interest in the relationships between pegagogy, social justice and equality.
Jones Irwin, Associate Professor in Philosophy and Education, Dublin City University

Published Volumes
Vol 1   The Practice of Equality: Jacques Rancière and Critical Pedagogy. 2019. 206 pages ISBN 978-1-78874-029-6
Vol 2   David Ridley: The Method of Democracy: John Dewey's Theory of Collective Intelligence. 2021. 230 Pages. ISBN 978-1-78997-337-2
Vol 3   Disrupting Education Policy: How New Philanthropy Works to Change Education. 2020. 222 pages ISBN 978-1-78707-688-4